The Shape of Art in the Short Stories of Donald Barthelme

The Shape of Art
in the Short Stories of
Donald Barthelme

Wayne B. Stengel

Louisiana State University Press
Baton Rouge and London

Designer: Patricia Douglas Crowder
Typeface: Linotron 202 Trump Medieval
Typesetter: G & S Typesetters, Inc.
Printer and binder: Edwards Brothers

Quotations from stories in *Come Back, Dr. Caligari* are made by permission of the publisher, Little, Brown and Company, copyright © 1961, 1962, 1963, 1964 by Donald Barthelme.

Excerpts reprinted by permission of Farrar, Straus and Giroux, Inc., from: *Guilty Pleasures*, copyright © 1963, 1964, 1965, 1966, 1968, 1969, 1970, 1971, 1972, 1973, 1974 by Donald Barthelme. *Unspeakable Practices, Unnatural Acts*, copyright © 1964, 1965, 1966, 1967, 1968 by Donald Barthelme. *City Life*, copyright © 1968, 1969, 1970 by Donald Barthelme. *Sadness*, copyright ©1970, 1971, 1972 by Donald Barthelme. *Amateurs*, copyright © 1970, 1971, 1972, 1973, 1974, 1975, 1976 by Donald Barthelme. *Great Days*, copyright © 1970, 1976, 1977, 1978, 1979 by Donald Barthelme.

Publication of this book has been assisted by a grant from the Andrew W. Mellon Foundation.

LIBRARY OF CONGRESS CATALOGING IN PUBLICATION DATA

Stengel, Wayne B.
  The shape of art in the short stories of Donald Barthelme.

  Bibliography: p.
  Includes index.
  1. Barthelme, Donald—Criticism and interpretation. 2. Art in literature.
I. Title.
PS3552.A76Z85   1985   813'.54   84-27856
ISBN 0-8071-1215-1

To my parents, without whose continual encouragement this book would have been impossible
And to my wife, Ellen, who believed in the project and saw me through

Contents

Acknowledgments

This study would have been impossible without the help of Bernard Duffey of Duke University, whose exacting reading and criticism of my analysis of Barthelme invaluably sharpened my writing and my perceptions. Equally important to its genesis was Louis Budd of Duke, who first convinced me to pursue this topic. I am particularly indebted to my typist and proofreader, Alfreda Kaplan of Durham, North Carolina, whose tireless speed at the typewriter, unfailing eye for detail, and youthful love of life have been a boon to countless writers in the Research Triangle area.

The Shape of Art in the Short Stories of Donald Barthelme

Introduction

Donald Barthelme is a fifty-four-year-old Philadelphia native, who grew up in Houston and has lived in New York City since the early sixties.[1] Over the last twenty years he has written more than one hundred short stories, many of them originally appearing in the *New Yorker*. These short stories have been published in eight books, *Come Back, Dr. Caligari* (1964); *Unspeakable Practices, Unnatural Acts* (1968); *City Life* (1970); *Sadness* (1972); *Amateurs* (1976); *Great Days* (1979); *Sixty Stories* (1981); and, most recently, *Overnight to Many Distant Cities* (1983). He has also written a children's book, *The Slightly Irregular Fire Engine* (1971), which won the National Book Award for Children's Literature; a book of parodies and satire, *Guilty Pleasures* (1974); and two novels, *Snow White* (1967) and *The Dead Father* (1975). During the last decade he taught creative writing at the State University of New York at Buffalo, Boston University, City College of New York, and the University of Houston.

In the early fifties Barthelme attended the University of Houston

1. Biographical information in this chapter on Barthelme has been compiled from three sources: Jerome Klinkowitz and Roy R. Behrens, *The Life of Fiction* (Urbana, 1977), 72–84; Jerome Klinkowitz, "Donald Barthelme," in *The New Fiction: Interviews with Innovative American Writers*, ed. Joe David Bellamy (Urbana, 1974), 45–54; and Jerome Klinkowitz, "Barthelme, Donald," *Dictionary of Literary Biography* (Detroit, 1978), II, 34–38.

and began his writing career as a reporter for the *Houston Post*. After serving in the army in Korea and Japan following the Korean War, he returned to Houston in 1957. In the next few years he became a publicist for the University of Houston's information office and founder and general editor of the *University of Houston Forum*, a periodical devoted to articles on contemporary literature and art. In 1959 he was appointed director of the Contemporary Arts Museum in Houston. In these roles the variety of Barthelme's interests began to coalesce. He showed an early affinity for art and typography and, as the originator of the *Forum*, was responsible for its layout and design. Always fascinated by lithography and graphics, he illustrated several of his early short stories with drawings that are surreal composites of human figures from several styles and periods wittily superimposed on one another. As a literary editor he chose to publish a wide range of contemporary writers, some of whom—Walker Percy, William Gass, and Alain Robbe-Grillet— would find a much larger audience after appearing in his magazine.

Barthelme's dual interest in modern art and contemporary literature has led him to search for the literary equivalent of modern art in the structure and language of his own writing. He frequently gives his tales a variety of typographical shapes on the page; on occasion he has numbered the sentences in a story, or sometimes he treats entire stories as interviews told exclusively in question-and-answer form. His concern with the physical shaping of his tales parallels his careful control of their language. As a former journalist and public relations writer, Barthelme is well equipped to demonstrate how the abuses of language and proliferation of clichés create propaganda and destroy valid communication.

This range of interests made Barthelme a fitting choice to become managing editor of *Location*, a periodical devised by Harold Rosenberg and Thomas B. Hess to chart the relationships between the contemporary visual and written arts. In 1961 Barthelme left Houston for New York and this job, but *Location* expired after only two issues, Spring, 1963, and Summer, 1964. With the magazine's demise, he gave up editing and publishing to devote all his energies to writing. Yet the influence on his writing of the artists and poets whose work appeared in *Location* remains important to any study of his career. Writers such as Kenneth Koch, John Ashbery, and Frank O'Hara and painters such as Larry Rivers and Richard Rauschenberg were published in the two issues of *Location*. These artists were already recognized as a group whose theories were influencing New York literary and art worlds. Known collectively as the New York School, the painters were abstract expressionists and the poets generally avoided impersonal or meditative poetry for narrative accounts of their partying and sexual lives in Greenwich Village. Frequently, a poet and a painter collaborate as in Frank O'Hara's long narrative poem, "Second Avenue," in which O'Hara describes, in exacting detail, the physical and psychological atmosphere of the Second Avenue loft in which Larry Rivers lived and worked as well as the friends, artists, and lovers who visited him there. Another example of this artistic collaboration between poet and painter is Kenneth Koch's poem, "George Washington Crossing the Delaware." Inspired by Rivers' nonrepresentational painting of the same title, this poem turns a courageous episode in American history into cartoon heroics full of buffoonery and slapstick. Editing these writers' work gave Barthelme a feeling for what contemporary art could contain rather than specific models for his own writing.

Like the work of the artists, Barthelme's stories show the domination of form over content and the recognition that the dramatization of the artist's personality in his art may constitute a large part of a work's style. Particularly from the painters, he learned to see the short story form as a canvas capable of displaying surreal art objects. His stories are frequently concerned with how enormous, unlikely objects of contemplation—a balloon or a glass mountain—can be presented to an audience. Frequently, his writing becomes a cartoon of reality in which characters and situations make exaggerated, jerky entrances and exits. He has likened his own short stories to what *New Yorker* art critic Harold Rosenberg has called "the anxious object," that contemporary museum piece which does not know whether it is a work of art or a pile of junk.[2]

2. Klinkowitz and Behrens, *Life*, 75.

Though short, Barthelme's time as managing editor of *Location* thoroughly grounded his writing in the New York poetry and art world of the 1960s. From there, however, it has moved and expanded. The influence of the *Location* artists is clearly seen in "After Joyce," a statement of aesthetics Barthelme wrote for the second and last issue of the magazine, published in Summer, 1964. This essay also shows his desire to go beyond his immediate artistic circle, still applying its principles to his own prose experiments but discovering new techniques in the process.[3] In "After Joyce," Barthelme calls for a literature in which the reader actively participates, as one would in a sport or game. The audience, perceiving the relationship between itself and the art work in terms of play and sport, must reconsider what constitutes an art work. Recognizing that a Campbell's soup can as well as enlarged photographs of Marilyn Monroe have been regarded as serious art objects in our time, Barthelme feels that any object, no matter how mundane or vacuous, can be transformed into a work of art if the artist so desires and an audience accepts the artist's signs and signals. With the artist open to new ways of playing with the public's expectations, art is now free to ask its audience new questions: how do you wish to play with the objects in your environment; what can you bring to your encounter with such objects to make this experience aesthetic; and what do you think of a society that values soup cans or Marilyn Monroe as art?

This self-reflexive quality is what Barthelme seeks and what he claimed to find in Kenneth Koch's novel *The Red Robins*, an excerpt of which was printed in the first number of *Location*. Koch's work parodies boys' books like the Rover Boys stories or Tom Swift adventures. Furthermore, *The Red Robins* mocks styles and conventions of novel-writing itself to comment on the traditional novel's inability to convey a contemporary world defined not by laws and hypotheses but by theories of relativity and principles of uncertainty. Specifically, Barthelme feels *The Red Robins* excels in three valuable aesthetic tasks: the destruction of sentimental

3. Donald Barthelme, "After Joyce," *Location*, II (Summer, 1964), 13–16.

cliché; the use of narrative form as a field of linguistic play in which language, not events, becomes the content of the novel; and the random assembly of objects, commodities, and attitudes that distorts the normal associations a reader makes with these objects and forces him to reconsider and restructure the materials of his own environment. These three attributes Barthelme praises in Koch and uses for his own purposes.

Because of Barthelme's abstract, innovative conception of art and the artist-audience relationship, any study of his short stories must find a strategy for confronting the specific problems his writing poses. His stories are frequently under ten pages in length, jocular in tone, and governed by the objects they examine, such as a dog falling from an apartment window onto the protagonist's back in "Falling Dog," or a glass mountain suddenly rising in the middle of Manhattan in "The Glass Mountain." These stories can appear as facetious or trivial—hardly worthy of critical examination. Reading the range of Barthelme's writing as it has appeared in his eight collections, however, yields evidence of a unity of idea and technique that establishes him as a writer of consistent vision and serious intention. Consequently, a possible way to approach his disparate subject matter and bewildering point of view would be to consider the full range of short stories in these collections and to group them according to type. Only a few critics have made efforts in this direction, and their work has been limited. Neil Schmitz sees Barthelme as a modern satirist, and he groups the overtly comic or satiric stories together to demonstrate Barthelme's attempt to ridicule an imperfect world. Dividing the stories into the ludic, or playful, and the representational, Alan Wilde distinguishes between the fanciful and the more realistic elements in Barthelme's writing. Yet these critics consider only a limited number of stories and fail to investigate enough varieties to offer a case for the artistic coherence of his writing.

In an effort to present an analytic system for the short stories, this study will develop a typology or classifying procedure, which will consider the one hundred plus tales that make up the whole. Sixteen types or categories will be considered. As a beginning principle, this typology classifies the stories by theme into four categories. The first division consists of tales dealing with identity or a fictional character's concept of self. The second deals with stories depicting an exchange or conflict between two individuals dramatized in dialogue. The third involves tales of groups of individuals in the social fabric that holds them together. The fourth embraces stories in which an object in the physical landscape—a dog or a museum, for example—becomes the subject of an essayistic description of the uses for this object in society. These four thematic divisions form the vertical axis of a grid on which the stories to be analyzed are placed, schematized, and described.

The stories in each of these categories can then be cross-divided into four classes based on Barthelme's development of his topics. In the first horizontal classification he seems to be playing with such concerns as the self, the dialogue, society, and objects in the landscape. Barthelme's play resembles that of a child's discovery, exploration, or evasion of an object he finds in his environment. This playfulness, found in the jocular tone of a narrator or the unrestrained actions of a protagonist, is a mental energy that constantly prods the objects and provokes the antagonists the child encounters. If play at first seems a juvenile or whimsical process, further examination shows that Barthelme believes his jokes produce a meaningful vision of his themes. In a second mode of storytelling Barthelme is intent on knowing, perceiving, or establishing some form of understanding of one of his four thematic concerns. The third variety of process occurs in stories in which the self, dialogue, society, or physical objects are trapped, turned in on themselves, and forced to repeat the same actions obsessively, without change or renewal. The fourth and final category includes stories in which Barthelme or his characters create a means of escape from these cycles of repetition. When all divisions and categories are considered, a typology of stories with a gridlike pattern of sixteen positions emerges.

Even this systemization is hardly complete. It excludes at least twenty stories that have no logical place anywhere on the grid.

Still, each of the sixteen junctures of theme and process suggests a method of description applicable to a large number of tales, and the entire system embraces the larger part of Barthelme's short-story writing. Several stories could satisfactorily fill more than one of the sixteen positions on the grid, and perhaps a dozen stories develop to the extent that they overlap four or five categories. The stories listed in each box beneath the most important story, the title of which is italicized, are similar to it in theme and quality and are discussed in conjunction with it. Even though only one story has been chosen as a representative type for each position on the grid, examining related tales stresses further correspondences. The word above each process on the horizontal axis of the typology describes a tone found frequently in stories developed by that process; the nouns below a particular process describe a subject recurrent in stories developed through that process. Each story has been chosen because of its suitability to a specific position on the grid regardless of when it was written. My interest is in classification rather than chronology and in particular combinations of form and content. This typology is a study of aspects of Barthelme's overall production and not an investigation into his development or evolution as a writer. The final typology, then, complete with stories selected for analysis, appears in the grid.

In developing my arguments, I will use the sixteen stories with italicized titles on the grid as the focal points for discussions of Barthelme's conception of the themes on the vertical axis. These discussions will also analyze and allude to the auxiliary stories listed in each box of the typology as well as the four processes for developing the theme of each chapter. For example, Chapter I of this study discusses the theme of identity as developed by play, the effort to know, repetition, and creation in the stories listed on the first horizontal row of the typology. Congruently, Chapters II, III, and IV discuss the themes of communication, contemporary social relationships, and modernist art objects as developed by the four processes of the horizontal axis in those stories on the three succeeding horizontal rows of the typology. Before beginning Chapter I

	Humor Play Underground Man	Futility Effort to Know The Collage	Stasis Repetition Education	Affirmation Creation The Artist
Tone: **Process:** **Subject:**				
Chapter I The Self Identity Stories	*Hiding Man* Phantom of the Opera's Friend Temptation of St. Anthony City of Churches	*See the Moon* My Father Weeping Brain Damage	*Miss Mandible* The Sergeant The School The Educational Experience	*A Shower of Gold* Paul Klee Daumier
II Communication Dialogue Stories	*The Explanation* The Reference	*Margins* The New Music	*The Catechist* Morning	*Kierkegaard Unfair to Schlegel* The Leap
III Society Social Fabric Stories	*To London and Rome* I Bought a Little City The Captured Woman	*Will You Tell Me!* Edward and Pia Moments of Waking and Sleeping	*Perpetua* Critique de la Vie Quotidienne The Party	*City Life* The Indian Uprising Paraguay
IV Art Objects Objects of Speculation Stories	*The Balloon* Police Band Police Ball	*RFK Saved* The Genius On Angels	*Glass Mountain* Nothing The Bodyguard	*Tolstoy Museum* Falling Dog Flight of Pigeons

Horizontal Axis Processes

Vertical Axis Topics

and an analysis of the theme of identity in Barthelme's stories, the reader can benefit from a more thorough description of the processes of the horizontal axis.

Of the four processes of development on the horizontal axis of the typology, the first, play, takes the greatest number of forms and thus becomes the most difficult to define. Barthelme's sense of play is humorous. His narrators or protagonists mock, ridicule, evade, escape, or hide from their own identities, conversations with others, their society, or objects that intrude on their world. His narrators play jokes on the reader, and his protagonists play games, toy with, and tease their antagonists, confusing and misleading them. A flippant tone emerges in these tales, but Barthelme nonetheless sees these jocular stories as meaningful insights into the ways various individuals manipulate their world. In some instances by using play as technique, the central character of a tale withdraws from society to become a skeptical underground man, an outcast who defines his identity by his position on the fringes of society. Many of Barthelme's tales play with the flow of conversation between two characters, each trying to outwit and flee the designs of the other. Another subgroup of stories examines the social play of contemporary life, including the buying and selling of luxurious items, services, and even other human beings within an affluent, amoral social set, whose insatiable desire for travel, novelty, and escape also functions as a form of play. In a final case play becomes the relationship between the modern artist, the art object he makes and places on view, and the audience that responds to it. Many of Barthelme's stories, like much contemporary art, present abstract groupings of their artists' feelings and impressions whose meaning lies sheerly in the exuberance of their language or in the creative juxtapositions formed by the arrangement of their parts. Sometimes Barthelme invites his audience to play further with the surface meaning of his work by placing a potentially artistic object in an environment that is openly hostile or, at best, indifferent to it.

Whereas play is a self-sustaining activity, knowing for the Barthelme protagonist or narrator serves as an active, aggressive search in which he observes, questions, or investigates phenomena, situations, or internalized feelings he does not understand or cannot explain. The unvarying sense of Barthelme behind the characters he creates is that of a thorough skeptic who is amused by his characters' efforts to know a world that offers few definite explanations for any event. If, in Barthelme's view, conclusive knowledge does not exist, he nonetheless admires individuals who never relinquish the desire to know, and he scoffs at those who feel that knowledge in any one area is definitive or complete. For Barthelme, the desire to know must be an ongoing process, which, though impossible to attain, remains forever necessary to establish a sense of individual purpose and identity. Many of Barthelme's stories incorporating the desire to know form verbal collages in which the narrator's or protagonist's life is fragmented into a series of discontinuous pieces. The protagonists of these collages attempt to fit the elements of their lives together in an effort to know themselves. Yet their lives have been so ravaged by time and change that their desire for self-knowledge can never be fulfilled.

This desire to know, the second form of story development, often emerges as the effort to appraise or measure using the conventional yardsticks of science, religion, or history. It may be an attempt to categorize or classify relying on the generalities and prejudices of social convention, or it may result from the drive to understand the self, others, or one's society. Barthelme's stories demonstrate that all these attempts are necessary but futile, and thus they can be satirized in the frustrations and false assurances of the individuals who pursue them.

Though it takes different forms in different stories, repetition, the third developmental process on the horizontal axis of the typology, is the most self-explanatory of the four. In the identity stories repetition becomes synonymous with a return to the past or to past educational experiences—grade school or military training, to give two examples—that instill patterns of behavior in an individual which continue for life. These stories see education as a trap committing individuals to learned responses that promote and reinforce their failure in the adult world. These stories seem static and deterministic because they reduce life to a treadmill of acquired gestures, which, once performed, become addictive habits regardless of the destructive pattern they induce. Repetition also functions as a static, ineffectual process in those dialogue stories which envision conversation as an endless echoing of stock phrases and responses performed for civility's sake or to avoid boredom and desperation. Conversation in these dialogues has been reduced to a stereotyped script allowing the participants to avoid actual communication or to evade the control one speaker desires over another. Repetition here seizes upon the latest mode or manner of a narcissistic culture, which, in striving to create the newest vogue, forever repeats itself. Repetition throughout Barthelme's tales is a self defeating flight from weariness with the conventional by the pursuit of what seems new. In a particular set of stories repetition becomes a scrutinizing or itemizing of the properties of a particular object, much as a zealous art student might list the qualities of a museum exhibit. Though repetition here again is static, as these stories continue, it becomes a quest that can never be satisfied or exhausted, and the reader can find an obsessive fascination in its ability to redescribe the objects it examines and aestheticizes.

Creativity is the most inclusive and the most important of the four processes on the horizontal axis of the typology. Barthelme's stories using this process incorporate play, the desire to know, and repetition as well as creativity in developing the themes on the vertical axis. Creativity, however, transcends the first three techniques in its depiction of the artist who goes beyond the merely humorous, satiric, or static tones associated with the other processes to affirm a vision of life created in his or her art. For Barthelme, creativity thus becomes a moral action in which the artist not only can re-imagine the world but also can devise surrogate selves who function successfully in any crisis or dilemma. The tales developed through creativity are among the most high-spirited, original, and lunatic he has written. Their narrators and protagonists appear as driven or inspired men and women who refuse to let the attitudes and social conventions of an insistent, compulsive world destroy their own beliefs. Indeed, they respond with a near madness of their own. Creativity for these characters is the unleashing of their wills on the aggressive, demeaning forces of modern society that demand conformity, regimentation, or silence from its citizens. Haunted by the failures of their pasts, these artists nevertheless create imaginary pasts enabling them to live in the present. These worlds are immune to the mistakes of the artists' own lives and free from the violations of intruders.

Many of Barthelme's artists conclude that the conditions of modern life are so hostile to the creation of art that they have only one legitimate function: the criticism of modern life. Creativity for these figures is the use of irony to attack and destroy those elements of the modern world which have cluttered contemporary existence without adding to its beauty or meaning. Yet these artists face a huge dilemma: they must learn to turn the essentially negative force of their irony into a creative, affirming value rather than allowing it to become another caustic voice adding to the debris it castigates. In a related set of stories, creativity thrives on the social environment in which the artist works. For some of Barthelme's narrators and protagonists, the modern city serves as a huge reservoir of energy and possibilities, which allows shrewd citizens to avoid the abuses and punishments of metropolitan life by fusing their talents to the city's drive and tempo. Other artists in other tales find certain urban environments such vast swamps of corruption with such broken lines of communication that their creativity is stifled and dies. In the final subset of stories, artistic creativity lies in the choice of distinctively artistic subject matter. Burdened by the past, the contemporary artist lies in the shadow of great artists of earlier times whose certainty of vision and majesty of style are entirely inappropriate to the depiction of mangled, disruptive modern life. Creativity for the contemporary artist exists in affirming his or her vision of life in subjects that suggest the uncertainty and contradictions of contemporary reality while anticipating the restlessness and desire for sensation of the modern audience. Creativity, then, becomes the strategic, ingenious, and inspired use of imagination, irony, environment, and subject matter to will and affirm a new reality.

Chapter I

The Identity Stories

In the four identity stories whose titles are italicized on the horizontal axis of the typology, Barthelme depicts four egos who are nearly destroyed by a glut of competing values. These four selves have been alienated by pasts that offer no explanation for their present roles and by other individuals, frequently authority figures, who insist on foisting unusable concepts of reality on them. Each of the protagonists discovers some activity through which he attempts to recover a sense of identity. One protagonist plays with various beliefs, past and present, to outwit the priest who threatens to return him to Catholicism. For another, the desire to know the meaning of his life causes him to juxtapose its fragments into a collage of memories that becomes his autobiography. A third returns to his sixth-grade classroom, doomed to repeat his secondary education until he masters the beliefs that will enable him to function in an adult world. Such protagonists fail to determine who they are, for Barthelme's view is that human identity is a shifting, ever-changing succession of roles eroded by time and personal history. The individual who limits himself to one role or personality in an effort to define himself misunderstands the meaning of identity. These egos are correct in thinking that identity is a process, an ongoing activity, but incorrect in relegating this activity to one specific function such as play, knowing, or repetition. Since creativity in fact incorporates play, knowing, and repetition in addition to invention, the ego most successful in establishing a sense of identity in these stories is the one who attempts to fathom the nature of his life through artistic creation. In such a tale a Barthelme character realizes he must disregard all the beliefs that the world would force on him. Merely by believing in himself, he creates a past, present, and potential future in which to flourish.

More specifically, the battered protagonists of all four stories search for identities not only by performing a particular activity but also by pitting themselves against hostility. Frequently here, Barthelme demonstrates that the self is defined in its conflicts with an authority figure—a priest, a father, a boss, a teacher, or even the president of the United States. Such encounters are among the most crucial in the identity stories. In each of these conflicts, the self discovers that it must stop worshiping such icons; in fact, it must destroy the respect it holds for these figures so that it can gain its own vision of reality, not one derived from superiors. The only belief worth holding is that which originates in the self.

In their desire for unity, the egos in these stories clash with their superiors and with elements within themselves. This struggle is the logical result for personalities who feel betrayed by the passage of time and by such dramatic changes in their personal histories that the beliefs and values they have honored in the past have little credibility in today's world. The past looms large in all of the stories, dividing each protagonist into several factions that seek coherence. Yet Barthelme's final view in all four stories is that the past is no source of aid or comfort, whereas alienation from it is only a reflex, not a creative enough response to merge the fragments of any one identity into a unified self. Since a proliferation of beliefs has split the modern self into so many warring camps, Barthelme ultimately recognizes that the fusion of the ego into a whole can occur only when an individual creates his own beliefs. Playing with others' beliefs, attempting to know or understand others' beliefs, or ritualistically repeating a society's beliefs is only a partial measure for developing a concept of the self. Identity is an ongoing activity or process. An individual can truly be said to possess identity only when he creates his own beliefs. Character must not only construct its identity but also posit a sense of values appropriate to this artistic task, and these stories constitute Barthelme's moral solution to a meaningless world. Some of his protagonists find life in the world by perpetually reimagining it, and these create themselves anew in every moment and situation. The self is not a static idea but a dynamic organism in constant turmoil and evolution.

No story so vividly demonstrates Barthelme's conception of identity sought through the process of play as the first on the typology, "Hiding Man." Here play becomes instrumental to the search for identity in three ways: one character seeks his identity in the play of his memory and imagination over his real and imagined roles in the past; another allows his play of mind to transform his beliefs and identity; and each of these characters forms an identity in the play of language and wit that flows between them.

In "Hiding Man," two men meet in a deserted movie theater in a decaying inner city as a horror film flickers on the screen above them. Burlingame, from whose point of view the story is told, is instantly suspicious of Bane-Hipkiss, a black man wearing dark glasses, who engages Burlingame in uneasy conversation and moves slowly closer to him across the empty seats. Bane-Hipkiss says that he recognizes in Burlingame a fellow hiding man, and Bane-Hipkiss proceeds to reveal his own past, composed of so many conflicting identities as a confidence man, a dealer in souvenirs, and a trader in notions that he wonders if he has any unified sense of self at all. His seemingly honest confession unleashes a similar response in Burlingame, and Burlingame describes an adolescence in which he fled Catholicism, not because he did not believe in its rituals but because Father Blau, his athletic parish priest, attempted to turn Burlingame into a basketball star. Burlingame feels totally alienated, brought to this climax when told by another priest that he is sought by a band of clerics pursuing former Catholics and seeking to return them to the church. Burlingame's response to this information is to go underground, to spend his days and nights haunting the decaying movie palace and suppressing the rituals of Catholicism for a new faith in the minutiae and trivia he sees in the horror movies. As Burlingame talks nervously and agitatedly to Bane-Hipkiss, he spouts vast numbers of scenes, situations, and details from countless horror films. These movies have become Burlingame's surrogate religion.

Bane-Hipkiss moves increasingly closer to Burlingame as the latter describes his transformation from religious faith to a belief in the rites of the horror movies. When Burlingame concludes his tale, Bane-Hipkiss rips off a black mask to reveal his true identity as a white man and one of the priests in search of the lapsed. Burlingame is seemingly nonchalant about Bane-Hipkiss' theatrics. He chooses to ignore Bane-Hipkiss' taunt that if Burlingame will not come with him quietly he will take him by force. Calmly, Burlingame advises Bane-Hipkiss to look at the rituals and revelations on the screen before them. When Bane-Hipkiss reaches Burlingame's seat, Burlingame takes a hypodermic needle from his pocket and injects it in Bane-Hipkiss' neck. Bane-Hipkiss is quickly unconscious. In only moments, Burlingame assures us, Bane-Hipkiss will be barking like a dog. Barthelme ends an improbable story with an impossible twist. Fleeing a priest who wishes to inflict him with religious zeal, Burlingame uses his vast knowledge of the horror movies to become a mad scientist and to turn his present assailant into a dog. His own belief in these movies has given him a means to action and a device for destroying Bane-Hipkiss' power over him.

Doubtless, "Hiding Man" is a story about men who play humorously with their own sense of identity and with their roles in relationship to one another. Still, the story, like many of the play stories on the typology, has a tone that encourages the reader to ask how much of its situation is a joke and how much has serious implications. Is the audience to believe that Bane-Hipkiss is a priest in disguise who has waited for this moment to return Burlingame to the church? Similarly, has Burlingame actually become a wizard who has learned from horror films how to turn men into dogs? Barthelme never answers these questions, and in leaving "Hiding Man" with an ambiguous ending he plays with his readers as much as his characters torment one another. Whatever his current role, Bane-

Hipkiss is a man who moves from role to role in search of his identity. As he tells Burlingame in the darkened theater:

My real name (how can I say it?) is Adrian Hipkiss, it is this among other things I flee. Can you imagine being named Adrian Hipkiss, the snickers, the jokes, the contumely, it was insupportable. There were other items, in 1944 I mailed a letter in which I didn't say what I meant. I moved the next day, it was New Year's Eve and all the moving men were drunk, they broke a leg on the piano. For fear it would return to accuse me. My life since has been one mask after another, Watford, Watkins, Watley, Watlow, Watson, Watt, now identity is gone, blown away. Who am I? Who knows?[1]

While Bane-Hipkiss is obsessed with roles and masks as forms of identity, his counterpart, Burlingame, is fascinated with the beliefs that have transformed his identity. He is willing to believe in the rituals and celebrations of *Blood of Dracula* and *Amazing Colossal Man* and yet still fears the nuns and priests on patrol tracking down lapsed Catholics like himself. The difference in their forms of identity is what creates both tension and playfulness between them and what causes Burlingame to lecture Bane-Hipkiss on the value of belief:

But there is more, it was the first ritual which discovered to me the possibility of other rituals, other celebrations, for instance "Blood of Dracula," "Amazing Colossal Man," "It Conquered the World." Can Bane-Hipkiss absorb this nice theological point, that one believes what one can, follows that vision which most brilliantly exalts and vilifies the world? Alone in the dark one surrenders to "Amazing Colossal Man" all hope, all desire, meanwhile the bishop sends out his patrols, the canny old priests, the nuns on simple errands in stately pairs. I remember the year everyone wore black, what dodging into doorways, what obscene haste in crossing streets.[2]

The play of mind that made Burlingame a devout Catholic makes him a zealous worshiper of horror movies. Likewise, the fear and paranoia that religion instilled in him transform the nuns and priests in pursuit of his soul into ghouls and zombies. In "Hiding Man" Barthelme suggests that any contemporary search for iden-

1. Donald Barthelme, "Hiding Man," in *Come Back, Dr. Caligari* (Boston, 1964), 30.
2. *Ibid.*, 34–35.

tity has become difficult because there are so many forces in modern life demanding belief.

The conflict in the story between Burlingame, who manipulates identities from his beliefs, and Bane-Hipkiss, who gains and loses his many identities from the changing roles he assumes, can never be resolved. Their menacing, highly charged play makes identity a tug of wills between two selves, each defined in terms of the other and each terrified of being revealed, lest he prove the more vulnerable. This endless childlike game of tag is what Burlingame and Bane-Hipkiss play, particularly in conversation with one another.

"Then what are you doing here?" Friend sits back in sliding seat with air of having clinched argument. "Surely you don't imagine this is a suitable place?"

"It looked good from the outside. And there's no one here but you."

"Ah, but I am here. What do you know about me? Nothing, absolutely nothing, I could be anybody."

"So could I be anybody. And I notice that you too keep an eye on the door."

"Thus we are problematic for each other." Said smoothly, with consciousness of power. "Name's Bane, by the way." Lights pipe, with flourishes and affectations. "Not my real one, of course."[3]

Their mutual unwillingness to disclose their identities turns their relationship into a game of blindman's bluff. The goals of the game are power and control gained through lying and intimidation.

However the reader finally interprets "Hiding Man," Burlingame seems the victor in his contest with Bane-Hipkiss. As the story concludes, Burlingame believes he is turning Bane-Hipkiss into a dog. Bane-Hipkiss may or may not be a member of the army of priests who Burlingame believes lies in wait for failed Catholics, but Burlingame's ability to believe completely in his concocted faith is finally seen as superior to the masks that Bane-Hipkiss superimposes on his shapeless personality. Yet Barthelme depicts Burlingame's triumph with comic ambivalence. Burlingame forges an identity by destroying the threat that Bane-Hipkiss poses and by relying on his faith in horror movies to help him. But Burlingame

3. *Ibid.*, 27–28.

originates no beliefs of his own in doing so. The lore of the horror movies is an established set of conventions, like Catholicism, and one to which Burlingame conforms in changing Bane-Hipkiss into a dog. Burlingame merely mimics the beliefs offered by his society. Failing to create or imagine his own values or beliefs, he becomes a man in flight, a man who would rather hide than acknowledge his inability to produce a distinctive identity.

Like each of the sixteen stories with italicized titles in the typology, "Hiding Man" is one in which the basic central situation recurs. In this particular type, a tale about identity generated through play, the protagonist is a harassed outcast forced by prevailing social standards to live on the fringes of society or in an extreme situation within it. The three stories in the box with "Hiding Man" are "The Phantom of the Opera's Friend," from *City Life* (1970), "The Temptation of St. Anthony," from *Sadness* (1972), and "A City of Churches," also from *Sadness*. The element of play that all four stories emphasize is hiding or evasion. Each story is about a man or woman who is unable to establish a functional social identity and attempts to hide or to evade identity by becoming a recluse or outcast from that society. These stories, like many of Barthelme's tales developed through play, are humorous in tone, but their humor is frequently unpredictable. Often the reader feels that not only is the protagonist hiding his identity but that Barthelme is as well. One frequently wonders where Barthelme's sympathies lie in any particular story. In "Hiding Man," Barthelme seems to sanction Burlingame's ultimate power over Bane-Hipkiss, but Burlingame's triumph is at once ridiculous and impossible. The last sentence of "Hiding Man" illustrates the contradictions of the story. As Burlingame says, while waiting for the transformation of Bane-Hipkiss to begin: "People think these things are jokes, but they are wrong, it is dangerous to ignore a vision, consider Bane-Hipkiss, he has begun to bark."[4] Each of the four stories in this box on the typology could be considered as a joke with vision. Yet whatever vision each of these isolated figures projects, their views are lonely,

4. *Ibid.*, 37.

suppressed reactions to a hostile world. Moreover, how serious are these visions when their protagonists playfully search for identity by making each story simultaneously a view of reality and a parody of that view?

Briefly analyzed, each of the humorous stories about outcasts, stories concerning human identity developed through play, reveals additional, unexpected affinities. In "The Phantom of the Opera's Friend," the outcast figure is the mythical phantom of the opera. Implored by a close friend, who is the narrator of the story, to leave the underground caverns of the Paris Opera Theater where he has lived in self-exile for forty years, the phantom cannot decide whether to remain in his underground existence or to leave his dungeon to join the respectable life above. The narrator tries to convince his friend that with plastic surgery to transform his grotesque facial appearance he could become a normal citizen, an esteemed musician, or even a husband and father. Still, the phantom decides that giving up the vintage wine he steals from the private cellar of the opera's Board of Directors or the large monthly stipend he extorts from the directors is hardly worth the joys and privileges of normal society, especially because he already savors many of these pleasures by himself in his basement apartment. Superficially, "The Phantom of the Opera's Friend" is a dialogue between conventionality and an alienated critic of conventional society, who has been literally driven underground by his disaffection. The irony of this joke with a vision is that the identity the phantom playfully makes for himself in his underground life, like Burlingame's worship of the horror movies, is as conventional as the world he evades.

"The Temptation of St. Anthony" develops a similar stituation from a slightly different perspective. The hiding man in this story is the Roman Catholic martyr, St. Anthony, who arrives in a contemporary American city of one hundred thousand people to practice his sainthood. The conventionality that he rejects, or that actually rejects him, is the suspicion and bigotry of middle-class America, which has no place for saintliness or miracles within its mundane values. The story of the saint's transgressions in this community is told by a staunchly respectable citizen, who, though sympathetic to St. Anthony's goodness, is a representative voice for the burgher mentality that sanctions individual differences only as long as they do not disrupt the spirit of the community. Soon after St. Anthony arrives, the citizens begin to hound and harass him, attempting to prove that he is a fake or to find some flaw in his holiness. The temptations that originally drove St. Anthony into the desert are thus repeated in this metropolis.

St. Anthony may or may not have put his hand on the leg of an attractive, intellectual woman who was sent to talk to him by local tormentors, but the incident generates so much controversy that he once again banishes himself to the desert. As in "The Phantom of the Opera's Friend," the temptations that the outcast figure cannot resist are those of ordinary bourgeois life. Like the phantom who had to remain hidden underground with all his comforts to maintain his alienated identity, in "The Temptation of St. Anthony," Barthelme's joke with a vision is that a saint must banish himself for commonplace sins to retain his identity as a man who is one of the common people yet somehow superior to them.

The problem posed by the individual who wishes to form a unique identity in a conforming society without assimilating the vulgarized values of this society into his or her individual identity is examined once more in "A City of Churches," the fourth and last identity story in this square. Cecelia, the protagonist, comes to Prester, a perfect town, to manage its only car-rental agency. Discovering that every resident owns a car and therefore no need for a car-rental agency exists, that every building in Prester is a church, and that she must rent an apartment in a church, Cecelia vows to fight the repressive monotony of the town by declaring her own identity. Capable of willing her own dreams, Cecelia decides she will become an outcast in Prester by dreaming sexually licentious, anarchic adventures and recounting them to all those who visit her car-rental agency. In "A City of Churches," as in all four stories on the typology about identity developed through play, Barthelme's amused but highly ambiguous point of view effectively hides the author's attitude to his story, its characters, and its conclusion. Superficially, he would seem to favor Cecelia's resistance to the stifling uniformity and religiosity around her, but Cecelia's only response is to play with the power of her subconscious so as to torment the inhabitants of Prester. Moreover, her solipsistic identity, complete with its sexual fantasies, is just what this physically perfect but psychologically discontented town secretly desires and perhaps one of the reasons it hired her. These fantasies are the conventional alternative to the standardized code which Cecelia mentally escapes. Yet they are certainly inferior to experience itself and just the sort of bourgeois daydreaming in which the Phantom of the Opera or St. Anthony would indulge. "A City of Churches" concludes without clarifying Barthelme's attitude to Cecelia. Is Cecelia a martyr or a dupe, an avenging angel or a source of psychic energy for Prester? This joke with a vision plays with the alternative possibilities of Cecelia's identity without claiming she has developed any one of them.

Critical opinion on Barthelme's attitude in his short stories supports the contention that he wants to hide or evade identity in his own tales. Critic Betty Flowers sees him as such a chameleonlike presence: "Not only is the reader discouraged from making any identification with the characters, but he is also prevented from forming any sort of sympathetic alliance with the narrator. . . . The reader . . . can find neither the center of Barthelme's world nor even Barthelme himself." Flowers likens the relationship between the reader and author to that between a frustrated psychoanalyst and an incoherent patient. The reader cannot maintain the role of analyst because the author does not maintain the role of patient. Aware of a critical observer, Barthelme concocts an elaborate disguise within which he hides his real identity and feeling.[5]

An evasive authorial presence is only one of many qualities that "Hiding Man," "The Phantom of the Opera's Friend," "The Temptation of St. Anthony," and "A City of Churches" share, giving such humor about outcasts numerous common denominators. These tales also possess the parodist's ability to imitate other prose styles.

5. Betty Flowers, "Barthelme's *Snow White*: The Reader-Patient Relationship," *Critique*, XVI (1975), 38.

The style of "The Phantom of the Opera's Friend" mimics Edgar Allan Poe at his most grotesque, and "The Temptation of St. Anthony" is told in the unadorned American vernacular of a character like the narrator in Thornton Wilder's *Our Town*. Yet none of the stories maintains one style. Each has several styles that are continually intruding on one another. In analyzing this quality in Barthelme's tales, Betty Flowers returns to her metaphor of the author as the disturbed patient attempting to hide from his analyst, who is any reader of these stories trying to find meaning and coherence in them. She believes that the clashing styles of any story demonstrate Barthelme's effort to confuse readers and to make their efforts in discovering his attitudes toward his characters an impossibility: "The basic similarity among the different styles lies in the fact that they are all parodies of themselves yet no single style provides an underlying tone to which the reader can orient himself. The object most consistently parodied is the reader-analyst himself, the victim of Barthelme's ever changing but always mocking narrative masks."[6] In these four stories Barthelme is likewise a parodist who mocks the idea of reading a text to determine authorial design. His success is in his ability to elude his reader's search for his characters' strategies and motivations.

The chief aim is play. Barthelme plays with time by bringing one famous phantom and one famous religious martyr out of their own times and into contemporary life. He plays with his reader's credulity by ending a story with the magical transformation of a man into a dog or by envisioning a city in which every building is a church. Science fiction or fantasy is another example of his endeavors to play with his audience, to distance and alienate them from his identity and that of his characters. By perpetually and humorously playing with his outcasts' sense of identity, Barthelme suggests that play, closely associated with evasion and hiding, is an insubstantial and uncertain way to forge a strong, independent sense of the self.

Moving, now, horizontally across our typology, we find "See the

6. *Ibid.*, 39.

Moon," an identity tale developed by the desire to know. The narrator of this collage of memories attempts to know or understand several things about himself. He wonders why his past life appears meaningless in relation to his present and why he suddenly becomes "moonstruck," leaving his wife, child, and job for a new life. He is puzzled by his delight in his impending fatherhood because his previous ambivalence at childrearing and his unsatisfying relationship with his own father might disillusion him. Above all, he cannot explain his continual fascination with science and all fields of knowledge.

Knowing in this tale takes several forms. The narrator attempts to know his life by collecting the fragments into which it has shattered. This process becomes the act of telling the story. Knowing for this narrator is also the process of measuring. The protagonist measures his past against his present and finds few chains of causality between the two. He also measures a priest and close family friend, Cardinal Y, to determine what gives the cardinal his belief. The narrator uses many medical and psychological tests, but to no avail. No scientific test can explain what makes the cardinal a believer. The narrator thus looks to science and religion as bodies of knowledge, as well as using collecting and measuring as tools of knowledge in his efforts to understand himself and others.

Although fragments from various aspects of the narrator's life appear throughout the story in random order, elements of his identity can be easily, if arbitrarily, divided into two groups based on chronology. The first group includes incidents involving past life or family history. In the second group are the narrator's present situations involving his impending fatherhood and the two new branches of knowledge he has invented to help himself understand and appreciate his fatherhood, which he calls "cardinology" and "lunar hostility studies." Cardinology is his study of Roman Catholic cardinals, and his examination of lunar hostility investigates why the moon hates mankind.

The narrator's analysis of some of the fragments from his past leads to and explains his present investigations. Graduating from college with honors and desiring success, the narrator is quickly drafted for the Korean War. His plans for career training sidetracked, he encounters the tedium and meaninglessness of army life. When he returns to the United States from active duty, the narrator's sense of displacement intensifies. Skyscrapers have risen across America, and suburbanites build patios and exude affluence. He goes to the placement office of his alma mater, takes a job writing public relations copy for the university president, and soon discovers that the atmosphere at the university is not as he remembers it from his undergraduate days. The faculty is interested in drinking and social climbing, and the students pursue suntans and athletics. Nonetheless, he settles into a job writing speeches full of double-talk for the president, marries, and has one child. One day, after a few years of a stultifying existence, he is suddenly moonstruck.

Plagued by the disparity between what he intended for his life and what it has become, and tormented by the changes in history that have made the phases of his life so incompatible, the narrator sees through the hollowness and corruption of his life. He becomes lightheaded, divorces his wife, and quits his job. He begins to spend hours observing the moon while collecting the pieces of his disintegrated life so as to know and understand who he is. This collection of fragments is the story the narrator presents to the reader.

All of the events in the story are told from a point years after the narrator's first contact with moonlight. By this time he has remarried and, expecting a second child by his second wife, is reminded of his troubled relationship with his son Gregory and his combative relationship with his own father. His father, a flagmaker for third world nations and once a cheerleader at a great eastern university, staunchly believes in school spirit, patriotism, and a pragmatism that sells to emerging countries the colored flags of their choice. The narrator finds his father's beliefs anachronistic, inconsistent, and completely fraudulent. Yet he differs with his own son nearly as much as he does with his father. Gregory is a curious MIT student, who believes that science will eventually solve man's problems, whereas the narrator argues that science, despite his own attraction to it, is as fallible as the men who enlarge its boundaries. Fighting both son and father because he cannot believe the ideals they represent, the narrator wonders why he once again rejoices over his impending fatherhood and what remains in the world for him and his new child to believe in together.

This search for belief prompts the narrator's obsessive investigations of cardinology and his lunar hostility studies in the last third of "See the Moon." The narrator's fascination with science and all forms of knowledge, even bogus sciences of his own invention, derives from his desire to forge an identity from his beliefs and knowledge. He carefully examines a Catholic priest, Cardinal Y, who is an old friend, in an effort to discover what causes the priest to believe. If he can scientifically isolate this factor, perhaps he can transmit it to himself and his newborn child. The narrator scrupulously measures the cardinal's response to a battery of medical and psychological tests as well as some tests of his own devising, such as the Minnesota Multiphastic Muzzle Map for ego strength.[7] These inventions satirize contemporary psychology's efforts to know and measure the unmeasurable. Here the narrator's measuring seeks the legitimacy of modern scientific procedure.

The tests given Cardinal Y offer no scientific explanation for his belief. In response to the protagonist's earlier questioning, the cardinal replies that everything that occurs in the world is accidental. Yet the cardinal's good works and faith belie his remark. Ultimately, there is no scientific or religious explanation for belief, knowledge, or identity. Likewise, the narrator's lunar hostility studies ridicule a further perversion of human knowledge. "See the moon, it hates us," says the narrator.[8] He is moonstruck because he realizes that the moon, once an object of romantic contemplation, has become the subject of scientific investigation and conquest. The moon, like humanity, has been subjected to every imaginable form of scientific inquiry, and yet we know no more about the moon, or ourselves, as a source of wonder than before science intervened. The narrator's tests and questions have developed the sciences of cardinology and lunar hostility for other men to pursue, but science and religion,

7. Donald Barthelme, "See the Moon," in *Unspeakable Practices, Unnatural Acts* (New York, 1968), 167.
8. *Ibid.*, 156.

like collecting and measuring, are limited, partial ways of knowing the self or establishing an identity.

Such detailed recounting of the contents of "See the Moon" is still insufficient to analyze the story thoroughly. Like all stories about identity developed through the desire to know, "See the Moon" is a collage, and Barthelme's collages gain their meaning more from their form and the relationship between their elements than from their surface content. Barthelme sees collage as a pasting together of unlike fragments of reality to form a new, completely original object. The narrator of "See the Moon" describes this technique while using it to tell the story of his life. He hopes that his life will become an abstract expressionist mosaic composed of the souvenirs he is collecting from the beliefs that have failed or eluded him. In the passage below, Sylvia, the narrator's first wife, symbolizes all the narrator believed before he was moonstruck, and Cardinal Y's red hat represents his inability to know what makes certain men believe:

It's my hope that these . . . souvenirs . . . will someday merge, blur—cohere is the word, maybe—into something meaningful. A grand word, meaningful. What do I look for? A work of art, I'll not accept anything less. Yes I know it's shatteringly ingenious, but I wanted to be a painter. They get away with murder in my view. Mr. X on the Times agrees with me. You don't know how I envy them. They can pick up a Baby Ruth wrapper on the street, glue it to the canvas (in the right place, of course, there's that) and lo! people crowd about and cry, "A real Baby Ruth wrapper, by God, what could be realer than that!" Fantastic metaphysical advantage. You hate them, if you're ambitious. The Ant Farm instructors are a souvenir of Sylvia. The red hat came from Cardinal Y. We're friends in a way. I wanted to be one, when I was young, a painter. But I couldn't stand stretching the canvas. Does things to the fingernails. And that's the first place people look. Fragments are the only forms I trust.[9]

Since many of the incidents in "See the Moon" parallel incidents in Barthelme's life, and fragmentation, in some form, occurs in a large number of Barthelme's stories, the temptation arises to make fragmentation the central force of Barthelme's aesthetics. Furthermore, like the narrator of "See the Moon," he is a writer who has

9. *Ibid.*, 156–57.

refused to stretch the canvas of his art, to put his short stories into the neat containers that the conventions of short-story form and practice have previously dictated. Yet in a published interview he has emphatically denied that the artistic opinions of the narrator of "See the Moon" belong to anyone but that character in those circumstances.[10] Fragmentation, he suggests, is the vision of the individual who once believed in grand designs and guiding principles that have been made worthless by time and change. Fragmentation is the final vision of all his characters, who, in attempting to know themselves, eventually discover that they can only hope to know pieces and elements of their identity or their world. As the narrator of "See the Moon" expresses this phenomenon, "Here is the world and here are the knowledgeable knowers knowing. What can I tell you? What has been pieced together from the reports of travelers. Fragments are the only forms I trust."[11]

As the language of "See the Moon" demonstrates the futility of knowing anything but fragments of the self or the world, the language of the story also specifies that measuring as a tool of knowledge, and science and religion as areas of knowledge, will not enable men to know themselves or others with certainty. After applying an elaborate range of physical and psychological tests to Cardinal Y, and carefully measuring the results, the narrator still does not know Cardinal Y, nor can he explain why this man has chosen to believe. Moreover, the narrator begins to understand his relationship to the priest only after his scientific efforts to examine the man have failed. The narrator suspects that, in trying to know the cardinal, he has partially assumed his role so as to become a model of belief for his infant son. The narrator explains the process in the midst of collecting the fragments of his life: "Cardinal Y. One can measure and measure and miss the most essential thing. I liked him. I still get the odd blessing in the mail now and then. Too, maybe I was trying on the role. Not for myself. When a child is born, the focus of one's hopes . . . shifts slightly. Not altogether, not all at once. But you feel it, this displacement. You speak up, strike

10. Klinkowitz, "Donald Barthelme," 53.
11. Barthelme, "Moon," 157.

attitudes, like the mother of a tiny Lollobrigida. Drunk with possibility once more."[12] This passage explains the one remaining mystery of the narrator's life: his inexplicable joy in becoming a father again even though he and his first child are frequently at odds. Children create hope for the future, and the narrator feels his entire identity shifting to accommodate the possibilities that a child engenders. Identity, the narrator discovers, is not a static concept but a dynamic, evolving entity. Likewise, his effort to know his identity is a demanding and unending struggle.

Such effort to know occurs also in the two remaining stories of this group, "Views of My Father Weeping" and "Brain Damage." All three are collages piecing out identity and are characterized by a satirical tone that questions whether self-knowledge is possible. All three depict a world so divided and torn by change and conflict that fragments of reality or the self may be the only forms an individual can know or assimilate. To analyze "Views of My Father Weeping" and "Brain Damage" as related types is to see Barthelme's stylistic fragmentation not only as the deconstruction of reality but also as a possible reconstruction of it. The narrators of these stories have to place the jagged pieces of their lives together in unusual juxtapositions and nonchronological order to see patterns, unity, and their identities emerge although, chronologically, only chaos is apparent. Many readers and critics have clearly misunderstood Barthelme's purposes. Joyce Carol Oates, for example, in the June 4, 1972, *New York Times Book Review* attacked Barthelme's fragmentation and stereotyped his fiction as lacking design or purpose:

Fragments are the only form I trust. This from a writer of arguable genius whose works reflect what he himself must feel, in book after book, that his brain is all fragments . . . just like everything else. Passive, drifting, witty, melancholy—hilarious, surrealist (though nearly seven decades have passed since Alfred Jarry wrote "Ubi Roi") . . . even the construction of his sentence is symptomatic of his role: It begins with "fragments," the stern healthy noun and concludes with the weak "I." But there is a point in history at which Wilde's remark comes horribly true, that life will imitate art. And then who is in charge, who believed himself cleverly impotent, who

12. *Ibid.*, 168.

supposed he had abdicated all conscious design. . . ? If you refuse to make choices, someone else will make them for you.[13]

Oates's moralistic attack not only makes the simplistic mistake of identifying the narrator of "See the Moon" with Barthelme, but her criticism refuses to acknowledge that a fragmented vision of reality may be an artistic, meaningful, and carefully composed vision as well. This view does injustice to a writer who places the fragments of his collages with great care, ensuring that the pieces produce original vision. Consistent with his practice, Barthelme, in a published interview, defines the best collages as subtle, complicated works of art: "The point of collage is that unlike things are stuck together to make in the best case, a new reality. This new reality, in the best case, may be or imply a comment on the reality from which it came, and may be also much else."[14]

Both "Views of My Father Weeping" and "Brain Damage" create the new reality that Barthelme envisions here. They are responses to identities known, at best, by a careful reconstruction of their elements. First "Views of My Father Weeping" and then "Brain Damage," discussed in this manner, show their affinities to "See the Moon," and all three define a form of Barthelme collage recurrent throughout his short stories.

"Views of My Father Weeping" takes two different but related situations and shuffles and reshuffles them on the page until some form of new reality emerges. One of these elements is the narrative of a protagonist's search for the aristocrat whose carriage ran down his father and left his corpse on the roadway. The narrative has the language and style of an English translation of such nineteenth-century Russian realist writers as Ivan Turgenev or Nikolai Gogol. This thread of the story is continually interrupted by another voice, that of a contemporary Texan, who sees his father in various tableaux in which the man is weeping or assuming childish, histrionic poses. This modern speaker describes a senile, pathetic old man who sticks his fingers into freshly iced cupcakes and amuses him-

13. Joyce Carol Oates, "Whose Side Are You On?" *New York Times Book Review*, June 4, 1972, p. 63.

14. Klinkowitz, "Donald Barthelme," 51–52.

self by shooting a water pistol into the air. Both of these collage elements ask the same unanswered questions: how can a son ever know his father, and how can one know his own identity? Both voices attempt to answer the questions by searching others or themselves for memories of their fathers.

After an intricate hunt, the first narrator locates the coachman whose coach and horses ran down his father. The coachman's account is that the narrator's father attacked his coach and team in a drunken frenzy, causing his own slaughter. As the coachman completes his account, a beautiful, dark-haired woman turns to the narrator and tells him that this tale is a total fabrication. At precisely this point, "Views of My Father Weeping" ends. The structure of the first narrator's story, even with its consistent interruption by the other voice, has the blind alleys, false clues, and sudden revelations of a detective novel, without the corresponding resolution. Just as the narrator never learns whether his father's death was self-inflicted, or whether his father was the drunken, enraged man the coachman claims, the narrator's gravest fear remains unconfirmed: he wonders if he resembles his father and contains the same capacities for drunkenness and anger. As in "See the Moon" and all Barthelme's collages, the attempt to know others and the self is folly. The fear that the son may become the father is the factor that links both halves. The Texan feels pain and embarrassment at his father's ridiculous pranks and antics. His contradictory desires to help the old man, to implore him to stop performing, and to remove him from his sight are all signs of the speaker's identification with his father and his anxiety that one day he may be a facsimile of this buffoon. Nonetheless, the son's refusal to accept the father as he appears is symptomatic of his inability to accept himself. As in other of Barthelme's collages, knowing another individual or seeing elements of one's own identity in another is not a guarantee of self-knowledge or self-acceptance.

Acknowledging that both threads of this collage are linked does not necessarily form the new reality that Barthelme desires for the best of his collages. What makes "Views of My Father Weeping" an original art work in collage form is the author's ability to distance and neutralize its painful personal experience within an interpolated literary style. One-half of this story is the anguish a garrulous, senile old man causes his son, interspersed among episodes of a Chekhovian detective story in which a potentially drunken, self-destructive son searches for the cause of his drunken, self-destructive father's death. Barthelme believes neither half of the divided son can ever know his father because each contains his father's warring possibilities. In searching for the causes of a father's ruin, both men invariably run from the sources of their own destiny. Only by carefully placing two fathers and two sons from vastly different times and social milieus side by side in collage form can Barthelme reveal what neither son can know about his own identity.

A Barthelme collage can thus reconstruct as well as deconstruct reality. "Views of My Father Weeping" satirizes individuals' efforts to understand their identities while parodying the styles and conventions of Russian realist writing and the detective story, the two elements of its collage effect. Pulling apart only to pull together, "Views of My Father Weeping" suggests that men in completely unrelated societies share the grief of the father's weeping and the grief of their own tears.

If "Views of My Father Weeping" is a fabric woven from two strands of narrative or situation, "Brain Damage," from *City Life* (1970), is a collage composed of at least three elements. The most important of these is the voice of the narrator of the prose segments of the story, an individual attempting to know his own identity and to separate it from the collective, engulfing force of contemporary society. This voice comments on at least three aspects of contemporary society: the role of the humanist in the modern world; the relationship between truth and identity; and the hierarchical, servile nature of many men and women in society. Intersecting the narrator's concerns, which are most frequently expressed as vignettes or anecdotes, are two other strands of the collage. The first is the large boldface printing of the collective activities by which society drowns individual identity or initiative. Some of these activities include MURMURING, YAWNING, RHYTHMIC HAND-CLAPPING, and SEXUAL ACTIVITY. These words and phrases interrupt the narrator's anecdotes with periodic regularity and are printed in groups of three and four at each interruption. Alternating with these activities and the narrator's incidents is the third element of the collage, Barthelme's ink engravings taken from nineteenth-century designer source books. Here we find pictures of human heads severed from their bodies and crying out in misery, several complete bodies chained to a rock and one another, a woman seated in an armchair covering her head in grief, and children playing at blindman's buff. Paralleling the collective social responses in boldface type, each of these pictures suggests paralysis, the atrophy of the senses, or physical and psychological inertia. Using both verbal and visual elements, "Brain Damage" is a sketcher's as well as a writer's collage.

The central question "Brain Damage" raises is how a humanist can know and declare his identity amid the chaos of modern life. In the opening prose segment of the story, the narrator acknowledges that he is deeply concerned about his fellow man, but rather than state his specific views he chooses to stay in what he calls that gray area where nothing is done but one endlessly vacillates, thinking about the problem. Already the reader can sense an equivocation on the part of the narrator, who is so overwhelmed by the complexity of the issues confronting him that he wishes to ponder rather than take a position on them. At this point in his considerations, the narrator is interrupted by Barthelme's insertion of four collective responses: CROWD NOISES, MURMURING, MURMURING, YAWNING. This juxtaposition of elements of the collage creates additional meaning here. Society will dilute individual beliefs within its generalized roar of opinion unless the individual resists and defines his identity by acting on his beliefs. The responses in boldface type are immediately followed by an ink drawing of three woeful heads resting on pedestals. The picture dramatizes the plight of the head severed from the body, endless speculation disassociated from action. As critic Josephine Hendin has observed, "Brain Damage" is about the destruction of the individual consciousness; and Barthelme fluidly uses not only the three elements of this collage but also the meanings he creates from the juxtapositions between them to depict the society always waiting to devour individuality and the fate of those individuals who have been devoured.[15]

The narrator of the prose segments of "Brain Damage" is concerned not only with his identity as a humanist but also with his ability to know truth from lies. In one of the narrator's segments he recalls his days as a newspaper reporter and his failure to report the truth. This fragment of collage is quickly followed by society's responses to his dilemma—RHYTHMIC HANDCLAPPING and SLEEPING—and then by a drawing of figures resembling Greek statues chained to a rock and to one another. This quick succession of images apparently gives the narrator two options. Since society is bored by the search for truth and reacts to it with sleep or perfunctory applause, the narrator must either value truth and ignore society or become enslaved to its false values, as have the chained figures. Not coincidentally, the anecdotes the narrator tells in his prose sections are filled with individuals who are enslaved to their jobs and to other human beings. The narrator tells stories of waiters passing large tips to headwaiters and of elevator girls passing expensive gifts among themselves. Social obligations and confusions are so great in the distorted world depicted in "Brain Damage" that the narrator or any reader has great difficulty knowing what, if anything, is a meaningful reaction.

The total effect of reading "Brain Damage" is to experience a world in which humane values or respect for individuality is completely absorbed by the noise and confusion of the crowd and by its collective social impulses. The narrator of the story finds knowledge of his identity, his society, and the relationship between the two impossible to fathom in a world in which social values continually intrude on individual thought and action. In "Brain Damage" form becomes content, and Barthelme cleverly uses collage to illustrate the chaos of a world forever divided between the self, others, and the behavior found acceptable by the masses. The story therefore satirizes individual efforts to know the self or one's place

15. Josephine Hendin, "Angries: S-M as a Literary Style," *Harper's*, February, 1974, p. 89.

in society as well as the impossible situation of an artist, who, like Barthelme, in wanting to attack the disease becomes infected by it. The curious irony of the story is that one cannot know the truth about brain damage or renounce it without becoming contaminated by it. As the narrator acknowledges, "Brain damage caused by art. I could describe it better if I weren't afflicted with it."[16]

Unlike "See the Moon," in which the narrator uses collage to attempt to put the pieces of his life together, or "Views of My Father Weeping," in which Barthelme places the relationship between two sets of fathers and sons so that the reader can know what fathers and sons can never know, "Brain Damage" denies that its pieces of reality can ever cohere. "Brain Damage" dramatizes the disassociation of a society divided between the primal responses of collective social behavior—MURMURING, HANDCLAPPING, CONSUMPTION OF FOOD—the moans and grimaces of individuals who are totally dependent on social gesture and approval, and the vacillating, humane individuals who know so much they cannot act. In "Brain Damage" the effort to know does not put the fragments of modern life together but insists on their continued separation.

Still within the realm of the identity story, we move on to a new technique, that of the realization of identity by repetition of a common experience. The major story analyzed here, "Me and Miss Mandible," from *Come Back, Dr. Caligari* (1964), appears on the horizontal axis of the identity stories under the process of repetition. "Me and Miss Mandible," like the other three stories in its box on the typology, is a tale about the educational process developed in a static, plotless manner. Repetition in these stories is a return to the past, and in each tale Barthelme examines a common past experience, such as grade school or military training, as a learning experience. He concludes that education is a vast system of signs that promises rewards only to renege on its promises. Education in these stories is a trap, which commits individuals to the repetition of patterns of behavior that do not necessarily lead any-

16. Donald Barthelme, "Brain Damage," in *City Life* (New York, 1970), 146.

where. These stories examine identity as this series of repetitions, and these tales become static in their repetitions of the processes the protagonists undergo in achieving their education.

In "Me and Miss Mandible," the narrator, a thirty-five-year-old insurance adjustor, is fired by his boss when he files a claim in favor of an elderly policyholder rather than the insurance company she is suing. The narrator's boss, Mr. Goodykind, believes the narrator's action demonstrates a basic failure to understand the insurance business and the pragmatic American values on which it is based. Accordingly, Mr. Goodykind arranges for the narrator to be sent back to a sixth-grade classroom and to repeat his secondary education so he can be schooled once again in the values an adult needs to survive in competitive American society. The narrator of the story is pleased with Mr. Goodykind's unusual effort because he believes that his return to the sixth grade will reveal where he has gone wrong. The comic technique of "Me and Miss Mandible" thus juxtaposes the narrator's attempts to appear as a child among children with his vivid memories of his failures as an adult in the adult world. In the process the narrator discovers that his adult life has not foundered because he rejected the skills and beliefs of the educational system, but rather that he has been proved incompetent because the teachings he learned all too well are inadequate to confront adult life. The protagonist of "Me and Miss Mandible," by repeating one stage of his miseducation, soon sees that the values of his teacher, Miss Mandible, and his classmates are as empty as those of the Great Northern Insurance Company. Moreover, the failure of his life and his identity, like those of so many adults of his generation, is not in rejecting or ignoring the lessons of his education but in futilely attempting to apply them to reality.

Not surprisingly, the static and reductive quality of a story in which a man repeats his past makes "Me and Miss Mandible" a tale with little narrative development. The narrator describes the daily routine of sixth grade life: the calling of the class roll, the studying of fractions, and the longing glances that Miss Mandible gives him, suggesting that she knows the narrator is a man and not a child. As the days drag by, the narrator lives in anticipation of what will happen when Miss Mandible eventually succumbs to his adult sexuality. When Miss Mandible's passions finally erupt in the cloakroom, another student is a witness to the event and reports her teacher and fellow student to the principal. Pleading guilty to being seduced, the narrator argues that he is to blame because he is as much an adult as a child. Yet even this episode does not cause the narrator's final expulsion from the classroom. Barthelme has not devised a means to end "Me and Miss Mandible," which is the point of the story. Sentenced to the tedium of a representative American education because he could not function in adult society, the narrator must repeat the experience of the classroom endlessly or until he learns to ignore its lessons. These same lessons in their straightforward earnestness and moral oversimplification doomed him to failure originally.

The irony of the series of repetitions that occur in "Me and Miss Mandible" is that one variety proves no more constructive than another. Mr. Goodykind, the narrator's boss, hopes to stop the pattern of failure and defeat that has plagued the narrator's adult life by returning him to grade school and instilling in him a pattern of schoolboy pragmatism and naive optimism. The narrator, on his second trip through, begins to see that this determination to apply a system of right and wrong, rewards and punishments, to the complexities of life has caused entire generations of Americans to lose a sense of identity. The narrator craves the reeducation that he believes will solve his problems while sensing that this education is what has caused them.

A ruined marriage, a ruined adjusting career, a grim interlude in the Army when I was almost not a person. This is the sum of my existence to date, a dismal total. Small wonder that reeducation seemed my only hope. It is clear even to me that I needed reworking in some fundamental way. How efficient is the society that provides thus for the salvage of its clinkers!

Plucked from my unexamined life among other pleasant, desperate, money-making young Americans, thrown backward in space and time, I am beginning to understand how I went wrong, how we all go wrong. (Although this was far from the intention of those who sent me here; they require only that I get right.)[17]

17. Barthelme, "Me and Miss Mandible," in *Come Back, Dr. Caligari*, 107–108.

The perpetually circular, repetitive nature of the narrator's dilemma—finding a cure to his failure that is itself the cause of the failure—forces him into a more systematic analysis of his own failings and the misconceptions of individuals he has known in his lives as a sixth grader and as an insurance adjustor. The narrator observes the constant confusions of Miss Mandible; a fellow student, Sue Ann Brownly; his wife, Brenda; and Mr. Goodykind. Like himself, all of these individuals have been conditioned to respond to signs that frequently fail to bring them the rewards they have been taught to expect. The narrator's recognition that many of the signs on which he and others act are not reliable is the great discovery of his return to the sixth grade. By returning to grade school the narrator learns to distrust education and the promise that any sign offers.

We read signs as promises. Miss Mandible understands by my great height, by my resonant vowels that I will one day carry her off to bed. Sue Ann interprets these same signs to mean that I am unique among her male acquaintances, therefore most desirable, therefore her special property as is everything that is Most Desirable. If neither of these propositions works out then life has broken faith with them.

I myself in my former existence, read the company motto ("Here to Help in Times of Need") as a description of the duty of the adjustor, drastically mislocating the company's deepest concerns. I believed that because I had obtained a wife who was made of wife-signs (beauty, charm, softness, perfume, cookery) I had found love. Brenda, reading the same signs that have now misled Miss Mandible and Sue Ann Brownly, felt she had been promised that she would never be bored again. All of us, Miss Mandible, Sue Ann, myself, Brenda, Mr. Goodykind, still believe that the American flag betokens a kind of general righteousness.

But I say, looking about me in this incubator of future citizens, that signs are signs, and that some of them are lies. This is the great discovery of my time here.[18]

In "Me and Miss Mandible" the narrator is trapped between a reductive, static pattern of repeating his adult failures or relearning the childish values that will ensure more failure. Returning to his past, he realizes that his education is useless and that many

18. *Ibid.*, 109.

signs are lies. Therefore, the narrator is left without any legitimate means of establishing his identity or determining that of those around him.

Correspondingly, a great source of confusion in the narrator's life is his conception of love. In one of the best articles on Barthelme's use and interpretation of signs, John Leland investigates the link between the narrator's idea of love and the false signs of love that society provides for mass consumption. Leland uses a sentence from the quoted passage of "Me and Miss Mandible" just above to make his point:

"I believed that because I had obtained a wife who was made up of wife-signs (beauty, charm, softness, perfume, cookery) I had found love." (MM, 81) With the sign, with the process of signifying love, something has gone wrong. In the sometimes melancholy humor of this and other of Barthelme sentences, we sense an alienation from historical/cultural signifieds, an intimation that some things are no longer plausible, including the standard and conventional signs offered up for our consumption by contemporary culture. Between the promise and the lie of signs lies the play space of Barthelme's fictions.[19]

From this excerpt Leland sees Barthelme as an author who fears that the modern ego may well be destroyed by unlimited numbers of false signs and clues which the individual cannot absorb or digest. The irony of this contemporary dilemma, which Leland fully acknowledges, is that the short story, the book, and literature itself are networks of signs that are lies as well. One of the purposes of Barthelme's attention to signs and clues throughout his fiction is to reshape his reader's conceptions of those formalized lies known as literary conventions and to offer literary techniques and devices that are more mimetic approximations of reality. If reality deluges the individual with false signs and if literature merely reproduces them, where does meaning reside in life or literature? Leland feels this is one of Barthelme's central questions:

Although literature as rationalized within the institution of the Book is assaulted by Barthelme, the assault is also a form of liberation; for litera-

19. John Leland, "Remarks Re-marked: What Curious of Signs!" *Boundary 2*, V (Spring, 1977), 796–811.

ture, if we accept Barthelme's epistemology, can never be a thing like a stone—resilient, self-contained, closed to becoming. Neither is literature a proprietary right of the author of special sensibilities, vision, imagination, etc. Instead, literature is a constituted object of our understanding, a making of a way-to-be-of remarks, a way of reading and deciphering signs. And in a special way—within the mode of irony—Barthelme opens up to us a new way of reading signs, including the sign literature. By subverting the quietude of meaning, Barthelme's writing poses to us again and again the same question—What fixes, determines, or delineates meaning?[20]

Rather than regarding "Me and Miss Mandible" as a story about a man returned to his past, Leland's interpretation suggests that Barthelme sees the story as the experience of many individuals who arrive at blocks in their lives because their past educations prove worthless and many of the signs they have been taught to believe fail them. This paradigm of experience applies as well to the dilemmas of the protagonists of "See the Moon" and "Hiding Man," the major identity stories on the typology analyzed earlier. As Leland contends, Barthelme refuses to see his short stories as linear structures defined by pages and print; rather, he wishes them to be experienced as open-ended explorations of the uncertainty of the signs that bombard many lives. Similarly, he offers his readers a dimensional concept of character. The self need not be a rigidly defined, permanent entity but can become a fluid, adaptable force that is highly sensitive to the pressures of its environment. The protagonist of "Me and Miss Mandible" becomes trapped because he cannot develop new responses either to his present or his past. As Leland states, Barthelme believes human identity should not be a book, a self-enclosed text, but should become a dynamic, evolving organism capable of change and flexibility. Without these qualities, individuals are doomed to the despairing cycles of repetition the protagonist suffers: "I take the right steps, obtain correct answers, and my wife leaves me for another man."[21] Clearly, Barthelme sees repetition, however prevalent a way of solving problems in our society, as an insufficient means to establish one's identity.

Next analyzing the three stories in the same box on the typology

20. *Ibid.*, 807.
21. Barthelme, "Mandible," 110.

as "Me and Miss Mandible"—"The Sergeant," "The School," and "The Educational Experience"—we see that not only are all four stories concerned with a definition of human identity misdeveloped through repetitive actions, but that each story deals with the educational process and unfolds in a static, unchanging manner. The similarities between these stories do not end here. Each demonstrates how the misuse of education can misshape an individual's expectations of reality and his future. All of the stories illustrate the role of authority in educational experiences and see power and intimidation as means of keeping human beings as perpetual children. Most consistently, the stories reveal that a return to the past could never correct the errors of the present. The solution to current failure is to break from the continual patterns of repetition in which the protagonists of these stories are trapped and to live, not in the past or the present modeled on the past, but now. Briefly interpreting first "The Sergeant," next "The School," and last "The Educational Experience" displays the stories' affinities to one another and to "Me and Miss Mandible," as well as the pattern of frustration in attempting to establish an identity through repetitive acts.

"The Sergeant" is the story most like "Me and Miss Mandible." In this tale the protagonist is mysteriously returned to a southern army post from which he was honorably discharged twenty years earlier and is forced to resume the responsibilities and drudgeries of an army sergeant's routine. He trains recruits, teaching them how to pull the pin from their hand grenades and how to keep a barracks clean. Yet he is subject to the same harassment and orders from officers that he gives to enlisted men. The lieutenant of his training company convinces the sergeant that their relationship will remain friendly if the sergeant lends him fifty dollars, for example; and when the sergeant forges a weekend pass, as all the recruits in his barracks have done, he is caught by two MPs and sent back to the company headquarters because the razor in his AWOL bag is dirty. The sergeant is both an authority figure like Miss Mandible and a figure trammeled by authority like her students. Unlike the narrator of "Me and Miss Mandible," the sergeant does not know why he has returned to an existence he hated, but twenty years have passed since his initial time in the military and he is now forty-five. Insisting that a huge mistake has been made and that he will be discharged once the error is discovered, the sergeant is clearly a man stuck between his past fears of authority and a present life that is allowing those past fears to tyrannize him.

The final vignette of "The Sergeant" dramatizes the desperate nature of the sergeant's impasse. Ordered by a commanding officer to open fire on a civilian walking through the company area, the sergeant refuses to comply with this purposeless directive. The officer gives the sergeant an alternative order: he must stuff eight hundred thousand cans of olives with cocktail onions for the general's martinis. Allergic to onions, aghast at the incalculable boredom of the task, the sergeant is nonetheless stuffing olives as the story concludes. Locked between a detestable role and a ludicrously demeaning one, or between his past and his present, the sergeant chooses his present, which is no choice at all but merely a repetition of the same static compliance with orders and authority that has always motivated him. Real freedom for the sergeant would be to choose neither role, to violate the orders and authorities that he has been educated to fear, and so to establish his own identity.

In "The School" the reader hears a voice similar to that of Miss Mandible. The narrator, Edgar, is a smiling, officious grade-school teacher who relates how every group of plants or animals that the children in his class attempt to nurture has died. As the narrator's story unfolds, we see that a repetitive pattern of mishap and death has spread from the plants and animals to a Korean child the class adopts through the Help the Children Program, even to an extraordinary number of parents of children in the class. After two of the children's own classmates die when some wooden beams fall on them at a building site, the class demands that Edgar explain why everything around them is dying.

Edgar is a teacher totally unable to answer his students' question. Essentially a nervous, petty bureaucrat, Edgar follows his lesson plans at all costs. Even when he suspects that the snakes and tropical fish on the agenda for class study cannot survive the under-heated classroom, or the puppy the class names Edgar will surely die in its makeshift house in the supply closet, Edgar smiles and continues teaching. Knowing the truth, Edgar is an authority figure who refuses to share knowledge with his students, who desires to keep them children for as long as possible. Edgar is an insidious tyrant, who actually believes he acts in his students' best interests. Paranoid about criticism of the school, his class, or his teaching, Edgar is the symbol of all that is deadening and stagnant in a standardized, preprocessed education. Edgar is the death that stalks his classroom.

With death everywhere and no explanation coming from the teacher, Edgar's students ask him for some assertion of value. They ask Edgar to show some sign of love for Helen, the attractive teaching assistant who works in the classroom. He begins to embrace Helen but is interrupted by a knock at the door. Edgar opens the door, and to the delight of the class, finds a new pet gerbil, which walks into his classroom. This conclusion to the story is another example of Edgar's ability to manipulate his class. As a man frightened of his own emotions, particularly his sexual emotions, Edgar wants to discontinue making love to Helen and, once more, to start the class on its series of live collections that previously have ended in so many deaths. Edgar's discovery of the gerbil in his doorway epitomizes the ability of death-obsessed education to repeat and reinforce itself endlessly under the command of a domineering teacher. Edgar's only identity is his continual, static repetition of the lessons that contaminate and kill everything in the classroom, from the smallest house plant to the children themselves.

Whereas the speaker of "The School" brings death to his grade school classroom, the voice that narrates "The Educational Experience" describes the deadening process of mechanized, assembly-line college education. In this story college matriculation is reduced to students passing through a cultural museum and quickly stopping at the booths and exhibits that momentarily divert their attention. As if on a conveyor belt, a steady stream of students continually passes in and out. Emotionless, void of any sustained interest in the cultural artifacts, scientific inventions, and reproductions of historical events before them, the students are told that these objects will make them more beautiful or more employable once their tour is finished. "The Educational Experience" describes a process—static, unchanging, and hopelessly sterile. The story attacks the modern failure of the imagination that has turned colleges into factories and students into automatons, wearily proceeding through rote steps to receive degrees and jobs.

The narrator of "The Educational Experience," who functions as the traffic director of this academic shopping mall, personifies the imaginative bankruptcy of this world. He presides over an educational wasteland that has been further gutted by the enormous explosion in the quantity of human knowledge. So much information exists in the rubbish heap of contemporary civilization that educators as well as their students are at a loss how to correlate facts and ideas into a synthesis. The narrator thus coddles the students, promising them exciting rewards and favors if they do the work he avoids and establish relationships between the miscellaneous data in the museum: "Here is a diode, learn what to do with it. Here is Du Guesclin, constable of France 1370–80—learn what to do with him. A divan is either a long cushioned seat or a council of state—figure out at what times it is what. Certainly you can have your dangerous drugs, but only for dessert—first you must chew your cauliflower, finish your fronds."[22] In describing this museum, the narrator also describes the modern world beyond it in which nothing connects with nothing.

Lacking the necessary understanding of their chaotic society to teach the students to comprehend the world, the narrator and the directors of "The Educational Experience" attempt to replace a meaningful education with a highly energized one. They transform their pupils' trip through their funhouse into a multimedia experience, which incorporates elements of military basic training and of the grade school playground with smatterings of the classics, nuclear physics, and Dante added for good measure: "Oh, they were

22. Donald Barthelme, "The Educational Experience," in *Amateurs* (New York, 1976), 126.

happy going through the exercises and we told them to keep their tails down as they crawled under the wire, the wire was a string of quotations, Tacitus, Herodotus, Pindar. . . . Then the steady-state cosmologists, Bondi, Gold, and Hoyle, had to be leaped over, the students had to swing from tree to tree in the Dark Wood, rappel down the sheer face of the Merzbau, engage in unarmed combat with the Van de Graaff machine, sew stocking masks. See? Unimpaired vitality."[23] This passage exudes the pride of a teacher who has made his students' mastery of unrelated pieces of knowledge in different disciplines into a series of track events. This instructor is delighted with his ability to make such difficult study so palatable and attractive. The passage also reveals an educational philosophy interested in visible results and physical sweat and indifferent to intellectual stimulation.

Every aspect of the narrator's view of education is practical. Lines are particularly long at the exhibits he devises to teach the students how to put stamps on letters, how to take out the garbage, and how to use the on-off switch and the belt buckle. If the story satirizes educational institutions that instruct adolescents in frills without providing them with basic knowledge, it also ridicules curricula that offer students the opposite trend: absurdly rudimentary courses, such as finger painting or personal growth, that might be worthy of summer camp or Transactional Analysis but seem hardly suitable for college credit.

After being herded through this educational environment, the students are finally as pragmatic and cynical as their instructor. As they approach the rear entrance of the museum, a noticeable change occurs in their instructor's lesson. He suggests that they learn the values of relaxation and spontaneity as guides to a satisfying life. The students' reaction is to smirk at the uselessness of these virtues. They sneer at qualities that will not make them more prosperous, attractive, healthy, or clever. Their teacher is a Dr. Frankenstein, who has molded monsters. When they laugh or display an emotion different from what he has recommended, he becomes as

23. *Ibid.*

defensive as Edgar or Miss Mandible, accusing them of defying their entire educational experience.

"The Educational Experience" is a sad parable on the vulgarity of much present-day higher education. Like "Me and Miss Mandible," "The Educational Experience" is about the relationship between a corrupt, confused society and the education that trains individuals for it. Both stories contend that many of the signs we are taught in school are lies. By honoring those signs in adult life, we merely reinforce the social degeneration that has deeply infected the educational process.

The typology contains one more major identity story to be analyzed. "A Shower of Gold" is a story about identity located on the vertical axis of stories developed through the process of creativity. Like the other two stories in its box on the typology, "Daumier" and "Engineer-Private Paul Klee Misplaces an Aircraft between Milbertshofen and Cambrai, March 1916," "A Shower of Gold" concerns artistic creativity that ultimately expresses an affirmative, optimistic perception of experience. "A Shower of Gold" and related stories contend that an individual cannot merely play with conceptions of the self, attempt to know what cannot be known, or endure an endless series of repetitive actions to establish the self. Rather than being discovered through any one of these processes, the self can be created only with a method that uses each of these aspects of play, knowing, and repetition. Anyone can become an artist of his own life by creating a vision of reality and then affirming this vision in his daily actions. This goal is precisely what the protagonists of "A Shower of Gold" and the other two stories about creative identity achieve. Analyzing the three stories individually reveals the creation of the self to be Barthelme's most affirmative and successful method for finding an identity in which one can live and grow.

"A Shower of Gold" is the most self-consciously absurd of all Barthelme's stories about identity. Hank Peterson, the protagonist, is a starving sculptor. To pay his bills, Peterson is forced to go on a television game show, "Who Am I?" the host of which questions his contestants much as an insistent psychiatrist might question his patients. In this story Barthelme examines the search for identity and the role that psychoanalysis and twentieth-century existentialist philosophy have played in this search in America in the sixties. Through the character of Peterson, Barthelme argues for the virtues of private identity as opposed to public identity as it is exposed on the television game show. At the same time, he dramatizes the limits Peterson must go to discover who he is, to create himself in a society that literally will not leave him alone.

As initially depicted, Peterson is a retiring man interested in starting a career as a sculptor and not at all concerned with problems of identity. After deciding to appear on "Who Am I?" however, Peterson is confronted with a series of individuals who reinforce the guilt and confusion that he feels for parading his identity on national television. His first of seven similarly related encounters is with Miss Arbor, who screens candidates for "Who Am I?" by asking them if they have ever been in psychoanalysis and if they are interested in absurdity. Miss Arbor has enormous lips smeared with a glowing white cream, and her interviewing technique patronizes and bullies candidates simultaneously. She is a figure of absurdity in her own right and is astounded when Peterson tells her he is not certain he believes in absurdity. In the next episode Peterson sees his art dealer, Jean-Claude, who chides him for appearing on "Who Am I?" for money and then tells him he can afford to display Peterson's latest sculpture only by sawing it in two pieces and selling each for half the price of the original. The physical world of the story is obviously full of such wild contradictions and absurdity as to send many individuals in search of their identities, but three or four additional threatening encounters are necessary to provoke Peterson into asserting that this world, for him, is also absurd.

The first of these occurs in Peterson's seedy artist's loft. After clashes with Miss Arbor and Jean-Claude, Peterson is brooding over his approaching television appearance. He seeks any rationalization for what he is about to do and remembers a recent remark by the president encouraging the arts. Yet surely, he surmises, the president, as an ultimate authority figure, would not approve of his becoming a contestant on "Who Am I?" even if this action enables him to pay his bills and produce his art. As if to pose a solution to his dilemma, the door to his loft bursts open and the president and a dozen Secret Service men run into the room. Without explanation, they divide Peterson's sculpture in half, just as Jean-Claude suggested. Then they smash the work into smaller pieces. Peterson's despair at this destruction sends him immediately to his barber, Kitchen. As Peterson's confidant, Kitchen is as close to a psychiatrist as the rationalistic, still calm Peterson will venture. Kitchen is a lay analyst and the author of four books entitled *The Decision To Be*. Like Miss Arbor, Kitchen exudes the popularized philosophical clichés about absurdity and alienation in fashion in New York artistic circles in the early sixties. The advice he gives Peterson is errant nonsense. Kitchen tells Peterson to break out of the hell of solipsism, to stop worrying about his relationship with the president, and to consider the president's relationship to him.

Concluding that any judgments he will be given about his life, his art, or his decision to go on "Who Am I?" will be as absurd as the philosophical absurdity he refuses to accept, Peterson attempts to remain alone in his loft. Nonetheless, the crazy, meaningless outside world forces Peterson from his solipsism just as Kitchen has. A tall, foreign-looking stranger walks into Peterson's loft without knocking and brandishes an open switchblade as he introduces himself. He informs Peterson that he is the cat-piano player, a demonic figure, who arrives to play his instrument, the cat-piano, whenever a kitten cries. Too poor to buy milk to feed his kitten, Peterson had lost his pet a few days earlier. Yet at exactly the moment the cat-piano player appears in his loft, Peterson's kitten returns home. Peterson's immediate, outraged response is to believe that the entire situation has been staged and that this intruder is an imposter. But the cat-piano player silences Peterson's outburst when Peterson's kitten begins to cry huge tears and the enormous switchblade the man carries proves to be his cat-piano. Snapping the blade of his knife back into its handle, he floods the room with chords of bizarre music. First refusing to believe in the cat-piano player or his cat-piano, Peterson gradually is discovering that he must somehow come to terms with the absurdity of the world.

A day later, yet more absurdity interrupts his exhausted efforts to evade it. Seeing an "Artist-in-Residence" sign posted outside his loft, three girls from California enter Peterson's apartment, hoping to stay with an artist until they find a better arrangement. Peterson tells them they have come to the wrong place because he is a minor, inauthentic artist. They respond by quoting Pascal on the wretchedness of the human condition, which is one of the comments Kitchen made to Peterson as the two discussed the mutilation of Peterson's sculpture. In Peterson's encounter with the girls from California he discovers that even the denial of his identity as a full-fledged artist is no refuge from the persistent onslaught of these sophomoric philosophical truisms. He is driven to the brink of desperation by a society that demands he admit life is absurd and that insists he find his identity in the philosophical wisdom one might hear at a cocktail party. After his exchange with the three girls from California, Peterson finally realizes the meaninglessness of an identity imposed on him by other people.

The grand finale of "A Shower of Gold" and Peterson's ultimate acceptance of absurdity occur as "Who Am I?" goes on the air. Peterson witnesses the torture of two other contestants, who, in answering the master of ceremonies' merciless questions about their pasts, lie to preserve some sense of undefiled identity. When Peterson's turn comes, he confronts the television audience with his realization that life is absurd. Nevertheless, he tells the audience, before one can be emotionally alienated, not merely philosophically alienated from present experience, one must value his past. Peterson counsels the audience to delve into their past experiences to find those moments before life became confused and threatening. Peterson then proceeds to use his own life as an example of his tenets. To escape the demands of others and their facile, philosophical alienation, he creates an idyllic past for himself that permits him to live without regrets in the present. His mother was a virgin, and his father was a divine shower of gold, he contends, gazing into the camera unflinchingly. His youth was pastoral, enriching, and perfect. As he continues talking to the television monitor and the story ends, the omniscient narrator of the tale recognizes that Peterson is both lying and not lying. Peterson has taken the perpetual option of the artist: creation. He borrows references from the Greek myth of the hero Perseus, who was sired when Zeus, disguised as a shower of gold, coupled with Danaë, a virgin of royal blood.[24] This autobiographical plagiarism gives him a past to protect him from the assaults on his identity delivered by the ongoing world; thereby, he creates a present that makes him receptive to experience, resilient to its absurdities, but never a victim of its shocks. In "A Shower of Gold" identity is not just playfulness, the desire to know the self, or the repetition of the learning process, but an act of creative will that ultimately makes the protagonist superior to a world in which he initially seems trapped. Peterson finally affirms that identity is not one quality but a force which he invents and believes. Acting on his newly found identity gives him heroic powers before the audience of "Who Am I?"

"A Shower of Gold" is markedly similar to Barthelme's other identity stories. The tale shows that authority figures such as Miss Arbor and Kitchen, who spout pretentious philosophical maxims, or Jean-Claude and the president, who wish to wrench one's art out of shape, must be denied if an individual is to gain a sense of freedom and integrity. Yet "A Shower of Gold" is different from the others in its optimistic, affirming belief that the individual can create his own imaginative identity, enabling him to withstand the tyranny of a coercive world. Identity in "A Shower of Gold" is a choice on Peterson's part to create and accept his life as it occurs. Choice is the crucial term in Peterson's definition of identity. Of all the people Peterson encounters in the vignettes of this story, the cat-piano player and the three girls from California are the most important for they remind Peterson of the choices he has made or will have to make to become a creator of his own life.

Particularly striking in this respect is Peterson's exchange with

24. Thomas Bullfinch, *Bullfinch's Mythology* (New York, n.d.), 91.

the cat-piano player at the moment when Peterson's cat returns to the loft. These two quickly engage in a discussion of choice and free will in which Peterson wants to deny that he has chosen to have the stray kitten live in his loft:

The kitten appeared, looked at Peterson reproachfully, and then rubbed itself against the cat-piano player's mechanical leg. "Wait a minute!" Peterson exclaimed, "This thing is rigged. That cat hasn't been here in two days. What do you want from me? What am I supposed to do?" "Choices, Mr. Peterson, choices. You chose that kitten as a way of encountering that which you are not, that is to say, kitten. An effort on the part of the pour soi to—." "But it chose me!" Peterson cried, "the door was open and the first thing I knew it was lying in my bed under the Army blanket. I didn't have anything to do with it!" The cat-piano player repeated his disingenuous smile. "Yes, Mr. Peterson, I know, I know. Things are done to you; it is all a gigantic conspiracy."[25]

Although the cat-piano player speaks in the same existentially synthesized language as Miss Arbor and Jean-Claude, unlike these characters he has a pivotal function in the story. His role is to make Peterson take responsibility for his own actions. He suggests to the sculptor that his willingness to allow the stray kitten to remain in his loft is itself a choice and that many acts of Peterson's own volition, rather than some gigantic conspiracy, have left him feeling cornered and compromised.

As the cat-piano player suggests to Peterson the importance of choice in creating his identity, the three girls from California in the episode that immediately follows remind Peterson of the specific choice he must make to create an identity. Peterson's initial response to more intruders in his apartment is identical to his reaction to the unsolicited visit of the cat-piano player. He wonders why he is being singled out for punishment. Whereas the cat-piano player never explicitly answers his question, one of the girls from California tells Peterson that they have come to his door because they recognized his loft as an artist's residence:

"Yes," Peterson said, "but why me?" "You're an artist," Sherry said sternly. "We saw the A. I. R. sign downstairs." Peterson cursed the fire laws which

25. Barthelme, "A Shower of Gold," in *Come Back, Dr. Caligari*, 179.

made posting of the signs obligatory. "Listen," he said, "I can't even feed the cat. I can't even keep myself in beer. This is not the place. You won't be happy here. My work isn't authentic. I'm a minor artist." "The natural misfortune of our mortal and feeble condition is so wretched that when we consider it closely nothing can console us," Sherry said. "That's Pascal." "I know," Peterson said, weakly.[26]

Once again, Peterson is forced to communicate with a society infatuated with the debased jargon of philosophical despair. In this exchange with one of the girls, however, Peterson, without succumbing to its vapid prattle, conforms to the bleak vision that this talk promotes. Trying to remove the girls from his doorstep, Peterson momentarily refutes not only their motive for desiring to stay in his loft but his own claim to an identity as well. Sherry's response to Peterson with a quotation from Pascal is a compounded irony. This quotation is one that Kitchen advised Peterson to consider earlier in the story, and in acknowledging his familiarity with the remark, Peterson discovers himself communicating in the facile pessimism and alienation he finds so fraudulent.

The cat-piano player and the three girls from California teach Peterson two valuable lessons: either he must choose the identity he wants in life or he will feel that this choice has been made for him; and his role in life should be to create the identity he desires as artfully as he sculpts his statues. Denying this second goal pushes Peterson closer to the estrangement that he finds simplistic and ridiculous in others.

This episode completes Peterson's education in the insanity of the world. Waiting for the master of ceremonies of "Who Am I?" to ask him the first question, Peterson considers all he has learned from his recent experiences. "I was wrong, Peterson thought, the world is absurd. The absurdity is punishing me for not believing in it. I affirm the absurdity. On the other hand, absurdity is itself absurd." Drawing on this conclusion and on his clash with the girls from California, who have convinced him of his identity as an artist, he proceeds to create an absurd, if artful, identity before the

26. *Ibid*, 180.

cameras and audience of "Who Am I?" Even though he may be a minor artist, Peterson tells the master of ceremonies, he may still create major realities in his imagination. "I am a minor artist and my dealer won't even display my work if he can help it, but minor is as minor does and lightning may strike even yet."[27]

In this statement Peterson shows his differences with the other guests on the show. Peterson refuses to indulge in maudlin memories of past failures and embarrassments, which seem to have immobilized these contestants. Though the master of ceremonies and the studio technicians try to move the camera away from Peterson, he still manages to instruct the audience to turn off its television sets, to stop questioning their identity, and, instead, to invent the persons they could become:

"Don't be reconciled. Turn off your television sets," Peterson said, "cash in your life insurance, indulge in a mindless optimism. Visit girls at dusk. Play the guitar. How can you be alienated without first having been connected? Think back and remember how it was. My mother was a royal virgin," Peterson said, "and my father was a shower of gold. My childhood was pastoral and rich in experiences which developed my character. . . ." Peterson went on and on and although he was in a sense lying, in a sense he was not.[28]

In "A Shower of Gold" Peterson plays with a sense of identity by creating a mythic past for himself while other characters in the story struggle in vain to know who they are or endlessly, repeatedly attempt to reexplore their pasts. The final words of Peterson, the artist, eradicate a painful past by creating a personal history and a surrogate identity that promote life and growth in the present.

Critics who have commented on the character of Peterson and his self-ordained fate in "A Shower of Gold" have noted that Peterson has consciously rejected public values in favor of personal, private definitions of his identity. William Stott, in an article on public versus private values in Barthelme's writing, comments on Peterson's espousal of the private and the personal as a means of creatively declaring his identity:

27. *Ibid.*, 182, 183.
28. *Ibid.*, 183.

The only answer to the pressures of publicity is to reassert harder the private. Peterson would have gotten money, celebrity, for laying himself bare—an interesting comment on success in our time. But he knew what he would lose. Barthelme's essential theme is the human cost of a society that values publicity more than privacy. He shows us quite simply the danger in what we Americans are doing to ourselves with our faith in other people's values, our collectivist pleasures, our encounter groups and groupings, our lust for self-exposure. The madness Barthelme satirizes, our madness, is real and urgent, no doubt about it.[29]

Stott is no doubt correct in analyzing the target of Barthelme's satire in "A Shower of Gold" as a social madness that inflicts self-exposure on even the most reticent members of a society. But the major theme of the story would seem not to center on the human damage done by such a society but on the artful, creative way an individual like Peterson finds to evade the prying nature of his world and still create a role for himself in it.

Neil Schmitz, in an article in *Partisan Review* on Barthelme's use of irony, describes Peterson's method for confronting his society's madness as almost a madness in itself. Schmitz says that Peterson "resorts to the subversion of fantasy, creating other selves, inventing experiences."[30] This quality of subversion, of artfully mocking the goals and values of a society and yet still creating an identity for oneself within that society, emerges in "A Shower of Gold" and other stories. This attribute characterizes the protagonists of "Engineer-Private Paul Klee Misplaces an Aircraft between Milbertshofen and Cambrai, March 1916" and "Daumier," both from *Sadness* (1972). These latter tales are the two auxiliary stories in the box on the typology containing stories about identity developed through a sense of creative expression. All three of these stories depict protagonists who veer between creativity and subversion in attempting to escape a world that threatens to engulf them. They have not fled to an underground existence, as in "Hiding Man" and the group of stories associated with it, but are potential artists who fight the domination of their lives with several strategies. They

29. William Stott, "Donald Barthelme and the Death of Fiction," *Prospects: Annual of American Cultural Studies,* I (1975), 382.
30. Neil Schmitz, "What Irony Unravels," *Partisan Review,* XL (1973), 486.

transform the drudgery of their daily tasks into works of art, and they create bizarre landscapes, subversive fantasies, or other selves which frequently seem as much crazed as artistic.

Not coincidentally, both of these stories are concerned with artists. "Engineer-Private Paul Klee" is loosely based on a period during World War I when the Expressionist artist Paul Klee was drafted by the German government and assigned to polish and paint aircraft. "Daumier" is related, but more tangentially, to the nineteenth-century French lithographer and cartoonist who caricatured and satirized Parisian society. Barthelme's Daumier is a caricaturist and a spiritual descendant of this man, but he is a twentieth-century artist. Both of these stories, like "A Shower of Gold," are defiantly modernist, even surrealist, in their view of the turbulence and disjunctures of the contemporary world. Yet in analyzing first "Engineer-Private Paul Klee" and then "Daumier," one also discovers a gaiety of vision in their affirmation of the power of the modern artist to create a private identity free from the madness of society.

In "Engineer-Private Paul Klee" Barthelme shows the ability of a great artist to create from the raw materials of a hostile world. Barthelme develops the tale from Klee's actual military experience in World War I. The story, however, embellishes an incident in which Klee, transferred from aircraft maintenance to aircraft transport, notices that one of the planes he is to escort between German cities has inexplicably disappeared from a transport train. Rather than despair, this calm, humane man, who hates war, the German cause, and his life as a soldier, takes pencil and paper and sketches the beautiful shape made by the canvas and rope on the floor of the empty flatcar. As Barthelme quotes the painter: "The shape of the collapsed canvas, under which the aircraft has rested, together with the loose ropes—the canvas forming hills and valleys, seductive folds, the ropes the very essence of looseness, lapsing—it is irresistible."[31] "Engineer-Private Paul Klee" celebrates the power of an art-

---

31. Donald Barthelme, "Engineer-Private Paul Klee Misplaces an Aircraft between Milbertshofen and Cambrai, March 1916," in *Sadness* (New York, 1972), 68.

ist to make an object of beauty from what is lost or missing, from what otherwise might be a source of distress or embarrassment.

The story is told in an alternating series of simple, declarative statements delivered by Paul Klee and by the voice of the German Secret Police who have constant surveillance over all soldiers and civilians in time of war. The Secret Police in this story represent social insanity such as William Stott finds throughout "A Shower of Gold." In "Engineer-Private Paul Klee" this policed madness drives a country to war and to attempts at total control over its citizens. If Klee is aware of the constant invasion of his privacy he does not acknowledge it. He responds to any threat to his identity by using his wartime experiences as the subject matter from which to mold his art. Demonstrating the artist's ability to create from unlikely perspectives and in threatening, demoralizing circumstances, Klee uses the canvas and rope to shape and texture his own sketch.

As certainly as Klee's resourcefulness permeates this story, his artful means for solving his dilemma reflects the vision of a man who has become the happy creator of his own reality. Realizing that he will be held responsible for the missing airplane, Klee decides that though the situation is ludicrous and his life as a soldier is absurd, he must respond rationally to the problem, not merely with a cry of alienation or self-pity. Klee realizes that to avoid punishment or demotion he must change the supply manifest, which lists the number of airplanes he is transporting. Likening his painter's skill to a forger's, Klee erases one airplane from his ledger. He artfully subverts the documented reality so that he can continue his private life as an artist at war with the dictates of his society. The Secret Police, always vigilant, watch Klee as he forges the roster. But they conclude that because their omniscience has failed to divulge who stole the aircraft or where it has been taken, Klee's subterfuge is sparing them the same harassment and penalties from their superiors that he attempts to avoid from his own. "Engineer-Private Paul Klee" concludes with Klee's affirmation of pleasure in his sketch of ropes and canvas composed in the midst of war. His triumphant belief is that an artful, creative life is a kind of forgery, which occasionally permits one to live in the imagination, even if reality is savage and destructive.

"Daumier" is the second auxiliary story in the box on the typology containing stories about identity developed through the creative process. The protagonist in this tale faces a different problem in creating his identity. Rather than being plagued by an insane society as is the hero of "A Shower of Gold," or attempting to create in the warring environment that hampers Paul Klee, the protagonist of "Daumier" fights to be free of the burden of his own personality. The creator strives to be rid of his self, which he calls "a dirty great villain, an interrupter of sleep, a deviler of awakeness, an intersubjective atrocity, a mouth, a maw."[32] With "Daumier" the tale of identity comes full circle. "Daumier" is one of the most ironic of all Barthelme's stories about identity in its insistence that the way for the artistic individual to create a sense of selfhood is through the total negation of his own needs, worries, and desires. As the protagonist contends, the urgings and fears of the self can never be sated. Only by artfully creating surrogate selves, whose wants and whims can be controlled and satisfied, can an individual ever discover his own potential, free from the immediate demands of his personality.

"Daumier" is much more than a mere statement of this premise. The protagonist of the story dramatizes his vision by creating two surrogate selves who have adventures of their own, even though their escapades are completely the product of the protagonist's imagination. The story is divided into titled sections in which the protagonist, a Daumier who resides in the twentieth century, creates another Daumier, described in the third person, who runs a female white slave operation and who lives in the swashbuckling nineteenth-century France of Alexandre Dumas' *The Three Musketeers*. The godlike protagonist also envisions a third Daumier, depicted only in the second person. This Daumier's function is to pursue a woman the protagonist fancies among his other surro-

32. Donald Barthelme, "Daumier," in *Sadness*, 169.

gate's current slaves and to bring her from the nineteenth to the twentieth century.

Though largely devoted to these three characters and situations, "Daumier" includes among its twenty-one titled episodes passages in which friends of the protagonist chide him for his insecurities. A segment also appears in which this Daumier describes, at digressive length and with absurd pomposity, a dinner of junk food that he carefully prepares for his newest lover, the woman from the slave trade. The total effect of this potpourri of assembled modes and tones is a caricaturist's world that parodies a variety of styles of writing.

"Daumier" takes its name from an artist who mocked the art and aspirations of his society. Dumas was a contemporary of Daumier's who was lionized by the public in his time. Barthelme makes the relationship between Daumier, the protagonist of this story, and Dumas, the French novelist, explicit at one point in the tale. Daumier's nineteenth-century surrogate self and accomplices gather together a new group of women they have captured and herd them across the countryside like so many cattle headed for a roundup. This surrogate is diverted from his loyalty to his white slavery business when he responds to the queen's cry for help. Her necklace has been stolen, and the first Daumier refers us to that portion of Dumas' *The Queen's Necklace* which explains why his surrogate abruptly leaves the slave caravan to help the besieged royal family. Throughout "Daumier" Barthelme imitates various forms of literature, from Dumas to psychological texts to self-help books, filled with ridiculous ideas and stilted conventions that have aided men in removing themselves from needless self-absorption.

Whatever else Daumier achieves through his creation of these surrogates, initially, at least, he curtails his destructive preoccupation with his own personality. Like Peterson's final identity in "A Shower of Gold," these surrogates function as ironic, imaginative selves who can escape the shrill pressures of a nagging, bellicose world. Yet rather than accept Peterson's dictum that reality is absurd but alienation from reality is itself absurd, Daumier circumvents the problem by creating his own worlds. In these he is both god and hero, and alienation would be ridiculous. This technique is what William Stott recognizes in Barthelme as the triumph of private over public values.[33] Carried to this extreme, the device becomes a total subversion of conventional literary reality, resulting in the bizarre, disconnected form that "Daumier" assumes on the page. "Daumier" revels in fantastic landscapes, other selves, and invented experiences that its protagonist creates, as well as in subversion of short-story form and the juxtaposition of wildly contrasting prose styles. "Daumier" recognizes the power of the artist to be free, however crazed.

Despite the skill of his mythmaking, a flaw nevertheless appears in Daumier's strategy. Near the end of the story, as Daumier elegantly ministers junk food to his newest love, Barthelme's ludicrously elevated rhetoric allows the reader to see that junk is finally junk, no matter how ornately or decoratively it is served. For Barthelme's Paul Klee, art is a forgery that allows the confirmation of his skills, even in a war-torn society. When Daumier forges inauthentic worlds, however, rather than freeing himself to become a different person, he reverts to past habits.

Despite the story's ambivalence about the role of the imagination in creating identity, "Daumier" is one of the zaniest, most high-spirited stories Barthelme has written. Although creativity may be no panacea for discovering the possibilities of the self, Barthelme feels that art is the only way men and women can occupy themselves while hoping to transcend their egos. This belief is expressed in the final sentences of the story: "The self cannot be escaped, but it can be, with ingenuity and hard work, distracted. There are always openings if you can find them, there is always something to do."[34] Compare this statement with one of Peterson's remarks before the audience of "Who Am I?" in "A Shower of Gold": "In this kind of world . . . absurd if you will, possibilities nevertheless proliferate and escalate all around us and there are opportunities for beginning again."[35] In these stories of creativity, the self and the ab-

33. Stott, "Donald Barthelme and the Death of Fiction," 382.
34. Barthelme, "Daumier," 183.
35. Barthelme, "Shower," 183.

surdity of life become the chief obstacles to the protagonists' struggles for identity. Regardless, these optimistic, affirming tales insist that the openings and possibilities are all men have—and may well be enough—to forget the self and defuse the absurdity for as long as needed to proclaim identity beyond their own time, circumstances, or personalities. The search of Peterson, Paul Klee, and Daumier for identity eventually becomes the urge to create a work of art. These three men come closer to discovering who they are than any protagonists in any other stories on the typology.

Identity takes many forms in Barthelme's short stories. Yet he obviously regards protagonists who assert their identities through some form of creative expression as achieving the most meaningful and constructive sense of self. But this chapter also contains Barthelme's hiding men and women such as Cecelia in "A City of Churches," St. Anthony, and the Phantom of the Opera. With these protagonists he creates characters who consciously frustrate a reader's conception of identity and thus with whom sympathetic identification becomes difficult.

Clearly, Barthelme intends all the stories discussed in this chapter to question and invert the conventional givens of fictional character. If "Hiding Man" and related stories are what Barthelme describes as jokes with a vision, this vision lies in their examination of the truisms of character as literary convention. These stories refuse to honor their protagonists' identities as easily translatable signs which elicit predictable responses in the minds of readers. Barthelme rejects a formula for identity in both life and art. His stories see character not as a static force but as a field of energy constantly changing in space and time. Therefore, character and the self must be malleable to the pressures of a changing world if they are to survive in it. Similarly, stories such as "See the Moon," "Views of My Father Weeping," and "Brain Damage" scrutinize identity by spilling fragments of their protagonists' lives in random, nonchronological order across the page, and then engaging these protagonists to put the pieces into some meaningful order. Barthelme has been criticized for declaring that these fragments are his only trustworthy artistic form. His goal in these and many other stories, however, is to use these concrete, known particles of identity to dissect ideas about character and the self. In deconstructing reality, he wishes to reconstruct it as well.

Barthelme's questioning continues in stories such as "Me and Miss Mandible," "The Sergeant," "The School," and "The Educational Experience" in which he examines the role of education in shaping an individual's life and expectations. In these tales educational systems, whether grade school, the military, or college, are seen as vast traps, collections of signs that promise rewards but fail to produce them. Thus those who repeat their pasts sadly discover that this return does not instruct them in ways to correct the mess they have made of their adult lives. Their error was not in neglecting their lessons but in failing to see that their training for society is as corrupting and inadequate as the world that upholds it. As always in Barthelme's stories, the conscious flight from the self inevitably returns one to the self.

Accordingly, Barthelme's characters must find a means to escape the circularity of the self while simultaneously expressing it. In stories such as "A Shower of Gold," "Engineer-Private Paul Klee Misplaces an Aircraft between Milbertshofen and Cambrai, March 1916," and "Daumier," Barthelme endows his narrators with an artistic gaiety of vision that enables them to create private worlds free of their own obsessions. In these tales the protagonists quickly learn that the act of creativity is a conscious choice on their part. Since society, the artist, and his past are in unending battle, these protagonists must will their creativeness against imposing odds. Despite the madness of the world and the ego, however, there are always possibilities and openings for the artistic sensibility. Hence creativity enables the individual to forget the burdens of identity while discovering its powers. Identity accepts few bounds or constraints. Absorbing past roles and expelling present ones overnight, the self is in perpetual ferment and transformation. For Barthelme, identity can never be defined by one action or mode. It flourishes best when that most versatile, godlike of human behaviors, creativity, is synonymous with the shapes it can and will take.

Chapter II

The Dialogue Stories

There are four central stories on the typology developed by dialogue between two voices whose tenuous control over their own identities causes them to fear contact with others as much as they desire an exchange of information. These tales depict a world in which the machinery of conversation has broken down and communication seldom occurs. Characters talk to themselves and ignore the comments and responses of their interrogators. The stories frequently describe power relationships pitting an authoritative questioner against a consciously weaker, more vulnerable respondent. The stronger character often represents technology or a computerized, futuristic society and attempts to persuade the other speaker to accept the machine and the brave new world that it inaugurates. The stories involve battles of will between scientific and humanistic sensibilities that refuse to debate with one another. When the artist figure in these tales does speak, he mocks or torments the scientist and his inquiries.

Barthelme envisions much modern conversation as a field of play that can be expertly used by the wily conversationalist who wants to evade the threatening, totalitarian powers of his interrogator or prevent this inquisitor from reading his mind. Not only the playful benefit from conversation in Barthelme's dialogue stories, however.

Many of the tales show two characters whose conversation, or failure to converse, is an effort to escape rationality. In these exchanges
one participant seeks to avoid categorization by rejecting his partner's classifications. Such figures are in flight from a bogus knowledge on the part of their antagonists which presumes to label them
before they have even spoken. A strong current against conventional logic exists in these stories, and the irrational becomes a defense against the putative insanity of a scientifically sane society.
Similarly, these stories celebrate the imaginative resources of individuals whose quick retorts or delaying tactics allow them to slip
through the verbal nets of those who wish to entangle them in any
system of ideas or beliefs. Befitting their sense of indirection, such
tales resound with explanations that do not really explain.

The last and most important function of the dialogue form in the
world posited by the dialogue stories is to divide the protagonist of
any story into two selves, questioner and answerer, prosecution and
defense. Repeatedly, the conversation stories seem not so much
two voices deliberating and contesting as one mind that has com-
partmentalized itself into pro and con, either-or, so as to examine
an issue or a phenomenon. The question-and-answer technique allows the mind to challenge itself, using irony to develop a point of
view and to criticize it simultaneously. By arbitrarily halving the
self, Barthelme demonstrates that the contrary aspects of a personality or an idea can coexist. Moreover, one of the ways conflict can
be harmoniously balanced out is by using this ironic dialogue with
the self as a tool for unifying the self. Thus irony can be a constructive force as well as a mocking, negating one.

The first of our four diagrammed stories is "The Explanation,"
from *City Life* (1970), a tale developed through the process of play.
It is told exclusively as a series of questions and answers. Q, the
questioner, who represents the forces of a computerized, scientific
world, attempts to persuade A, the answerer and an artist, to accept
and appreciate the beauties of machine technology. The technique
of the story uses play and the playful, devious ways A shapes the
interview form by refusing to answer Q's questions directly, by re-

peating Q's questions in rebuttal, or by asking Q questions about his questions. The subject of the story is the relationship between the scientific and the artistic imaginations, the former seeking explanations and reasons for all phenomena, the latter creating its own reasons or playfully subverting the effort to find explanations in its search for a different truth. "The Explanation," like all the dialogue stories developed through play, is richly humorous, depicting the struggle of the evasive underground man, here the artistic sensibility, to escape the domination of a scientific spirit that has become the pervasive force of contemporary society. As a result of A's rejoinders and Q's fallibility, an additional joke within the story is the ease with which Q is led to reexamine his insistence on the superiority of technology. Much of the humor of "The Explanation" lies in its portrayal of a futuristic, technologically efficient society that cannot explain itself.

Although the tone of "The Explanation" is superficially humorous and playful, the structure of the story affords interpretive complications. There are three subjects of conversation: Q's efforts to persuade A of the value of the machine; A's description of a beautiful woman whom he watches undress as Q insistently questions him about what he sees; and a series of nonsensical, simple sentences exchanged between Q and A that could be found in any introductory grammar. Throughout "The Explanation" each of these conversational forms appears, running from four or five lines to a page in length and occurring in random order with printed separations between them. "The Explanation" has no plot and no sense of progressive development. Whatever rising intensity it possesses is supplied by Q's growing determination to convince A that the machine is capable of humanity and even sex appeal. A counters this argument by continually returning to the woman he is watching undress, while Q demands to know specifically what A can see. Q consistently reveals much greater interest in sex than in whatever titillation is offered by technological sublimation. These two forms of repartee are occasionally interrupted by the nonsense sentences bantered between Q and A that express not only deterioration of communication but the malfunctioning of the question-and-answer form. Resembling the stories whose characters play with a concept of identity, "The Explanation" demonstrates that dialogues in which the participants play at communication can end only in evasion and hiding. Much like a psychiatrist who wishes to label and classify his patients, Q presents A with a Rorschach figure, a black box, at several points in the story, and asks A what he sees in the figure. A, however, is too wily and too playful to be trapped by the humorless mechanics of psychiatry. If his fanciful turns of conversation suggest the free association of a damaged brain that Barthelme has described in other stories, at least A escapes the sexless, reductionistic world of systems and technology in which Q's questions attempt to snare him.

Barthelme begins "The Explanation" with Q offering A just such a square-shaped Rorschach for his scrutiny, and immediately Q attempts to trick A with it. In a group of three conversations Q tries to convince A that a buttonless, dialless, perfectly square machine could be a tool for political change, and even if it is not, any machine, such as a bicycle, will outlast a work of art like the novel.

Q: Do you believe that this machine could be helpful in changing the government?
A: Changing the government . . .
Q: Making it more responsive to the needs of the people?
A: I don't know what it is. What does it do?
Q: Well, look at it.

A: It offers no clues.
Q: It has a certain . . . reticence.
A: I don't know what it does.
Q: A lack of confidence in the machine?
Q: Is the novel dead?
A: Oh yes. Very much so.
Q: What replaces it?
A: I should think that it is replaced by what existed before it was invented.
Q: The same thing?
A: The same sort of thing.
Q: Is the bicycle dead?
Q: You don't trust the machine?
A: Why should I trust it?
Q: (States his own lack of interest in machines.)[1]

A refuses to be impressed by the machinery of Q's questioning or the machinery of his technology, particularly when Q cannot explain the specific function of his black box. Q's appeal to A's artist's sensibility in the third conversation is particularly clever. Here Q attempts to draw a partial analogy between art and the machine. If art forms die, as A readily admits the novel has died, but some machines, like the bicycle, never lose their utility, Q urges, the machine and technology are more lasting and of greater permanent value than art. Because of Q's manipulative logic, A is quickly aware of the scientist's efforts to trap him into admitting that tech-

1. Donald Barthelme, "The Explanation," in *City Life*, 69–71.

nology is superior to art. A, however, adamantly refuses to do so. Rather than be led into a false conclusion by Q's specious reasoning, A does not respond when Q asks him rhetorically if the bicycle is dead. In this situation and others, both Q and A rewrite our conventional expectations for the question-and-answer form. What adds to the humor and humanity of "The Explanation" is Q's willingness to admit his own uncertainty about technology. A's integrity in questioning the premise of Q's argument that one should have implicit trust in the machine prompts Q to admit that even though he is a spokesman for technology he finds machines uninteresting. Like the novel, the question-and-answer form as a dialogue form is a dead or dying means of communication. Yet in "The Explanation" Barthelme demonstrates how all the signs and conventions of conversation and storytelling can be revitalized by an imaginative sensibility.

Barthelme's imagination and A's playful skepticism are most evident in another series of three conversations midway in the story, which uses all three forms of dialogue found in "The Explanation." Continuing to ignore A's dissatisfaction with the machine, Q insists on teaching him the language in which a computer thinks. As Q proceeds through a long list of the language of computer programming, A recognizes that his opponent has no emotional interest in this terminology but wants to return to A's account of the woman he is watching undress. These conversations begin to degenerate when, in the second conversation, A describes the woman not in erotic terms but as self-absorbed, and A tells Q that his own self-absorption in this form of play will prevent Q's scientific sensibility from reading his artistic mind.

Q: I have a number of error messages I'd like to introduce here and I'd like you to study them carefully . . . they're numbered. I'll go over them with you: undefined variable . . . improper sequence of operators . . . improper use of hierarchy . . . missing operator . . . mixed mode, that one's particularly grave. . . .
A: I like them very much.
Q: There are hundreds of others, hundreds and hundreds.
A: You seem emotionless.

Q: That's not true.

A: To what do your emotions . . . adhere, if I can put it that way?

Q: Do you see what she is doing?

A: Removing her blouse.

Q: How does she look?

A: . . . Self-Absorbed.

Q: Are you bored with the question-and-answer form?

A: I am bored with it, but I realize that it permits many valuable omissions: What kind of day it is, What I'm wearing, What I'm thinking. That's a very comfortable advantage, I would say.

Q: I believe in it.

Q: She sang and we listened to her.

A: I was speaking to a tourist.

Q: Their chair is here.

A: I knocked at the door; it was shut.

Q: The soldiers marched toward the castle.

A: I had a watch.

Q: He has struck me.

A: I have struck him.[2]

The third conversation in this group represents a complete wrenching of language from thought and communication as foreshadowed in the preceding two conversations. Realizing they are forever at solipsistic cross-purposes, the artist and the scientist can only deliver meaningless declarative sentences to each other. Self-absorption has overwhelmed the dialogue form, and the language of computer errors becomes as meaningful as any other statement. Ironically, the farthest reaches of technology only return man to his most primitive states of communication. As the reader watches the tools of expression disintegrate before him, Q and A devolve toward outright conflict.

The antagonism comes to intimations of violence because at this point, in the middle of the story, A is already succeeding in playfully eluding the traps Q has laid for him. At this juncture, both men realize they are enemies. Despite their intermittent hostility, however, the conversations of "The Explanation" exude a sense of

2. *Ibid.*, 73–74.

boredom and lassitude. Q realizes that A is as weary of his descriptions of the sensuous woman as he is with his own list of computer errors. Both men seem to have short attention spans, but a pivotal difference exists in their attempts to control one another. Q lacks the self-obsession to use the question-and-answer form for his own purposes. He finishes the second conversation with A above by proclaiming that he believes in the conventions of questions and answers. A, on the other hand, announces that he will appropriate the strategies of this device to evade and to play with Q's every effort to discern what he is thinking. For example, A feigns affection for the scientific language of Q's error messages in the first conversation here, allowing Q to express his emotional detachment from them by contrast. As a result, A guides Q away from Q's effort to indoctrinate him in the virtues of technology and toward thoughts of the woman A is watching. The game of cat and mouse that Q and A play here is the clash between two very different men. One believes in the conventions of debate as well as scientific technology. Another so values his own integrity or, like Daumier, becomes so preoccupied with it that he invents selves to escape the role imposed upon him. A finds himself in a characteristic situation for the modern artist: his self-absorption allows him to escape the petty dictates of his society at the expense of failing to communicate with the individuals within it.

"The Explanation" dramatizes the destruction of communication when one man brings a sense of mockery and play to his conversation with another. A is the underground hiding man who flees the questions of Q, a man who wishes to convert A to a belief in technology and social conventions. The story convincingly demonstrates that A's playful sense of humor, which inverts and challenges Q's questions, will always allow him to escape the ideologies of a man who foolishly believes in the ability of an atrophied question-and-answer form to transmit communication. As in "Hiding Man," A resembles a clever psychiatric patient and Q, his bewildered doctor. This story demonstrates, however, that two individuals can never develop communication based exclusively on play because A frequently delights in reversing roles and playing doctor to Q's confused patient.

Moving horizontally across the row of dialogue stories on the typology, we proceed to "Margins," from *Come Back, Dr. Caligari* (1964), a story concerning a conversation between two men, which is motivated and developed by one man's desire to know and understand another. As in all the stories concerned with knowing or the desire to know, "Margins" expresses the futility of attaining complete certainty. "Margins" illustrates the failure of a white man to use the generalizations and abstractions of his society to understand the black panhandler he confronts on a street corner. The tale also reveals the unreliability of the shifting, evasive dialogue form for granting Edward, the white man, any knowledge of or control over Carl, the black. Its tone of futility satirizes the assurance of white assumptions about black attitudes and black about white, while its conversation between Edward and Carl becomes a collage of meaningless, unlinked questions and answers unified only by the conventions of the dialogue form. As in "The Explanation," in "Margins" conversational communication deteriorates because it proves too deceptive a form to allow understanding.

Summarizing the story unfolds its absurdist vision of one possible type of interracial dialogue. "Margins" is a grotesque, angry encounter on a New York City street corner between Carl, a black panhandler, and Edward, a white man, who professes a need to know what makes an itinerant black like Carl function as he does. Yet for all Edward's supposed concern in discovering Carl's inner reality, Edward is obsessed with applying ridiculous, superficial tests of white values to Carl's character. As the story begins, Edward is examining Carl's penmanship on the sandwich board advertising his largely invented, traumatic childhood. Edward looks at the letters Carl has shaped along the right- and left-hand margins of his appeal, and with the aid of a handwriting analysis book he carries with him, he evaluates Carl's character. Fixated on appearances, Edward continues to judge Carl by the length of his unkempt hair and the shabbiness of his frayed suit. Edward's real desire is to know

Carl by transforming him into a well-groomed, socially mobile white man. Carl responds by denying that he believes in Edward's criteria, yet he indulges Edward's ludicrous efforts to label him. Furthermore, Carl develops a strategy of his own. Disdaining Edward's desires to talk about race, Carl constantly refers to books that might appear on the syllabus of an Ivy League college humanities course, works far removed from mainstream black culture. Carl's ploy is to emerge in conversation as a literate, self-consciously educated black, contradicting his physical appearance as an itinerant panhandler. The educated white world can be prevented from categorizing him only if Carl bewilders the power structure by appearing to possess an education equal to its own. "Margins," like most of Barthelme's dialogue stories, is a description of power relationships and power plays; the story suggests that knowledge gained through conversation becomes not so much the effort to understand another person as a means to classify and control him. Correspondingly, Carl confuses his superficially more powerful foe by sounding stereotypically white and offering opinions on modern culture, despite his shabby clothes and the color of his skin.

Carl's technique for eluding Edward succeeds so well that, midway in the story, Edward's annoyance at his prey flares into anger. Since Carl has consistently appeased his tormentor, he glibly follows Edward's embittered lead and falsely admits to shoplifting and petty thievery. Edward wants to find criminal traits in blacks regardless of their individual demeanor. The closest these men come to experiencing each other's feelings occurs when Carl, leaving the street corner to relieve himself, asks Edward to wear his sign. Edward finds the placard surprisingly heavy, and its straps cut sharply into his shoulders. The story concludes in a burst of unexpected violence as Carl returns to the street and each man strikes the other's face. "Margins" thus asks how racial barriers can ever be overcome if individuals, aping or inverting the stereotypes of their society and their races, have so thoroughly lost a sense of self. The concluding violence, like the implied violence between Q and A in "The Explanation," is a metaphor for this loud and futile dialogue that, completely failing to communicate, must explode. This sparring takes the following shape:

"Are you a drug addict?"
"Edward," Carl said, "you are a swinger."
"Are you a Muslim?"
Carl felt his long hair. "Have you read *The Mystery of Being* by Gabriel Marcel? I really liked that one. I thought that one was fine."
"No, c'mon Carl, answer the question," Edward insisted. "There's got to be frankness and honesty between the races. Are you one?"
"I think an accommodation can be reached and the government is doing all it can at the moment," Carl said. "I think there's something to be said on all sides of the question."[3]

As the story continues, their empty bantering becomes more belligerent. Carl suddenly begins to mix insults with his flattery of Edward. Edward alternates between declaring his racial superiority to Carl and adopting a tone of self-deprecation that still allows him to be worthier than Carl. Edward traps Carl with this recognition whenever Carl agrees with Edward's self-effacement. The only moment of spontaneous feeling occurs in the following passage from midway in the story, when Edward dejectedly senses that Carl speaks too glibly and wishes to appear too well-read to be the minstrel show straight man he sometimes plays:

"You're kind of boring, Edward. To tell the truth."
Edward thought about this for a moment. Then he said: "But I'm white."
"It's the color of choice," Carl said, "I'm tired of talking about color, though. Let's talk about values or something."
"Carl, I'm a fool," Edward said suddenly.
"Yes," Carl said.
"But I'm a white fool," Edward said. "That's what's so lovely about me."
"You are lovely," Carl said. "It's true. You have a nice look. Your aspect is good."
"Oh, hell," Edward said despondently, "you're very well-spoken," he said. "I noticed that."
"The reason for that is," Carl said, "I read. Did you read *The Cannibal* by John Hawkes? I thought that was a hell of a book."[4]

3. Barthelme, "Margins," in *Come Back, Dr. Caligari*, 143.
4. *Ibid.*, 143–44.

In "Margins" Barthelme creates a world in which individual identities have been so effaced by masks and poses that these protagonists cannot converse or communicate. The effort to know another person in this world results in a bizarre dialogue, premised on a basic confusion between appearances and reality and full of assumed attitudes, sudden assaults, and unmotivated retreats. The story examines a society in which stereotypes regarding racial differences have made dialogues between blacks and whites virtually impossible. Conversations between human beings who represent only ideas to one another, and outmoded or incomplete ideas at that, can end only in violence, and dialogue consistently resists the designs of those who attempt to use it to gain knowledge of the other speaker.

We move on in the typology to "The Catechist," a dialogue tale developed through the process of repetition. It presents a conversation between a priest and his superior, an older clergyman who hears the younger man's confession in a dialogue much the same as those in "The Explanation" and "Margins." Despite the endless questioning, conversation again evades communication. Largely ignoring one another, each of the priests talks only to himself. Nonetheless, their exchange has all the formality and convention of the Catholic catechism, a form that the older man frequently consults to discover techniques for controlling his wayward students.

Catechism—fixed, carefully scripted, and resistant to change—becomes a paradigm. Just as a faithful parishioner follows the liturgy, this tale repeats the same conversation that has been exchanged daily for as long as the younger priest can remember. The story also manages to reiterate the boredom and monotony of such experiences. "The Catechism," like the other dialogue stories, demonstrates obsession and is a perfect fusion of form and content because its subject is its form. Again, it is a tale about the power relationships between its two speakers. As the elder priest attempts to make the younger bow to the authority of the church, the younger man daydreams of the woman he loves.

A brief synopsis reveals the patterns of repetition in which the younger priest is trapped. In the story the two priests meet daily at the same location. The older priest hears the younger's confession of love for a woman whose own confession the younger man hears. Every day the older priest gives the younger the same sermon, attacking modernization of church rites while questioning the younger man's motives for joining the church. The love-smitten clergyman is thoroughly bored with this ritual. As he complains: "There is no day on which the conversation is not held and no detail of this conversation which is not replicated on any particular day on which this conversation is held."[5] Still, the ceremony continues unabated and the story examines why this conversation between the faithful and the wayward has not ceased. The tale suggests that both priests feel the need to communicate their feelings, but the question-and-answer catechismal form that enslaves them does not permit any exchange of ideas or feelings. Therefore, each, bored with the static quality of his role, tries to trick his opponent into adopting his own position. The older priest repeatedly attempts to trap the younger into saying that his love affair is a sin, while the younger, sensing this ploy, recurringly urges that the only love he knows is divine love. When the older man stubbornly persists, the younger interrupts him with an account of the thousands of confessions of adultery he has heard since he was first ordained. He contends that adultery, like his own love affair, should be recognized as a human impulse and not a sin. As demonstrated in this exchange, the older priest initiates a strategy to inveigle the younger in his snare, but the younger man, like A, the answerer, and Carl, the black panhandler, inverts his inquisitor's logic to prove his own point.

He says: "When were you ordained?"
I say: "1950."
He says: "These sins, your own, the sins we have been discussing. I'm sure you won't mind if I refer to them as sins although their magnitude, whether they are mortal or venial, I leave it to you to assess in the secret places of your heart—"
I say: "One sits in the confessional hearing confessions, year after year,

5. Barthelme, "The Catechist," in *Sadness*, 126, hereinafter cited parenthetically in the text as "TC."

Saturday after Saturday at four in the afternoon, twenty-one years times
fifty-two Saturdays, excluding leap year—"
   "One thousand and ninety-two Saturdays—"
   "Figuring forty-five adulteries to the average Saturday—"
   "Forty-nine thousand, one hundred and forty adulteries—"
   One wonders: "Perhaps there should be a redefinition?" ("TC," 126, 127)

In tabulating the number of Saturdays the younger priest has given
confession and the number of incidents of adultery he has heard
confessed, the older man adopts the role of responsive singer to the
younger priest's own catechism, and, in a sense, waxes sympathetic
to the younger's plea for toleration. The two protagonists of "The
Catechist" frequently sound one choric voice that questions their
differences and asks why men of such persistent faith must be in
continual conflict.

Beyond the ambiguous contest it contains, "The Catechist" also
dramatizes another trait. Its speakers live in despair without realizing the degree to which they are trapped. The older priest reads
from his sermon concerning the incessant hatred of Sunday, the day
of the Lord, throughout the world. Yet he cannot understand why
this text, read daily for years, bores the younger priest and does not
inspire him to greater religious enthusiasm. To escape the older
man's catechism, the younger priest turns his thoughts to his lover.
The older priest does not recognize that this weakness of the flesh—
what impels the younger priest to take a lover—is the same force
that makes men hate the call to devotion and self-sacrifice which
Sunday represents the world over.

He says: "Sunday, the day of rest and worship is hated by all classes of men
in every country to which the Word has been carried. Hatred of Sunday in
London approaches one hundred percent. Hatred of Sunday in Rio produces
suicides. Hatred of Sunday in Madrid is only appeased by the ritual slaughter of large black animals in rings. Hatred of Sunday in Munich is the stuff
of legend. Hatred of Sunday in Sydney is considered by the knowledgeable
to be hatred of Sunday at its most exquisite."
   I think: "She will press against me with her hands in the back pockets of
her trousers."
   The catechist opens his book. He reads: "The apathy of the listeners.
The judicious catechist copes with the difficulty." He closes the book.

I think: "Analysis terminable and interminable." I think: "Then she will leave the park looking backward over her shoulder." ("TC," 125)

These priests are forever mired in their own weaknesses and failings acquired through instinct and education. Both fear the authority of the church and the catechism, but the younger man manages to flee complete control by imagining some responses to the catechism that encompass his lover and not his awe of religion. The barriers to effective dialogue here are the men themselves, both victims of their education as priests and of their dependence on catechismal form as a means of communication. In their apathy and their penchant for analysis both men are trapped in repetitive, static patterns of speech and action.

"The Catechist" does have other than a circular, reductionistic vision of its character or situation. A slightly different quality emerges in moments when the elder priest, playing psychiatrist to the younger man's patient, asks his adversary why he became a clergyman.

"Would you say, originally, that you had a vocation? Heard a call?"
"I heard many things. Screams. Suites for unaccompanied cello. I did not hear a call."
"Nevertheless—"
"Nevertheless, I went to the clerical equipment store and purchased a summer cassock and a winter cassock. The summer cassock has short sleeves. I purchased a black hat." ("TC," 126)

Having relaxed the other man's inhibitions, the older priest next asks him what the husband of his lover does for a living.

"And the lady's husband?"
"He is a psychologist. He works in the limits of sensation. He is attempting to define precisely the two limiting sensations in the sensory continuum, the upper limit and the lower limit. He is often at the lab. He is measuring vanishing points."
"An irony."
"I suppose." ("TC," 126)

This man's occupation serves as a model for both these priests and all those individuals locked by habit, education, and instinct into roles in which they can only repeat but never seem to escape their past performances. This series of questions and answers establishes the haphazard nature of many modern lives and illustrates how individuals develop ironic commitments to roles simply by reenacting them.

Life and communication in "The Catechist" evolve into a grotesquely boring effort to keep oneself functioning on a low threshold of feeling. In responding to others, men's abilities to measure their own enfeebled sensations have become so poor that they do not realize their lives function only as meaningless, repetitive traps. The ironic nature of their vocations and the insufficient education that lead to these pursuits give them their only values. Yet these ironies offer negative value at best. Despite burlesque qualities inherent in its situation, "The Catechist" describes a thoroughly static and pessimistic world.

The central dialogue story remaining on the typology is "Kierkegaard Unfair to Schlegel," from *City Life* (1970), and it moves on to the question of creative energies. It can be seen as a continuation and expansion of "The Explanation." In "Kierkegaard," however, the conflict no longer resides between Q and A, the scientist and the artist, but between Q and A, the scientist and the ironist. The ironist, also identifiable as a jokester or humorist, finds much of his experience so ironic or absurd that he wonders if the destructive force of his laughter can create an artistic vision capable of withstanding the intimidating threats of a technological, omnipotent society. In "Kierkegaard" Q again insists that A accept the marvels of technology, and A declines by refusing to answer Q's questions. But A does not attempt to communicate with Q in "Kierkegaard" merely by playing with and evading his questions. Instead, he uses his most imaginative skills to find means of transforming his absurd answers into an ironic art that creates rather than destroys and so offers an alternative to the perils of technology.

"Kierkegaard" uses the other three developmental processes on the typology—play, the effort to know, and repetition—in its depiction of the creative acts that enable A to affirm his artistry. In an anecdote early in the story, A describes a house that he and his family rented, which was filled with board games, athletic equipment, and every imaginable apparatus for play and recreation. Reverting to his typically ironic stance, A observes that the owner of the house had succeeded in finding a cure worse than the disease of boredom that plagued him. Yet as soon as A makes this statement, he realizes his witticism functions only as that, a joke that hardly becomes the sort of artful communication he intends. Still, the emptiness of all these objects of play, as well as this quip, is added to the repertoire of techniques he evaluates in trying to transform his humor into art.

Likewise, repetition is incorporated into A's drive to transcend mere mockery. Drawing on methods he uses in "The Explanation," A, once again, describes to Q the beautiful woman he is watching undress so that he can divert Q from his continuing attempt to convert him to a belief in technology. Correspondingly, Q repeats his familiar ploy of inserting his black Rorschachlike machine into the conversation at a particular moment, suggesting to A that the machine easily, painlessly solves dilemmas which irony or art cannot. Renewing their strategies of persuasion from "The Explanation," A and Q fail to convince each other of their rival philosophies, despite these repetitions. A also learns that repeating previous gestures will not produce art, although these actions do lead to a more spontaneous communicative dialogue, revealing to A the source of his potentially ironic art. In striving to know how his irony works, A reads Kierkegaard's essay, "The Concept of Irony," and A's description of the details of this aesthetic statement forms the centerpiece of the story, gives the tale whatever plot it possesses, and shows how A uses the third element of creativity, the effort to understand or know, in his struggle to become a comic artist.

A attacks Kierkegaard because the philosopher criticizes A's own role as an ironist and flippant critic of human pretension. He forcefully denies such negative allegations by citing Kierkegaard's criticism of Schlegel's novel, *Lucinde*—that the work offers such an unfalteringly romantic, prettified vision of existence that, like a form of irony, it triumphs over reality. Yet, as A cautions Q, Kierkegaard misses the point, misunderstanding other aspects of *Lucinde*. The novel creates relationships between its characters, situations, and elements of its language—an objecthood—that has little to do with its status as a prescriptive text telling its readers how to live.[6] In this respect, A insists, Kierkegaard treats Schlegel unfairly. More personally, and A's personal outrage provides the real impetus for his rebuke of Kierkegaard here, A feels the philosopher does an injustice to ironists like himself, as well as to romantics like Schlegel. A believes irony can create as well as destroy, can surround itself with diverse tones and points of view. Therefore, its placement and juxtaposition with other devices can mitigate its conventionally negative view of life. In the right context, A contends, his own irony can achieve a reconciliation with reality.

A proceeds to prove these views in conversation with Q:

What is interesting is my making the statement that I think Kierkegaard is unfair to Schlegel. And that the whole thing is nothing else but a damned shame and crime!

Because that is not what I think at all. We have to do here with my own irony. Because of course Kierkegaard was "fair" to Schlegel. In making a statement to the contrary, I am attempting to . . . I might have several purposes—simply being provocative, for example. But mostly I am trying to annihilate Kierkegaard in order to deal with his disapproval.

Q: Of Schlegel?
A: Of me.

    6. Barthelme, "Kierkegaard Unfair to Schlegel," in *City Life*, 89–90, hereinafter cited parenthetically in the text as "KUS."

Q: What is she doing now?
A: She appears to be—
Q: How does she look?
A: Self-absorbed.
Q: That's not enough. You can't just say, "Self-absorbed." You have to give
   more . . . You've made a sort of promise which . . .
A:
Q: Are her eyes closed?
A: Her eyes are open. She's staring.
Q: What is she staring at?
A: Nothing that I can see.
Q: And
A: She's caressing her breasts.
Q: Still wearing the blouse?
A: Yes.
Q: A yellow blouse?
A: Blue. ("KUS," 91)

A loses his cool, ironic stance only for seconds. He regains his
mocking demeanor to construct an artful, ironic conversation,
which tantalizes Q with its suggestiveness and annoys him with its
ellipses, silence, and lack of stimulating detail. This sensuous,
veiled vision of a beautiful woman exemplifies the art attained by
the ironist who uses his irony's ability to create and destroy in the
same portrait. Self-absorption compounds the obscurity of this
creation: A's self-absorption in developing the conversation lan-
guidly at best; the supposed self-absorption of the woman who assumes the focus of A's vision; and Q's salacious self-absorption in
wanting to imagine a provocative view of the woman, whatever A's
description. The conversation suggests the reflective, remote irony
of much modern art and the clamoring demands of portions of its
audience that it somehow be more explicit.

But self-absorption finally destroys A's art in this tale. Q realizes
that A's love for irony has become an end in itself and thus can be
exhausted. Accordingly, Q makes one last assertion that A could
substitute a preoccupation with technology for irony's diminishing
returns. Once again, A quickly loses his ironic, detached emotional
balance, and in this instance his anger builds. Unable to recover his

irony, A cannot create a droll, self-absorbed conversation with Q. This second, far more hostile, altercation establishes the warring note on which the story concludes.

A: But I love my irony.
Q: Does it give you pleasure?
A: A poor . . . A rather unsatisfactory. . . .
Q: The unavoidable tendency of everything particular to emphasize its own particularity.
A: Yes.
Q: You could interest yourself in these interesting machines. They're hard to understand.
A: I don't like you.
Q: I sensed it.
A: These imbecile questions.
Q: Inadequately answered. . . .
A: . . . imbecile questions leading nowhere . . .
Q: The personal abuse continues.
A: . . . that voice, confident and shrill . . .
Q (aside): He has given away his gaiety and now he has nothing. ("KUS," 93)

What this bellicose exchange lacks defines just those elements which can transform A's jokes into art. His failure to create a smooth, manipulative conversation once his anger flares and his irony subsides reveals his customary reliance on maintaining some emotional distance from his fellow conversationalist. A also depends on his irony's ability to destroy his antagonist's pretensions. Although juxtaposed against other elements in the dialogue, A's irony creates quizzical, questioning responses as well as merely destructive ones. Yet A needs a veneer of gaiety, mockery, and intellectual disdain. Stripped of these qualities, as Q observes, A loses the self-absorption which enables him to mask his own identity. In its place, he reveals the petulant bitterness of self-absorption coarsened into self-obsession.

Because of the bitterness and insults between A and Q in this concluding conversation, the speakers shatter the conventions of genteel, diplomatic conversation. In wrenching dialogue form and all pretenses to artful expression, A and Q communicate their feelings and frustrations more effectively than at any other point in this story or in "The Explanation." This final situation proves the supreme irony of "Kierkegaard Unfair to Schlegel." A infuses his irony and jokes with creative energy to transform his humor into art. As the story ends, however, A discovers that he must lose this self-conscious irony to experience creative communication.

Much of the conversation in modern life, Barthelme implies, and much contemporary art resemble A's description of the beautiful woman to Q and Q's feverish demands that A tell him more. Glib, ambiguous, and empty, these words and visions reflect speakers, or artists and audiences, who appear so passive, self-absorbed, and emotionally estranged that only anger and hostility force them into meaningful communication. "Kierkegaard Unfair to Schlegel" seems to instill a dichotomy between art and conversation on one hand and heated, volatile communication on the other. Yet the story also suggests that contemporary concepts of irony and creativity need energy and vitality to bridge the growing abyss between thought and feeling. In its radical form and content, "Kierkegaard Unfair to Schlegel" advocates destroying conventional conversation in order to discover new modes of communication and creativity.

Nonetheless, "Kierkegaard Unfair to Schlegel" emerges as among the most creative tales of any on the typology. In using the creative process to test the strengths and limitations of his irony, A becomes an artist of his own life who almost learns to communicate meaningfully in his dialogue with Q. By momentarily ignoring those sources of his creativity that have produced artful, stilted conversations in the past, A creates a frank, if abrasive, exchange with Q that does communicate their feelings. Like Peterson, the protagonist of "A Shower of Gold," A learns that he must be connected to life before he can be alienated from it.[7] Thus the story examines the ability of irony to create and destroy, the possible mutual exclusiveness of art and communication—or art and irony—in modern life, and the necessity that the artist wear the mask of ironic gaiety, regardless of his attitude to a subject. In acknowledging that

7. Barthelme, "Shower," 183.

a creative speaker uses the other three processes of the typology—play, the desire to know, and repetition—in communicating with another, "Kierkegaard Unfair to Schlegel" presents a conversationalist who affirms his artistry, even when it mocks and ridicules the types of communication that conventional dialogue form contains. The story suggests that some contemporary dialogues are a modern art form in themselves, emotionally cold, uncommunicative, resistant to interpretation, and seeming to contradict the humanism that previous ages of art have exalted.

Many critics have noted Barthelme's use of the question-and-answer form throughout his stories and the frequently ironic effects the technique produces. Their observations relate and restructure the issues of the stories as previously developed. In his discussion of "The Explanation" and "Kierkegaard Unfair to Schlegel," R. E. Johnson, Jr., suggests that Barthelme's reliance on this form becomes a comment on the state of narrative values in contemporary writing and on the condition of conversation in everyday reality as well. Johnson says: "The Q/A method is in a sense a structural paradigm for the dialectics of all narrative; it creates an anticipation for itself into which it moves; the reader asks the book's question and the book supplies the reader's answer."[8] Too often men and women live in a world in which individuals, and books, talk only to themselves. Barthelme's stories reflect this phenomenon. Realizing that conversation as communication has degenerated in life, Barthelme duplicates this condition in his dialogue stories. He produces conversations in which his readers anticipate communication that never occurs. The question-answer dialectic has survived, but it is an atrophied mechanism embodying functionless, empty rituals.

In "Margins" no communication can occur between the two protagonists because one man desires to know and understand another, an undertaking Barthelme always regards as futile. In "The Explanation" and "Kierkegaard Unfair to Schlegel," some responsive exchange occurs between Q and A, but only through trickery

8. R. E. Johnson, Jr., "'Bees Barking in the Night': The End and Beginning of Donald Barthelme's Narrative," *Boundary 2*, V (Fall, 1976), 84.

and subversion in the first story, or A's effort to create art from his irony in the second. No one communicates in these stories through the dynamics of questions and answers. In "The Catechist," both the older priest and his younger confessor are so bound by church law and their daily catechism that communication has become an impossibility. Only the younger priest's ability to feel and love beyond the rigid apparatus of his interrogation enables him to commune with the reader.

As Johnson recognizes, Barthelme's dialogue stories invite the reader to participate in their conversations only to confuse and mislead his anticipation of what will and should occur in a conventional dialogue. Like those identity stories developed through the effort to know, all of Barthelme's dialogue stories ask the reader to reexamine the signs and conventions of the question-and-answer form. These stories contend that the reader's expectations of formalized or literary dialogue have falsified his responses to conversational reality, constraining him in rigid, even dangerous, modes of thought and behavior. These stories illustrate the subversion or destruction of typical conversations that would be necessary to escape the tyranny imposed by a technological society, the white power structure, or religious authority. Juxtaposing art and life, their own texts, and the presumptions of the audience perceiving them, these tales offer a critique of conventional communication as well as new means of creating dialogues.

In appraising Barthelme as both critic and creator of forms of conversation, John Leland takes a position similar to R. E. Johnson's. Leland sees Barthelme's use of questions and answers in "The Explanation" as the author's device for forcing his audience to investigate literature as a form of reasoning or a way of making sense:

Although Barthelme does mock traditional literary expectations, his writing is also profoundly liberating, as we are forced to encounter again and again our conventions of making sense . . . to explain, Barthelme suggests in "The Explanation," is to "send the appropriate error message." Or
Q: What is the content of right reason?
A: The content of right reason is rhetoric.
Q: And the content of rhetoric?

A: The content of rhetoric is purity.
Q: Is purity quantifiable?
A: Purity is not quantifiable. It is inflatable.
Q: How is our rhetoric preserved against attacks by other rhetoric?
A: Our rhetoric is preserved by our elected representatives. In the fat of their heads.

Right reason shares for Barthelme a similar status with literature. Both are a function of cultural codes and conventions which prescribe our ways of thinking, seeing, being.[9]

Observing that neither modern life nor contemporary literature offers coherent patterns of meaning, Barthelme parodies this fact in his dialogue stories. Reason has disappeared from the world in these tales, and the stories become exchanges between questioners and respondents who seek explanations for others' actions, whether or not intelligible motives exist. Leland, like Johnson, realizes that these conversations symbiotically feed on current relationships between life and art. Thus to offer explanations in a meaningless world is to make the most socially acceptable rationalization or, in computer terminology, to send the appropriate error message. Furthermore, the search for rationality, as this passage on right reason, rhetoric, and purity demonstrates, transforms reason into a litany of nonsense, a ridiculous script in which one speaker avoids the other's questions with nebulous terms or comic, tautological definitions.

Barthelme does, however, offer a solution for the artist who seeks rationality within his dialogue stories. This speaker must divide himself into two voices: one persona who is actively involved in the power struggle of the conversation and another who stands outside the dialogue, observing it and rationally exposing its failure to communicate. Neil Schmitz in two articles on irony and satire in Barthelme's writing refers to this dualism as "the split between the writer who falls within the text and the writer of the text."[10] The first writer represents the artistic sensibility and the second the ironic, and this division between art and irony occurs whenever the artistic force in the dialogue uses irony to examine the illogicality of his verbal sparring.

9. Leland, "Remarks Re-marked," 806–807.
10. Neil Schmitz, "Donald Barthelme and the Emergence of Modern Satire," *Minnesota Review*, I (1972), 110.

Irony therefore assumes distinct connotations in the dialogue stories. Not only is it a means for one speaker to bring reason to the conversation, but Schmitz astutely shows how irony functions in "Kierkegaard" to bring other creative qualities to the story. Schmitz sees A's effort to attack Kierkegaardian theories because they destroy his own ironic role as an unexpected victory for A. Forced by Q into admitting that Kierkegaard was perfectly fair to Schlegel, A establishes that his own sense of irony has imaginative value. As Schmitz reads "Kierkegaard Unfair to Schlegel," "Irony distinguishes, ascertains value, does not destroy. The ironist who believes he has the 'magical power' to make objects cringe and disappear puts himself within the pale of his irony."[11] By momentarily removing himself from the exchanges of the dialogue, the ironic half of A, the artist, brings reason and an inventive irony to the story.

Throughout the story A attempts to discredit Kierkegaard's theory of irony and to replace it with an irony all his own. He achieves his goal by occasionally withdrawing from his debate with Q to verbalize his own perceptions and concerns. Before and after his factual presentation of the philosopher's views, A allows his mind to drift spontaneously over the range of his daily thoughts and actions. Again Schmitz assesses this strategy as A's successful effort to evade the oversimplifications of Kierkegaard's thought and the irrationality of Q's questions with his own inspired human consciousness:

The paraphrase of Kierkegaard is rammed home in short hard sentences, but its declarative intellectuality is subsumed fore and aft by the variegated plenum of experience, by the constant stream of relationships to things, speech, people, and art. It is this consciousness, always slipping away from the fixed locus of the abstract, this plastic consciousness which attends so uniquely and diversely to the world that Barthelme ultimately celebrates. For it is the discourse of that attuned consciousness that is at once his subject and his morality.[12]

The last two sentences in this passage contain the best critical summary of the subject of any Barthelme dialogue. All four dialogues celebrate the escape of a consciousness attuned to the world

11. *Ibid.*, 118.
12. *Ibid.*

from an interrogator who wishes to hold it in bondage to an abstract idea, system, or belief.

We move on to four auxiliary dialogues, "The Reference," "The New Music," "Morning," and "The Leap," in which the ironic escape of the human consciousness from irrational questions continues to shape the conversation. "The Reference," from *Amateurs* (1976), is a story like all on the typology centering in play. It is wildly humorous and concerned with an underground hiding figure. It depicts a long telephone conversation between an executive of the Arkansas State Planning Commission and a Mr. Cockburn, a reference given to this organization by a prospective employee. The executive attempts to discover whether a certain Shel McPartland has been a good city planner and whether he would make an effective employee for the commission. Quickly, the employer realizes Cockburn is playing with his questions, willfully confusing and subverting his efforts to determine McPartland's abilities and failings. Moreover, Cockburn camouflages his evaluations of McPartland beneath a facetious, outrageously funny slang that mimics the hip jive talk of jazz musicians. As their conversation continues, Cockburn's vernacular becomes infectious, and the executive, who has spoken decorously at first, soon composes his own free-form counterpoint to Cockburn's zany language. Their dialogue sounds most musical when the employer asks simple questions about McPartland and Cockburn echoes similar refrains.

"Is he fake?"
"Not more than anybody else. He has facades but who does not?"
"Does he know the blue lines?"
"Excellent with the blue lines."
"Does he know the old songs?"
"He'll crack your heart with the old songs."
"Does he have the right moves?"
"People all over America are sitting in darkened projection rooms right this minute studying the McPartland moves."[13]

Two underground hiding men are protected by this conversation. Cockburn's wiles thoroughly obscure Shel McPartland's skills and

13. Donald Barthelme, "The Reference," in *Amateurs*, 150–51, hereinafter cited parenthetically in the text as "TR."

liabilities as an engineer and city planner, and Cockburn's choice of
a flip, insouciant tone to answer serious questions about a man he
respects puts his own identity in doubt.

Beyond Cockburn's unwillingness to answer the personnel manager's inquiries, "The Reference" implies that a personality cannot
be reduced to a quantifiable commodity but represents uncertain
combinations of variable pressures. Cockburn defends his slang
from his interrogator's censure with a rebuttal: "Different folk I
talk to in different ways. I got to keep myself interested" ("TR,"
148). As in "The Explanation," the individuals here use conversation to play with their own personalities. Hence as the telephone
interview proceeds, the personnel executive learns less and less
about McPartland. Cockburn even gives a vague physical description of McPartland and delights in presenting him as all things to
all people. "He's got a certain common-as-dirt quality. That's right
under his laser-sharp M.I.T. quality" ("TR," 151). When Cockburn
praises McPartland for developing the artichoke composed of nothing but heart, which thus requires no peeling, his questioner re-
minds Cockburn that some people might still enjoy the layer-
by-layer unveiling. Cockburn, however, pretends to find levels of
meaning in human personality or those who would respect them as
incomprehensible.

The only consistent quality Cockburn gives to McPartland is
"warp." "He was and is warp" ("TR," 149), Cockburn proclaims
proudly. Yet just as the personnel manager grows wary of this mysterious trait, Cockburn defines warp as in "the warp to power"
("TR," 152). McPartland and he are enemies, Cockburn tells the executive, but he must acknowledge merit wherever he finds it. The
employer grows so impressed with Cockburn's arguments for Mc-
Partland that he agrees to hire McPartland at $50,000 a year, $10,000
more than he originally offered for the job. The final joke of this
wildly playful story turns on Cockburn's real identity. In one of his
last exchanges with the personnel manager, he reveals that he
is McPartland's employment agent. By fascinating his interrogator with McPartland, he has earned 10 percent of $50,000 for his
services.

Even as briefly summarized, "The Reference" shows direct affinities to our earlier tale, "The Explanation." Both have a zany, unpredictable humor, and both describe a man who hides from the sources of power and technology in his world by playfully conversing with a representative of this structured society. Each story reveals the impotence of power and the deterioration of language. Just as A, the evasive hiding man of "The Explanation," learns to transmit computer error messages that pretend to mean as much as words once did, so Cockburn ambiguously describes McPartland's quality of warp as the warp to power. Ironically, the personnel manager becomes so intrigued with McPartland's warp to power that he immediately hires him at an inflated salary with only a vague idea of what the phrase might mean. Power so fears its rivals that the planning commission eagerly consumes this man in its workings. Yet in both of these stories, as in "Hiding Man," presumed weakness outwits supposed power; the devious misdirection of a sly, calculating individual leads a scientific society or a bureaucracy astray. A and Cockburn triumph as the heroes of these stories. They possess the plastic consciousness that, attuned to the world, can evade the traps set by a technologically ordered society and devise its own snares in which their stolid foes quickly become enveloped.

Further resemblances between "The Reference" and "The Explanation" only substantiate the inability of the speakers in these tales ever to connect with one another. A's unwillingness to accept machine technology in "The Explanation" finds its parallel in Cockburn's refusal to tell the planning commissioner whether McPartland would be an indispensable employee, or whether McPartland's desirable warp makes him gifted but dangerously eccentric. Cockburn's fey retorts to the executive's initially sincere questions cast not only McPartland's reliability in doubt but impugn Cockburn as a dependable reference. Both stories suggest worlds of such increasing predictability and self-absorption that dialogue becomes the domain of conversationalists who playfully seek to escape themselves. Scientists and engineers would seem to have limited capacities for these games. Barthelme pinpoints these limitations in the last sentence of "The Reference." In his preceding remark the planning commissioner calls McPartland's engineering qualifications "a dream of beauty" ("TR," 153). Full of guile even in his final comment, Cockburn replies, "Not a dream, sir, not a dream. Engineers, sir, never sleep and dream only in the daytime" ("TR," 153). The engineers and social planners in Barthelme's playful dialogue stories qualify as diligent and hardworking but prove unromantic, unadventurous, and unimaginative. Therefore, the mind of a clever, artful individual can always elude the dulled collective thought of a scientific society that daydreams only to dissipate its boredom. Thus this method of escape becomes a recurring pattern in the dialogue stories.

Among the many patterns of similarity between these stories, some crucial differences nevertheless exist. In "The Explanation," A emerges as the unabashed free spirit, the humanist who refuses to yield the mysteries of his personality to the tyrannical corporate spirit represented by Q, the questioner. In "The Reference," however, A has become Cockburn, the professional colleague and representative of McPartland, the engineer who desires to become part of the bureaucratic planning commission. Though Cockburn effectively disguises his client and his own reasons for promoting McPartland behind his brash bantering, Cockburn's teasing answers function as advertisements for McPartland's skills, even with his warp. Unlike A, Cockburn does not use the dialogue form to escape the inducements of the modern industrial state. He becomes an agent and middleman for McPartland and thereby serves the state. Yet Cockburn possesses a redeeming, further contradictory trait. He has a penchant for satirizing the goals and aspirations of the planning engineer whose talents he sells. His remark that engineers never sleep and dream only in daytime reveals his willingness to dehumanize humanity. "The Reference" divides the traditional question-and-answer form of the dialogue story into one questioner, the planning commission employer, and two answerers, the absent McPartland and his loquacious representative Cockburn. In this way the tale enables Cockburn to be what Neil Schmitz has called the writer in the story and the writer outside of it,[14] criti-

14. Schmitz, "Irony," 487.

cizing the tale and judging its standards. Regardless of its affinities to "The Explanation," "The Reference," with its conception of the telephone reference as secret agent and employee of the job candidate, emerges like "Hiding Man" as a far more devious, cynical story than "The Explanation," with its clearly drawn battle lines between scientist and humanist.

Ultimately, "The Explanation" and "The Reference" belong in the same box on the typology because they describe in outrageously humorous terms underground hiding men who fail to communicate with the societies from which they have fled. Both of these men engage in dialogues, the question-and-answer interview in "The Explanation" and a syncopated counterpoint in "The Reference," that allow them to play with their antagonists while fleeing the insidious, omnipotent forces these men represent. Only by destroying the modes of their exchanges could these men communicate honestly and directly with their enemies. Unfortunately, rationality has left these dialogues. In "The Explanation" the scientist no more explains the purpose and function of his machine to the artist than the telephone reference in "The Reference" can explain why his enemy, who currently employs him, should be hired. Without explanations or reasons, only play persists, and dialogue, communication, and all ways of making sense deteriorate.

Locating the next auxiliary dialogue story, we find the tale "The New Music," from *Great Days* (1979), under the rubric of the effort to know. "The New Music" shares this box with the racial dialogue of "Margins," which presents a conversation that degenerates into a collage of disconnected remarks because of the futility of the desire of one of its speakers to know the other. Although "The New Music" has enough affinities with "Margins" to make it a clear choice for this position on the typology, the story contains several major departures from "Margins" or any of the previous dialogue stories. At its outset "The New Music" already has the sound of fragmented contrapuntal jazz. Yet the tale does not deteriorate because of the impossibility of its conversationalists to know one another so much as from their failure to know themselves and their pasts. "The New Music" begins nervously with the quick choral notes aired by its vocalists immediately achieving the rhythm and infectious flippancy that the conversation between Cockburn and the planning commissioner assumes midway in "The Reference." "The New Music" literally composes a new music for Barthelme.

Fascinated by various ways of knowing, "The New Music" depicts two brothers who reminisce in dialogue about their repressive ogre of a mother, a woman who constantly sought "knowledge of things unspeakable."[15] In the flight of their collective imagination, she becomes not just the stern matriarch of the old jazz song "Momma Don't 'low," but a high priestess of the Eleusinian mysteries of ancient Greece. According to Greek legend, during their ecstatic Dionysian revelries these priestesses could summon the earth goddess, Persephone, and her mother, Demeter.[16] Yet the brothers feel that the primal, forbidden knowledge their earth mother once coveted now seems ridiculous. Obsessed with her own magic, she denied them love and her permission to play their musical instruments. Their momma did not allow for their desires, and many years later these siblings recall the dark side of her domineering personality:

—Like when she played Scrabble. She played to kill. Used the filthiest words insisting on their legitimacy. I was shocked.
—In her robes of deep purple.
—Seeking the ecstatic vision. That which would lift people four feet off the floor.
—Six feet.
—Four feet or six feet off the floor. Persephone herself appearing.
—The chanting in the darkened telesterion.
—Persephone herself appearing, hovering. Accepting offerings, balls of salt, solid gold serpents, fig branches, figs.
—Hallucinatory dancing. All the women drunk.
—Dancing with jugs on their heads, mixtures of barley, water, mint—
—Knowledge of things unspeakable—
—Still, all I wanted to do was a little Krummhorn. A little Krummhorn once in a while.
—Can open graves, properly played.

15. Donald Barthelme, "The New Music," in *Great Days* (New York, 1979), 35, hereinafter cited parenthetically in the text as "NM."
16. Bullfinch, *Mythology*, 51.

—I was never good. Never really good.
—Who could practice?
—And your clavier.
—Momma didn't 'low clavier.
—Thought it would unleash in her impulses better leashed? I don't know.
—Her dark side. They all have them, mommas. ("NM," 35)

Unfortunately, Momma's behavior, or her sons' memory of it, has stereotyped their relationships with other women. Her cold severity with her children and her disapproval of their girl friends have made them aging bachelors who are proud of their sexual aloofness. Yet, once again, they are betrayed by a kind of knowledge. Congratulating themselves on escaping a bodily compulsion like alcoholism, they assume that sex belongs in the same class of potentially dangerous indulgences of the body. These boylike men believe that occasional sexual contact revitalizes the body, but frequent involvement might become compulsive. Fortunately, the body's wisdom exceeds their own. The body knows what the men do not: sex fulfills a natural physical need. The two men begin their discussion of these themes by returning to the old blues refrain about yet another pleasure that Momma did not allow them:

—As with much else. Momma didn't 'low Patrice.
—I remember. You still see her?
—Once in a way. Saw her Saturday. I hugged her and her body leaped. That was odd.
—How did that feel?
—Odd. Wonderful.
—The body knows.
—The body is perspicacious.
—The body ain't dumb.
—Words can't say what the body knows.
—Sometimes I hear them howling from the hospital.
—The detox ward.
—Tied to the bed with beige cloths.
—We've avoided it.
—So far.
—Knock wood.
—I did. ("NM," 34)

On one plane, "The New Music" details a classic oedipal example of the destructive force of an overly strong mother on her sons. On another level, these siblings are stunted by several varieties of knowledge which prove false or unattainable: their mother's primitive search for knowledge of things unspeakable, their own misconceptions of what the body knows and values, and, finally, the questionable knowledge offered by books about sexuality such as *The Hite Report*. This last kind of knowledge, like the other two, has lastingly damaged these men's relationships with women, and their dialogue reflects the brothers' fear of their girl friends' familiarity with the sexual standards legitimized by these books. One brother responds by making sexist male taunts to his girl friend, even though he realizes he and his brother are growing too old to rely on this dubious advantage. The other brother suggests that they use the new music, the latest fad or fashion, as one might use alcohol or a drug to forget that this spurious knowledge has harmed their sex lives:

—I have to tell you something. Susie's been reading *The Hite Report*. She says other women have more orgasms than she does. Wanted to know why.
—Where does one go to complain? Where does one go to complain, when fiends have worsened your life?
—I told her about the Great Septuagesimal Orgasm, implying she could have one, if she was good. But it is growing late, very late indeed, for such as we.
—But perhaps one ought not to complain, when fiends have worsened your life. But rather, emulating the great Stoics, Epictetus and so on, just zip into a bar and lift a few, whilst listening to the new, incorrigible, great-white-shark, knife music. ("NM," 36)

This passage epitomizes the qualities of the new music that the story reproduces. The tale records a collage of two voices that seldom respond or listen to one another. Nonetheless, they engage in a series of questions and reactions by which they attempt to know and understand the meaning of their lives. Frequently, these responses are heightened musical phrases such as "Where does one go to complain?" in the passage above, or, "Momma didn't 'low," from an old jazz song intoned throughout the story. The recurrence

of these motifs gives the story some sense of coherence but a tre-
mendous feeling of futility as well, particularly at those moments
when the brothers sense they are aging, so much time has passed,
and Momma's ways have left their mark. As the brothers conclude:
"The new music says, life becomes more and more exciting as there
is less and less time. Momma wouldn't have 'lowed it. But Momma's gone" ("NM," 37).

Like the narrator of "See the Moon," the central story in the box
above "The New Music" on the typology, the brothers realize they
can never completely know who they are, even if they consume
their lives with knowledge of *The Hite Report*, the Great Septuagesimal Orgasm, the great Stoics, and all the other bits of miscellaneous information that fill this story. Regretfully, they can know
and understand with certainty only the strange, atonal music in
which they communicate. Its composition serves as their latest
fad, even though their momma would not have allowed it. Because
momma has died, the story suggests that this dishonest, vulgar
music may function as a substitute for their unrequited love of the
woman. In evoking this sound, Barthelme produces the nervous,
jagged rhythms of a hedonistic society in which everyone speaks,
no one listens, and few have knowledge of themselves.

The new music continues in the next auxiliary story, "Morning,"
from *Great Days* (1979), located one box to the right of "The New
Music" on the horizontal axis of the dialogue stories. "Morning"
occupies the same box with the central dialogue story, "The Catechist," and both stories develop conversations through the process
of repetition. In "Morning," however, the manic, musical quality of
the tale intensifies its depiction of a dialogue as a series of repeated
questions and answers in which no communication results because
each speaker has heard the other's remarks so many times before.
Yet like "The Catechist," "Morning" faults individuals' education
for leading them into endless rounds of static observations and responses that pass for exchanges of information and feeling.

As the story begins, two nameless male voices awaken in their
apartment to the gray light of another day. Immediately, they begin

jabbering at each other. One insists that the other acknowledge his fears, while the speaker lists all the antidotes he possesses for his own anxieties. In this trembling, nervous fashion the story evolves. Virtually nothing happens in the tale because these men have been educated to react rather than to act, to talk without ever stopping to think about what they are saying, and to regard their own behavior as fluid and adaptable but thoroughly estranged from their motives. Accordingly, these men live in constant flight from themselves, their language, and each other, and fear dominates everything they do. The two work as professional researchers, and they need government grant money to survive. Yet they worry that the same failure of communication which exists between them has permeated all of society. They fear the vast proliferation of signs, symbols, and false social inducements that promise more than they can ever gratify. This phenomenon sounds familiarly like critic John Leland's description of the failure of the narrator's education in "Me and Miss Mandible," the central identity story also developed through repetition. These men most dread that even the basic relationships between signs and reality have gone awry and made their education and lives completely meaningless. This recurring nightmare prompts the following exchange in which the speakers attempt to reassure each other that, despite their fears, a few of the rudimentary signs they have been taught to acknowledge still justify meaningful interpretations:

—Think we can get some of that fine grant money?
—If we can make ourselves understood. If I applaud, the actors understand that I am pleased. If I take a needle and singe it with a match, you understand that I have picked up a splinter in my foot. If I say, "Have any of the English residents been murdered?" you understand that I am cognizant of native unrest. If I hand you two copies of a thesis bound in black cloth, you understand that I am trying to improve myself. Appeals to patriotism, small-boat warnings up.
—Say you're frightened.
—I'm frightened. But maybe not tomorrow.[17]

17. Donald Barthelme, "Morning," in *Great Days*, 125, hereinafter cited parenthetically in the text as "M."

Like this excerpt, all of "Morning" projects a great sense of static repetition, of two minds in constant agitation but moving nowhere. The speakers constantly repeat themselves, attempting to codify the signs they use into a fixed language. They desperately hope that, outliving their fears and another gray morning, tomorrow might be better. Their badinage has the hysterical monotony of the bad rock music which the more traumatized of the two describes to his similarly nervous compatriot. With the usual redundancy this speaker tells the other he does not fear that this once new music has become old music in his own lifetime, nor even that this fact fails to alarm him significantly.

—They played "One O'Clock Jump," "Two O'Clock Jump," "Three O'Clock Jump," and "Four O'Clock Jump." They were very good. I saw them on television. They're all dead now.
—That scare you?
—Naw that doesn't scare me.
—That scare you?
—Naw that doesn't scare me.
—What scares you?
—My hand scares me. It's not well.
—Hear that? That's wolf talk. Not bad, is it? ("M," 126)

The truly ominous quality of this passage does not lie in the one speaker's purported indifference to the passage of time or to his own aging. Rather, his admission that his trembling hand now jumps like the jittery, repetitious music he once enjoyed characterizes a man who lives in fear that he can no longer respond to many of the signs and dialogue and much of the music in the contemporary world. This man trembles because, like the dead members of the defunct rock band, he has lost his ability to connect with others, and fear consumes him. Even though his conversation tries to imitate the staccato percussion of the band's music, the repetitive questions and answers the two voices compose fail to establish good communication or even basic trust between them. In fact, the other speaker, violating the conventions of the dialogue, directly addresses the reader in the last line of the above passage. He doubts that his roommate tells the truth about his shaking hand. Accusing him of crying wolf, he nevertheless grants that his companion can concoct a credible lie. Here one again encounters the quality which critic Neil Schmitz defines as Barthelme's "split between the writer who falls within the text and the writer of the text."[18] Barthelme uses this device throughout his dialogue stories for ironic effect, and in this passage the technique demonstrates the failure of the static repetition of questions and answers to generate the atmosphere of good faith or sincerity necessary for honest, reciprocal communication.

The attempt to make responsive dialogue from static repetitions continues throughout "Morning." Of all the returns or repetitions that the tale criticizes, the return to one's home or original family environment proves most destructive to any sense of legitimate communication. As the speaker, who bemoans the death of rock 'n' roll and the inability of signs to indicate what they signify, once again answers his interrogator's obsessive questions, he reveals why home is one of the worst sources of his own and many individuals' education.

—Going home.
—No, thank you.
—You're afraid of it?
—Indeed, do I still live?
—What are you afraid of?
—One old man alone in a room. Two old men alone in a room. Three old men alone in a room.
—Well maybe you could talk to them or something.
—And say: Howdy, have you heard about pleasure, have you heard about fun? Let's go out and bust up a bar, it's been a long time. What are you up to, what are your plans? Still lifting weights? I've been screwing all night, how 'bout you? "You please me, happiness!" ("M," 128)

In this exchange, the refrain, "One old man alone in a room. Two old men alone in a room . . ." assumes the same gasp of death rattle that "One O'Clock Jump," "Two O'Clock Jump . . ." does in the immediately preceding passage. The speaker of these choral lamentations not only fears his own death and dying but the death of rock

18. Schmitz, "Irony," 487.

'n' roll and his immediate family, two of his most potent educational influences. His puritanical, upright family, like that of the two brothers in "The New Music," disdained the pleasures of its children's bodies. Consequently, he has spent his adult life in physical rebellion from this education. His pursuit of a sensual hedonism has made him restless yet enervated, constantly in motion, hence forever listless and incapable of maintaining the concentration and emotion necessary for conversation, friendship, or love. Note that his final comment in this passage, "You please me, happiness!" is addressed not to his questioner, his family, or even the reader of the story but to a highly ephemeral feeling that constantly changes its shape and pattern to meet the whims of society. Rejecting the signs and rules of their formal education, the protagonists of "Morning" blindly absorb their most hedonistic impulses, and the men's total license makes their daily communication a series of static repetitions. Frightened by their failure to reach one another, they constantly verbalize motion devising endless plans to escape their lives. As "Morning" begins and ends, another morning looms on the horizon; another round of repetitions emerges in which the new music, obsession, or pastime will look and sound suspiciously like the old.

Moving on to the final case, "The Leap," from *Great Days* (1979), we find one of Barthelme's successfully communicative dialogue stories. The creative process enlivens a lengthy exchange between two speakers, one of whom prepares to take the leap of faith necessary for his belief in God. In itemizing his reasons for deciding to believe, this voice confronts his antagonist, the other speaker, who describes himself "as an incorrigibly double-minded man."[19] The latter both encourages his sparring partner, seconding the other's evidence with proof of his own, and challenges him as well, playing with this evidence by demonstrating that the same views could be used with equal facility to deny the existence of God. In their frolicsome give-and-take, both men create a view of the world in which, if nothing else, God might exist. "The Leap" quickly be-

19. Donald Barthelme, "The Leap," in *Great Days*, 153, hereinafter cited parenthetically in the text as "TL."

comes Barthelme's happiest, most affirming dialogue story as the tale posits a Platonic universe in which God seems the probable artist of much beauty. In this tale man in his creative, imitative acts aspires to godlike, artistic heights. Like "Kierkegaard Unfair to Schlegel" and all of Barthelme's stories on the vertical column of those tales concerned with creative expression, "The Leap" depicts a character who becomes an artist through his creation of a vision that chooses to affirm a chaotic, confusing world rather than to deny it. In all the stories here the act of creativity encompasses the processes of play, the desire to know, and repetition, the three other modes through which the stories collectively develop.

A detailed reading of "The Leap" shows how skillfully its voices blend the techniques of play, the desire to know, and repetition, creating an argument for God's existence as they converse and legitimately commune with each other. The believer and the double-minded man agree that the trees make a good subject about which to contemplate the magnificence of a probable supreme being. Therefore, they begin quoting Joyce Kilmer's amusingly banal poem, "Trees," as proof of God's existence, or at least as evidence that the creative mind can believe in God.

—The trees. "I think that I shall never see slash A poem as lovely as a tree."
—"A tree whose hungry mouth is prest slash Against the earth's sweet flowing breast."
—Why "mouth"?
—Why "breast"?
—The working of the creative mind.
—An unfathomable mystery.
—Never to be fathomed.
—I wouldn't even want to fathom it. If one fathomed it, who can say what frightful things might thereupon be fathomed?
—Fathoming such is beyond the powers of poor ravening noodles like ourselves, who, but for the— ("TL," 147)

The choice of Kilmer's cloying, trite poem as a human equivalent to the beauty of God's creative powers indicates the enormous inferiority of man's artistic abilities compared with those of a potential omnipotent force. As this excerpt shows, however, the two speakers momentarily investigate the poem and the creative mind that composed it before the double-minded man speculates that creatures of God such as they might be should not even presume to understand creativity. A great sense of play, one of the components of the creative process, exists in these men's singsong recitation of the poem to one another, in their questioning of Kilmer's ludicrous word choice, and in their conclusion that the creative mind, perhaps like the mind of God, cannot be fathomed.

Repetition, the second component of creativity in the tales developed through this technique, also has a major role in this passage and throughout "The Leap." These men's repetition of the word "fathomed" and the quality of unfathomability illustrates their fascination with words and processes, regardless whether their continual invoking of a sound or an action explains to them the workings of the creative mind. Like all Barthelme characters caught on the treadmill of repetitive gestures or endeavors, they continue these performances despite their frustrations. Yet this sheer, repeated unfathomability of the creative mind makes these two acutely aware of the futility of their attempts to know Joyce Kilmer, themselves, God, or any other artist. Like all Barthelme's stories championing the creative process, "The Leap" assimilates play, repetition, and the effort to know into its techniques of development; and this tale, in confirming the mystery of the creative imagination much as do "A Shower of Gold," "Daumier," or "Paul Klee," affirms the privacy of artistic inspiration. In "The Leap," stressing the mystique of the artistic imagination suggests the existence of the greatest artist, God, even for an incorrigibly double-minded man. In this tale creativity springs from the inability to understand creativity.

This relationship between the mind of God, the supreme artist, and the imagination of man, an infinitely lesser creator, emerges again and again in "The Leap." As the conversation progresses, the believer appears to be a man willing to have faith in both God and the god of human intellect, science. His model for the means by which economic and social justice will be reached in an overpopulated world of the future explains how society might be governed if a benevolent God controlled the most advanced computer yet devised by man. With great delight, the double-minded man probes his friend, asking him if his plan is human or divine and if one plan must necessarily precede the other.

—So God's creatures, in your opinion, multiplying and multiplying as per instruction, will—
—Propagate fiercely until the sum total of what has been propagated yields a pressure so intense that every feature great or small of every life great or small is instantly scrutinized, weighed, judged, decided upon, and disposed of by the sum total of one's peers in doubtless electronic ongoing all-seeing everlasting congress assembled. Thus if one guy has a little advantage, a little edge, it is instantly taken away from him and similarly if another guy has a little lack, some little lack, this little lack is instantly supplied by the arbiters. Things cannot be otherwise. Because there's not going to be any room to fucking move, man, do you follow me? there's not going to be any room to fucking sneeze, without you're sneezing on somebody.
—This is the Divine plan?
—Who can know the subtle workings of His mind? But it seems to be the way events are—
—That's another thing. The human mind.
—Good God yes. The human mind. ("TL," 149)

This passage demonstrates some of the resemblances and differences between "The Leap" and "Kierkegaard Unfair to Schlegel," the central dialogue story in the same box on the typology with "The Leap." Whereas in "Kierkegaard" the scientific spirit attempts to trap the artist into believing in an electronic world, in "The Leap" the double-minded man persuades the scientist that technology could not exist if man, with his love of the mechanized and the mechanical, were not trying to imitate the mind of God, the greatest artist. In effect, the double-minded man represents a criticism of the Kierkegaardian ideal. This voice assumes the role of what critic Neil Schmitz recognizes as the writer in the text and the writer of the text,[20] both artist and ironist, who can never completely reconcile his two impulses and who senses it will take an unlikely fusion of both for him to believe completely in God. Lest this double-minded man appear as willingly acquiescent to the spirit of God as his leaping friend, this dialogue's most directly

20. Schmitz, "Irony," 487.

anti-Kierkegaardian moment reveals the continual dichotomy under which the artistic ironist strains.

—Purity of heart is to will one thing.
—No. Here I differ with Kierkegaard. Purity of heart is, rather, to will several things, and not know which is the better, truer thing, and to worry about this forever.
—A continuing itch of the mind.
—Sometimes assuagable by timely masturbation.
—I forgot. Love.
—Oh my God, yes. Love. Both human and divine.
—Love, the highest form of human endeavor.
—Coming or going, the absolute zenith.
—Is it permitted to differ with Kierkegaard?
—Not only permitted but necessary. If you love him. ("TL," 152)

This excerpt epitomizes all the believer and the double-minded man can fathom about belief, love, God, and art in the course of their musical exchange. Interestingly, the believer acknowledges love as a means of communication which alleviates the frustration of being forever torn between several points of view, while the double-minded man initially thinks only of masturbation and self-gratification as a solution to his problem. The believer's mention of love, however, suggests divine love to the double-minded man. He believes God's artistic gift of the natural world to humanity represents His divine love for mankind. Moreover, individuals in imitating God's artistry express love for their fellow man. But, insists the double-minded speaker, love means both artistry and irony. To love Kierkegaard's thought means one must dissect it, contradict it, and see through it.

This passage moves delightfully from a question about the nature of belief to its possible solution in love, to its corollary in divine love, and ends on the realization that love of the artistry of Kierkegaard's thought presupposes a belief in and love of God. In the process of this witty, graceful conversation two men fall in love with the possibility of an idea and, as is characteristic of Barthelme's stories developed through the process of creativity, actually communicate with one another. Delicately and humorously, this story affirms the creative artistry inherent in belief, God, the double-minded man, and the dialogue form itself.

In a final summary of the four central dialogue stories and the four auxiliary dialogue stories, their similar and contrasting views of reality become apparent. The central dialogue stories, with the exception of "Kierkegaard" developed by its sense of the creative process, project a vision of a far from satisfying, even paralyzed world. In each tale language has deteriorated, communication functions intermittently at best, and the question-and-answer form has become an outmoded convention used to evade rather than express thought and feeling. Despite their bizarre, frequent bolts of humor these stories seem grim because they posit a world dominated by power and power relationships. In "The Explanation" the power structure wants to absorb and destroy the individual artistic impulse. Yet it lacks an explanation for the function of its machines or why it should inherently prevail over humanistic reasoning. Correspondingly, a presumptuous, camouflaged bigotry forms the power structure in "Margins." The white man, Edward, wishes to use the conversational form to transform the black, Carl, into a presentable, achieving member of his own race, but Carl's wiles consistently defeat Edward's attempts to reduce and classify him. In a similar vein, "The Catechist" dramatizes the intractability of the power structure. Its seemingly endless series of question, comment, and digression forms a basic paradigm for all the dialogue stories. Mired in repetition and its own conventions, controlled by the authority and awe invested in one of the speakers, and meaninglessly continued because both participants have been educated in learned responses which seem impossible to eradicate, the tale virtually absorbs itself. With the final dialogue story, "Kierkegaard Unfair to Schlegel," contemporary conversation itself has become the ultimate power structure, yet some possibility for legitimate communication does emerge in the tale. A learns that to become an artist he must first become an artist of his own life. In turn, he realizes that only by communicating with others can he communicate in art, that his irony destroys as well as creates, and, finally, that art and communication may prove mutually exclusive in modern life.

The power plays that dominate the central dialogue stories have all but disappeared from three of the four auxiliary dialogue stories. These stories, "The New Music," "Morning," and "The Leap," all from *Great Days* (1979), represent a continued development of Barthelme's concept of the dialogue form. The insistent questions and devious answers exchanged by antagonists in the earlier conversations are not present here. The surly interrogators and wary, hiding men have been replaced by an addled but open counterpoint. In these tales relatives, friends, and roommates offer one another encouragement and support against their mutual enemy, fear. These speakers fear age, boredom, and failure. In their incessant urge to escape these anxieties they produce a nervous, jangled new music, which extends even to the more conventional power strategies of the fourth auxiliary story, "The Reference." Yet this music sounds anything but glum. Its persistent syncopation evokes a rehearsal hall filled with jazz musicians. The infectious rhythms of the tales keep returning to refrains from old songs or harmonies that link and tie the motifs of each story together. These tales at first seem flippant, but learning to appreciate their jazz brings a gradual understanding that these stories are jive orchestrations of a new age of anxiety.

Despite the music to be heard, far less communication occurs in these auxiliary stories than sheer noise. As in the central dialogue stories, language is used to hide and evade, and the glibness of this talk frequently camouflages and inhibits the speaker's feeling. These confidants form a sophisticated, brittle smart set, who clutter their hedonistic lives with the objects and trivia that their society values at the moment. Though their speakers adroitly manipulate clichés, these tales demonstrate how this empty facility with language finally erodes these voices' capacity for feeling.

This survey of both the central dialogue stories and the auxiliary dialogue stories displays the affinities that all eight share. The Kierkegaardian philosophy mentioned in two of these stories directly colors all eight of them. With his uncompromising views that belief requires a leap of faith, that purity of heart means to will only one thing, and that irony functions as a completely destructive, uncreative force, Kierkegaard presents a consistently either-or conception of reality. The yes-and-no, question-and-answer dialectics of conversational form smoothly accommodate his hypotheses. This view, however, finds opposition in the strong sense of irony that pervades all these stories. The ironic vision in these tales creates values as well as destroying them, contends that belief must be a double-minded process embodying skepticism as well as faith, and feels that purity of heart means willing several things without being able to choose among them. In these ways, irony attempts its own reconciliation with reality. This effort affirms uncertainty as a creative principle in its own right capable of sustaining belief in God and love of one's fellow man. This battle between the Kierkegaardian absolute and double-minded irony evolves in all the dialogue stories into a stalemate in which each speaker retreats into his own self-absorption. His boredom or his pride in the unresolved state of his irony continues to build. Finally, he can be provoked into communication only by anger or a violent verbal rebuttal from the other speaker.

Regardless of the state of contemporary conversation, Barthelme does find a victor in these debates: the speaker, who, independent of his antagonist, uses his imaginative, artistic consciousness to commune with the world while paradoxically trapped within the prison of arid questions and answers. This creative consciousness recognizes irony, contradiction, a resilient, malleable imagination, and a subversive assault on authority as its tools in removing established patterns of dialogue and replacing them with communication and art.

Chapter III

The Society Stories

This chapter examines in detail the four major society stories, with italicized titles, appearing on the typology, "To London and Rome," "Will You Tell Me?" "Perpetua," and "City Life." Before analyzing these stories, the auxiliary tales developed through the same techniques, and the criticism pertinent to specific stories, a brief assessment of the concept of society that emerges in these four tales will prove relevant to the considerations of the entire chapter. An appraisal of the world that each major story defines reveals Barthelme's vision of society throughout these tales and throughout the body of his short-story writing.

The society depicted in "To London and Rome" parodies the flatness and terror of Harold Pinter's theater of menace and presents a thoroughly debased world. "To London and Rome" becomes a morality tale because of its total lack of moral or humane concerns. The Necchi sewing machine that its protagonist buys his wife and the Rolls Royce that he uses to impress his mistress both have more life and more motivation than any of this story's characters. "To London and Rome" forms a rigorously mechanistic society, which manufactures perfect models of its world's nightmarish imperfections. In this society the myth of acquisition as fulfillment has made purchase a device for momentary release from other desires. "To London and Rome" serves as an apt title for a society constantly in motion, searching for stimulation that can always be bought but seemingly never enjoyed.

Likewise, the society posited by the second major society story, "Will You Tell Me?" developed through the desires of its characters to know their society, describes the homeless American vagabonds that Gertrude Stein called the Lost Generation, transposed from the twenties to the affluent sixties and placed on both European and American terrain. The young adults in this tale feel betrayed by the lies of their parents, the meaninglessness of language, and their inability to know themselves, one another, or their society. In rapid, elliptical leaps in time and scene that parallel the disassociation of their own sensibilities, this story charts their unsuccessful efforts to map the landscape of a society that would have meaning for them. In place of a humane society which they could comfortably inhabit, they discover the barren vision of T. S. Eliot or Pinter, which has ironically become the received culture of the contemporary postmodern world. From the perspective of the story, these characters seem emotionless, fickle men and women roaming the flattened contours of the modern world on which the snows of Montreal appear little different from the waters of the Black Sea. Attempting to escape the knowledge of their own wasteland while simultaneously fascinated with its debris, these people are in flight from themselves; "Will You Tell Me?" describes a world in complete disjuncture. From the voracious society of "To London and Rome," "Will You Tell Me?" takes the reader to more cities and locations around the globe but again depicts modern society as restless, self-obsessed, and confused.

The third major society story, "Perpetua," follows the exploits of a woman who attempts to make a society in her own image but finds instead a modern urban world composed of hundreds of thousands of individuals just like herself. "Perpetua" asks how spontaneity or individuality can ever survive in a society that automatically processes and merchandises those traits. The story focuses on the chaotic contemporary city as a place of refuge for its protagonist, who suddenly becomes bored with the routine and monotony of conventional married life. Quickly fascinated by the self-consciously new or distinctive, Perpetua enters the contemporary city, a world that reflects the transience of modern life. This city is a labyrinth full of cul-de-sacs and unmarked doors from which professional eccentrics emerge. All its social relationships have a random and coincidental quality. Its citizens meet, make love, and part as casually as pedestrians jostle one another in its streets at rush hour. These people seem like cardboard cutouts rather than three-dimensional human beings, and their affairs and experiences can only be lifeless and brittle. By duplicating the gestures and styles of all those around her, Perpetua fails to realize that originality cannot be reproduced. Her story develops as a repetitive fable, which demonstrates that a satisfying society must be created from the ground up. Using the rubbish of her new world to escape the debris of her past, Perpetua quickly becomes trapped in the city's fads and clichés. Attempting escape, distraction, and a surrogate existence, she constantly dresses her old self in instantly dated fashions. Moreover, the story implies that the trash formed from yesterday's refuse has taken on a life and value of its own, which society does not understand and cannot completely control. The voguishness of the city reduces much human activity to mere imitation.

By contrast, "City Life," the final major society story on the typology evolving through an investigation of the creative process, shows how creativity and the individual human imagination can be sharpened by constant contact with an urban environment. Ramona, a New Yorker and the protagonist of the story, gives birth to a child she fully believes has been conceived without sexual intercourse. The popular rock singer Moonbelly writes a song to commemorate this birth, entitled "Cities are Centers of Copulation." After Moonbelly receives a gold record for selling a million copies of the song, Ramona imagines channeling the collective energy of New York City so that all nine million residents would refuse to pay their inflated electricity bills. In this eccentric manner, "City Life" records the interrelationships between the individual human consciousness and the artistic process, with the city as a high-voltage charge inspiring both qualities. Unlike Perpetua, Ramona finds the city a place where she can accept diverse lives without allowing them to dominate her own. For Ramona, the city as a society becomes an enormous field of energy. She interprets her creative responsibility as finding a means of focusing this energy to influence artistic potential in those around her. Through her artistry and Moonbelly's she discovers that her urban society functions as a vast collage of possibilities for the creation of everything from pop art to her highly suspect announcement of a second virgin birth. In the endless, claustrophobic clash of citizen with citizen in this society, a huge array of signs, sign language, and sign systems undergoes continual transformation.

Naturally, this society has dangers. When its signs overwhelm their human receptors, the city becomes a jungle. The individual creative consciousness must control or regulate these signs or they will control the individual. At its most philosophical, "City Life" denies that the city, as such, exsits. The city, Ramona contends, represents nothing more than the conscious attitudes of all its residents toward it. Thus Ramona finds the city the ideal place for the consciousness to create art. The art can host the eternal, imaginative tension between men and women, tradition and originality, rage and vitality, form and content.

"To London and Rome" was included in *Come Back, Dr. Caligari* (1964). It describes two protagonists, Peter and Alison, a married couple, who try to evade the sterility of their relationship by using money to place themselves above their boredom and inability to communicate. Their ludicrously hedonistic lives thus form a social orbit of their own devising. Such play in Barthelme's identity and dialogue stories generally means a hiding and evasion from an authority figure who threatens the individual. Here it suggests activities commonly associated with a child's play: ceaseless restlessness and a desire for new pursuits and stimulations to avert boredom. Barthelme envisions a marriage whose partners base all their social actions on this concept of play. Peter and Alison, physical adults but emotional children, play with life by buying their way through it. Money fuels and propels their lives; it supplies the means by which they entertain themselves, avoid monotony, and remain insulated from the silences that engulf their relationship. "To London and Rome" constitutes Barthelme's theory of the leisure class in which a surrealistic Tom and Daisy Buchanan, buying increasingly larger, more expensive trinkets, must eventually buy the services and servants necessary to maintain their purchases. Their narrow, obsessive goals produce the story's flatly linear plot.

One day, Alison suddenly decides she wants a sewing machine more than anything else in the world. Peter buys her a Necchi and simultaneously buys a new Rolls Royce. Their spending momentarily dissipated, Alison and Peter are returned to one another's company and boredom. Quickly, they make an excursion to Aqueduct, buy a horse named Dan, who has just won a race, and ship Dan back to their residence in Milwaukee. Having forgotten they live in an apartment, Peter and Alison must next buy a new home in Milwaukee's best suburb, where they will have grounds large enough to keep Dan. Dan requires a jockey to exercise him, and their new house needs a gardener to plant trees similar to those they remember from the yard of their former apartment house. They also decide a grand piano will make the house more aesthetically pleasing. Sending for a piano teacher and a piano tuner, the couple greets Slim, a piano teacher, who states that his real career goal is to become a jockey, and Buster, a piano tuner, who admits his incompetence at his job. Peter and Alison eliminate the men's angst about their work by making Slim into Dan's jockey at $12,000 a year and transforming Buster into their gardener at a slightly lower salary. After resolving these financial arrangements, Peter continues an affair with his mistress, Amelia. Arriving at her home to impress her with his new Rolls Royce, Peter finds Amelia too busy playing a flute to admit him. Only when Peter offers to buy Amelia's attentions for $5,500 does she respond to his knocking on her door. Once business is settled, Peter and Amelia spend the afternoon making love. Peter's greatest excitement, which brings the story to its conclusion, is Dan's sudden illness. Discovering that the horse appears to be near death, Peter buys a large hospital nearby for $1.5 million and rushes Dan there. Dan has a miraculous and complete recovery. To celebrate, Peter gathers this cast of cardboard characters, his self-made society, around him and announces they will all travel with him and Alison to London and Rome on a Viscount jet he has just purchased.

Though this flat, reductionistic outline of a reductionistic story might make the tale appear too absurd to be amusing, the technique of "To London and Rome" gives the story a consistently imaginative sense of humor and play. Barthelme tells the story in a series of unpunctuated dialogues between Peter, Alison, and their assorted serfs and underlings. In a narrow column running down the left-hand margin of the page, he inserts playwright's directions, which tell the reader either how to interpret a particular conversation or what occurs before or after the current speaker's comment. These marginalia sometimes constitute responses to the conversations. In this left-hand column Barthelme prints all the long, short, frightened, or comic silences preceding and following conversations that make "To London and Rome" a parody of Pinteresque theater of the absurd. The materials of "To London and Rome" have conscious affinities with the emotionally sparse, laconic worlds of Pinter and Samuel Beckett, even though these writers often deal with the impoverished and the dispossessed, whereas Barthelme's subjects more frequently are the affluent and the overindulged. But though these writers instill their vision of society in their techniques, their styles reflecting a tense, anguished world, Barthelme makes his material self-consciously thin and then superimposes on it a prosaic vernacular style.

Barthelme's technical approach to the story consciously raises the question: if growing numbers of individuals form their only links with society or make their only connections with other human beings by buying and selling, how does innovative literature convey this reality without appearing to be simply refurbished absurdist drama? The column down the left-hand side of the page in "To London and Rome" forms a dialogue with the story proper and answers this question. In reasserting that the silences between the empty prattle represent actual silences, that these fictional people have countless vacuous counterparts in reality, the story recognizes that this society's decline taxes the descriptive powers of language. The story accomplishes a difficult task with a technique that consistently, playfully amuses. The hollowness of this society, its incessant urge to play, and the relationship between these qualities are mirrored in the story's humorous silences and pauses in its opening paragraphs.

THERE WAS A BRIEF PAUSE	Do you know what I want more than anything else? Alison asked. What? I said. A sewing machine Alison said, with buttonhole-making attachments.
THERE WAS A LONG PAUSE	There are so many things I could do with it for instance fixing up last year's fall dresses and lots of other things.
THERE WAS A TREMENDOUS PAUSE DURING WHICH I BOUGHT HER A NECCHI SEWING MACHINE	Wonderful! Alison said sitting at the controls of the Necchi and making buttonholes in a copy of the *New York Times Sunday Magazine*. Her eyes glistened. I had also bought her a two-year subscription to *Necchi News* because I could not be sure that her interest would not be held for that long at least.
THERE WAS A PAUSE BROKEN ONLY BY THE HUMMING OF THE NECCHI	Then I bought her a purple Rolls which we decided to park on the street because our apartment building had no garage. Alison said she absolutely loved the Rolls! and gave me an enthusiastic kiss. I paid for the car with a check drawn on the First City Bank.[1]

In "To London and Rome" Barthelme creates a world so uniformly one-dimensional that any single detail becomes as important as any other. The story becomes absurdist theater in prose and creates a vision of society as lifeless as much absurdist drama.

Whatever values Peter's world contains, it lacks a sense of morality. Therefore, a danger exists in misreading "To London and Rome" and other technically innovative Barthelme society stories. These tales do not function merely as pop art explorations of contemporary culture that refuse to judge their findings. The absence of standards of compassion and discrimination in these tales works as an indictment of the social systems Peter and other protagonists at-

1. Barthelme,"To London and Rome," in *Come Back, Dr. Caligari*, 161.

tempt to build through their avarice. For example, the story shows Peter's thoughts about Amelia's psychology as easily interrupted by his interest in the stock market, or his concern for her quickly transformed to his ability to persuade her to sleep with him. In "To London and Rome" Peter reduces the psychology of those with whom he plays to how they can best be manipulated, bribed, or seduced. Confusing sexual gratification with spending money, Peter tries to balance shopping sprees, a wife, and a mistress just as he balances several large checking accounts. When his strategies fail, he invents banks to avoid being overdrawn. As the following episodes reveal, the story humorously captures the ridiculous sense of playfulness in these people's lives and the bankrupt morality that lurks beneath it.

THE SOUND OF THE
FLUTE FILLED THE
SILENT HALLWAY

I knocked again but Amelia continued to play. So I sat down on the steps and began to read the newspaper which was lying on the floor, knocking at intervals and at the same time wondering about the psychology of Amelia.

Montgomery Ward I noticed in the newspaper was at 40½. Was Amelia being adamant I considered, because of Alison?

SILENTLY I WONDERED
WHAT TO DO

Amelia I said at length (through the door), I want to give you a nice present of around $5500. Would you like that?

AN INTERMINABLE
SILENCE. THEN AMELIA
HOLDING THE FLUTE
OPENED THE DOOR

Do you mean it? she said.
Certainly I said.
Can you afford it? she asked doubtfully.
I have a new Rolls I told her, and took her outside where she admired the car at great length. Then I gave her a check for $5500 on the Commercial National for which she thanked me. Back in the apartment she gracefully removed her clothes and put the check in a book in the bookcase. She looked very pretty without her clothes, as pretty as ever, and we had a pleasant time for an hour or more. When I left the apartment Amelia said Peter, I think you're a very pleasant person

which made me feel very good and on the way home I bought a new gray Dacron suit.

WHEN I GAVE THE
SALESMAN A CHECK
ON THE MEDICAL
NATIONAL HE PAUSED,
FROWNED, AND SAID:
"THIS IS A NEW BANK
ISN'T IT?"

Where have you been? Alison said, I've been waiting lunch for hours. I bought a new suit I said, how do you like it? Very nice Alison said, but hurry I've got to go shopping after lunch. Shopping! I said, I'll go with you!

So we ate a hasty lunch of vichyssoise and ice cream and had Buster drive us in the Rolls to the Federated Department Store where we bought a great many things for the new house and a new horse blanket for Dan.[2]

Play here embodies the recklessness and abandon with which individuals buy the goods and services of their world and eventually consume one another. Peter and Alison's wealth makes them, in effect, totalitarian sensibilities who can shape their society and the people they hire to their own desires. Yet through their continual play with money and spending they only deplete their energies and exhaust their relationships with others. Their play and domination fail to form a world in which they use imagination as well as power. This discrimination signifies the major difference between the underground, hiding figures of "Hiding Man," "The Explanation," and their auxiliary stories and the totalitarian spirit of Peter and Alison in this story and its auxiliary stories. In "Hiding Man," "The Explanation," and related stories, the hiding man uses his wit, guile, and imagination to evade even further the society he has fled. In "To London and Rome," Peter and Alison, in plain sight, use their monetary power to make a world in their own image. These totalitarians remain in complete mastery of a lifeless, reductive social system in which their talent for manipulation has defeated their imaginative sympathies and their feelings for other human beings.

Such a spirit continues in "I Bought a Little City" and "The Captured Woman," both from *Amateurs* (1976). Each of the tales directly parallels "To London and Rome" in depicting a male protagonist similar to Peter, who tries to assume complete control over a

2. *Ibid.*, 165–66.

city or a woman by buying or capturing the object of his fascination. In these stories possession becomes a form of control. Although the two tales develop with wryly humorous tones, they
nonetheless illustrate the failure of sheer play and gamesmanship
to accrue satisfaction. Ultimately, these protagonists lack the imagination to do more than play with their concepts of a world.

The imaginative limitations of the narrator of "I Bought a Little
City" provide the story with its bizarre events. The speaker of the
tale, a Texas real estate developer, decides to buy Galveston, Texas,
and play with it to relieve his boredom. Lacking any sensitivity or
vision, this city czar unintentionally menaces many of the residents. Thus the story satirizes corporate owners or professional
managers who make decisions from afar that throw individual lives
into unnecessary upheaval. For example, the owner decides to move
some city dwellers from a decaying middle-class neighborhood to a
modernistic housing complex. Benevolent in his dictatorship, he
foolishly grants the request of one of his uprooted citizens that
each lot in the new housing complex have the shape of one of the
pieces of a jigsaw puzzle the evictee shows him. Immediately receiving complaints that the new residents feel they are living in a
jigsaw puzzle, the manager allows those who wish to reshape their
lots to conventional rectangular specifications. Next, the owner,
believing that he has not exerted enough of the authority expected
of an individual who possesses power, shoots six thousand of the
unleashed dogs roaming the streets of Galveston. This action accomplishes nothing but shows the citizens that he can be a forceful
arbiter of his cruel decrees. Again he draws furious criticism. The
dogs' owners emotionally protest the slaughter of their pets, but
their ruler tells one of these visitors to his office that any violence
the man might perpetrate against him will be subject to investigation by the Galveston police and the local chapter of the American
Civil Liberties Union, both of which he owns. Despite this totalitarian's endless facility for power plays, the tale ends with the
man's recognition of his considerable vulnerability. In a final episode he falls in love with a local resident, who will not marry him
despite his power and influence. In despair, he sells Galveston at a

loss, realizing he has no imagination and should never have tried to play God. Furthermore, the continued gnawing pain he suffers in his unrequited love symbolizes for him the power of legitimate, imaginative possibilities to haunt his empty life.

Thus "I Bought a Little City" concludes as a fable about the impotence of the powerful. Extending the mindless consumerism of "To London and Rome" to gargantuan proportions, the narrator of "I Bought a Little City" not only purchases other individuals but commands an entire town. Yet without a goal for his possession and with play as his only means of development, the speaker discovers that his acquisitive desires have robbed him of humanity and imagination without giving him the woman he loves.

This same sense of subjugation and control pervades the sexual relationships in "The Captured Woman," the second auxiliary story. It dramatizes a series of discussions among a group men, each of whom has kidnapped a woman to hold as hostage. The humor of this story lies in the ability of its central protagonist's captured woman to invert the terms of her confinement until she eventually begins to hold her captor in bondage. Nonetheless, at the outset of the story, a reader might assume that this captured woman has been trapped in a stereotypically bad marriage ruled by a domineering male. Superficially, these women are enslaved by their mates' rituals, bound and gagged, and occasionally allowed to exercise on a long leash. Women initially seem the complete chattel of men in "The Captured Woman," but appearances in this tale prove thoroughly deceiving.

As the story progresses the sex and power roles conventionally associated with men's tyranny over women become blurred. The captured woman of the protagonist receives word from her husband that he and her daughter are doing well without her. Angered by the news, the woman asks her jailer to tie her in the bare room he has provided. She demands the oppression and humiliation that a kidnapper customarily gives his prey. Yet by the end of the story, after receiving a steady stream of these debasements, the woman resembles a scolding, surrogate wife who can find no value in anything her sheepish, husbandlike captor does or says. Further compounding the intricacy of their role playing, she seems reluctant to be a free woman again. When her purported assailant tells her she may leave whenever she wishes, she grows hesitant and delays her departure. At this moment, her supposed oppressor begins to do the dishes. He believes that performing menial, wifely chores will endear him to this thrall and convince her to stay.

These mercurial changes in both characters' strategies only serve as a preface to the major reversal of the story, which also functions as its climax. At this point the central kidnapper discovers L, a highly successful fellow abductor of women, in his captured woman's room. He asks L if he has managed to steal his captured woman from him in his own house. Before L can answer, the woman announces that she has changed the rules of this elaborate game and captured L herself. The next day, L vanishes as suddenly as he appeared. The woman acknowledges that L did some sketches of her that she found less than flattering. Her vanity will not allow a suitor to view her in a less than perfect light. Capturing L to capture the protagonist, the woman decides her keeper's jealousy confirms that she should be his permanent prisoner. Her plan works beautifully. A week later, she remains with her abductor; she is giving him orders, and he is dressing to please her.

The thread of events developed in "The Captured Woman" obviously forces the reader to ask who masters whom by the conclusion of the story. The tale characterizes contemporary courtship as a kidnapping in which the standardly more aggressive male subjects the presumably more passive female to his authority, while the female slowly takes control of the relationship. The story's skill emerges in its demonstration of how both men and women reshape sexual stereotypes to gain the leverage each wants in a household. "The Captured Woman" sees sexual chemistry as a taking or possession by the male. Eventually his actions become addictive, and he is willingly chained to his quarry, enduring her abuse and foiling her pretended efforts to escape. The totalitarian men of "The Captured Woman" trap themselves in nets of their own weaving. Playing abductors to women who intrigue them, they make worlds with more rigid codes and rites than the societies shaped by the protagonists of "To London and Rome" or "I Bought a Little City." Yet they soon learn that their women play their own game by ignoring the rules and changing accepted feminine roles at their whim. In "The Captured Woman" the process of play humorously spins a social fabric that only fitfully satisfies the possessive, manipulative men who initiate it and the wily women who subvert it.

All three of these society stories share a central concern: the progressively manipulative character of modern life and play as the means by which one person controls another in this society. Barthelme's artistic device for depicting the social structures in these stories avoids direct representation of the worlds that are criticized. By using models that serve as symbolic refinements of the actualities ridiculed, the tales demonstrate how alien contemporary social values have become to humane impulses and how closely modern man seems to be living in self-contained, oppressive nightmares. Play, once the domain of the child or the unrepressed spirit, is increasingly the action or rationalization by which the wealthy and the powerful harness the unprotected to their devouring impulses. Not only are these three stories models of the self-destructive system that modern society is quickly becoming, but each illustrates a world in which the players are never satisfied or finished with their manipulation. As John Leland says of Barthelme's writing: "Literature has lost its privileged status as the myth of its origins (the dream of fulfilling) is reduced to a mere filling . . . the desperate need of surrogation."[3] Thus in "To London and Rome" Peter and Alison are constantly embarking on a new trip or buying one more costly commodity without attempting to dissipate the drives that make them addictive consumers.

Turning again to the typology, we find "Will You Tell Me?", a society tale developed through the effort to know, occupying the second square on the horizontal row. Rather than examining an individual's search for self-knowledge as in "See the Moon," or a white man's efforts to know a black through interrogation as in "Margins," "Will You Tell Me?" describes the efforts of various members

3. Leland, "Remarks Re-marked," 806.

of a specific social circle to know and understand one another. Because the story evolves through an associationistic technique, "Will You Tell Me?" poses as many problems of interpretation as any tale Barthelme has written. It moves abruptly backward and forward through leaps in time and setting. This sense of elliptical discontinuity makes the tale a highly fragmented social collage whose artful confusions parallel the frustration its characters experience in attempting to know their society or even to piece it together. Thus, like all the stories in its vertical row on the typology, "Will You Tell Me?" achieves the effect of collage in a tone of futility. This tonal quality arises not only from the impossibility of its men and women ever understanding their world but also from the vacillation this uncertainty brings to their love for one another.

The characters of "Will You Tell Me?" continually question their feelings for one another and wonder if others actually care for them. Moreover, these people fail to express their emotions because they have little ability to use and control language. Abetting their dilemma, the conventions of literature parodied in the tale supply the characters with only stilted, artificial modes of expression. These people summarily reject their fragmentary knowledge of their society, their own capacities for love, and the power of language to evoke experience, while too often they accept the false expectations from life given them by literature. Nothing remains for them but their feverish urge to escape their immediate, incomprehensible world. Therefore, they travel the globe in flight from themselves. A superficial synopsis of whatever plot "Will You Tell Me?" possesses hardly does these themes justice, but the following outline will suggest the collage effect of the tale and the futility of the lives it portrays.

The story involves two families and various bizarre, ongoing relationships between them that have linked the families for several decades. Each of the members of this social community knows of these situations, yet they all fail to understand how the events have shaped their lives. Hubert and Irene have been lovers for a dozen years, even though Charles, Irene's husband and Hubert's best friend, has been fully aware of their affair. Desiring to please both his lover and his friend, Hubert presents them with the gift of Paul, a baby boy. When Charles and Irene ask Hubert where he obtained Paul, Hubert, a businessman, instantly replies, "from the bank."[4] Hence Paul's origin symbolizes not only the blatant materialism of a society that allows an infant to be bought at a bank but also the tangled relationships between Paul's purchaser, Hubert, and the parents who receive and own him. From this central event, the story follows Hubert, Irene, and Charles, their children, and their children's friends back and forth in time and around the globe. Everyone touched by news of Paul's background feels contaminated by it, yet they all abandon their attempts to understand their society in favor of escape, distraction, and self-pity.

In time, Paul, the adopted child, grows into an anarchist making bombs in his parents' basement. He creates these feeble explosives as a means for sons to frighten their fathers. Meanwhile, Paul believes he may be in love with Hilda, a friend with whom he travels around the world. They want to know that their love will be as true in Montreal as it seems in France. As a means of comparison, Paul makes love to Inge, a blond facsimile of Hilda, in Denmark. In the approximately twenty years depicted, Eric, Hubert's natural son, becomes a bitter outcast, who visits Paul's basement workshop so he can have a bomb to throw at his father. Eric's bomb misses Hubert, frightening him but resolving nothing. While still a college student, Eric commits suicide by putting a loaded gun to his mouth.

Like the other young people in the tale, Hilda slips into a state of despair as the story proceeds. At first merely a beautiful child, she matures into the sensual ideal not only of Paul but also of his adopted father, Charles. From a window of his home, Charles watches Hilda bite into the bitter fruit of the black pear tree and painfully grimace at its acrid taste. Infatuated with this nymphet, Charles cries at the sight of Hilda's displeasure. Hilda, whose vanity equals her beauty, eventually cuts down the black pear tree because its loveliness rivals her own. Thereafter, the black pear tree represents the pride that frequently destroys love between individ-

4. Barthelme, "Will You Tell Me?" in *Come Back, Dr. Caligari,* 41, hereinafter cited parenthetically in the text as "WY."

uals in this story. Charles's unrequited love for Hilda parallels the love of Ann, a friend of both families, for Paul. Ann responds to Paul's indifference by restlessly crossing the globe, scattering hyacinths wherever she goes. She frequently drops her flowers into the Black Sea.

No summary of this unique story can describe the tale's skill in distilling the sensation of aimless drifting that overcomes these people and their relationships. As these men and women flow in and out of this collage, the tale carefully controls its fragments. It composes a portrait of a group of world-weary Americans who resemble what Gertrude Stein called the Lost Generation of the twenties placed in a society as decimated and meaningless as that depicted in T. S. Eliot's *The Waste Land*. In the following passage Paul freely associates his thoughts with Ann's, and before Hubert can clarify an observation, Eric throws a bomb from Paul's workshop near Hubert.

Dialogue between Paul and Ann:
—You say anything that crawls into your head Paul, Ann objected.
—Go peddle your hyacinths, Hyacinth Girl.
—It is a portrait, Hubert said, composed of all the vices of our generation in the fullness of their development.
    Eric's bomb exploded with a great splash near Hubert. Hubert was frightened. What has been decided? he asked Eric. Eric could not answer. ("WY," 43)

This passage clearly posits a world in a violent state of anarchy, a society that has lost a basic ability to communicate. Even efforts in this world to appraise the failure of communication, such as Eliot's *Waste Land*, end in assaults between literary generations which resolve nothing.

If "Will You Tell Me?" dramatizes the precarious uncertainty of its people's lives, the story finds the continually shifting emotional and intellectual distance between these lives even more important. As Paul sits at his workbench mixing another batch of bombs, the story records his thought process. Seeds from a branch of the black pear tree whose fruit Hilda tastes fall into Paul's toolbox. Though the seeds remind the reader of Paul's tenuous affair with Hilda and

Hilda's vanity, Paul thinks of his own mysterious past. Through these associations the tale forms a conjunction between Paul's inability to understand the meaning of Hubert's words for Paul's origin, "from the bank," and Paul's inability to love Hilda completely. Thus in the following excerpt the powerlessness of language dissipates the force of emotion and, conversely, the enervation of feeling weakens individuals' capacities to communicate and love: "In the cellar Paul mixed the plastic for another batch of bombs. A branch from the black pear tree lay on his work-table. Seeds fell into his toolbox. From the bank? he wondered. What was meant by 'from the bank'? He remembered the kindness of Montreal. Hilda's black sweater lay across a chair. God is subtle, but he is not malicious, Einstein said. Paul held his tools in his hands. They included an awl. Now I shall have to find more Schlitz cans, he thought. Quickly" ("WY," 45). Paul's mind darts from one thought to another, resting for the moment on a comment by Einstein. Both the mental and physical worlds of "Will You Tell Me?" should suggest the relativity of an entropic universe. In the story all events occur contemporaneously and, as in "To London and Rome," any event, no matter how trivial or mundane, assumes the importance of any other. Torn between an endless number of disconnected thoughts, Paul decides to make more bombs to sever relationships he cannot understand.

Not merely Paul but all of the characters in "Will You Tell Me?" exemplify his compartmentalization of mind from feeling. The impulses and desires of these people are never expressed in their rush of thoughts or their bustling activity. This repression produces their nervous but unvarying habits: junkets around the world or admissions of their sentiments long after their most vital feelings have passed. Consequently, these men and women drift in the medium of their own self-pity and self-absorption. They quickly grow incapable of honestly knowing themselves, the dynamics of those around them, or the society in which they live. In a characteristic passage the story follows Ann, Paul, Eric, Irene, Hubert, Inge, and Rosemarie, Hubert's daughter, around the world linking their lives and malaise.

Ann looked over the ship's rail at the Black Sea. She threw hyacinths into it, not just one but a dozen or more. They floated upon the black surface of the water.

"But I can't stand the pain. Oh, why doesn't God help me?"

"Can you give me a urine sample?" asked the nurse.

Paul placed his new awl in the toolbox. Was that a shotgun Eric had been looking at in the hardware store?

Irene, Hubert said, I love you. I've always hesitated to mention it though because I was inhibited by the fact that you are married to my close friend, Charles. Now I feel close to you here in this newsreel theater, for almost the first time. I feel intimate. I feel like there might be some love in you for me, too. Then Irene said, your giving me Paul for a Christmas present was symbolic?

Inge smiled.

Rosemarie smiled.

Ann smiled.

Goodbye, Inge, Paul said. Your wonderful blondness has been wonderful and I shall always remember you that way. Goodbye! Goodbye!

The newsreel articulated the fall of Ethiopia. ("WY," 49)

Confessing his love for Irene in a newsreel theater, after she has been his mistress for some years, Hubert makes a gesture that typifies the reactions of all the characters in the story. Hubert's intense emotional constraint disappears only in a darkened room in a timeless, placeless world. As he watches a news account of a massacre that occurred several decades before the confused times in which he lives, Hubert suddenly feels at ease and capable of intimacy with Irene. Having relinquished all efforts to know their chaotic society, the characters of "Will You Tell Me?" seem able to assimilate events and live with their emotions only when they can distance reality as a news event on a movie screen.

Hubert's emotional thaw induces a similar response in Irene. She asks him the question that has been uppermost in her mind for twenty years: if Hubert really loves her, should his gift of a son to her and Charles be regarded as symbolic of Hubert's feeling? The story intends that Irene use the word "symbolic" in a literary sense for it quickly jumps to three of its characters smiling symbolically. Though characters have smiled enigmatically if purposefully in literature for centuries, "Will You Tell Me?" ridicules the symbols and conventions of literature that, like this passage, refuse to answer Irene's question about the difference between art and life. This tale indicts art for prettifying life and for contending that such prefabricated symbols exist in reality, when, as the story demonstrates, individuals smile and smile without communicating with one another in any way. Using symbolic devices to show how these techniques have betrayed individuals who expect them to appear in life, the tale has a nihilistic view of life and art. As the above excerpt reveals, the unknowable society of "Will You Tell Me?" functions as a joyless world whose inhabitants differentiate their lovers by nothing more than the color of their hair.

"Will You Tell Me?" concludes as it has developed throughout Irene and Hubert rush off to a tryst in the Virgin Islands and a new black pear tree germinates in exactly the same spot where Hilda cut down the old tree. The appearance of a new plant represents the perpetual struggle between the strong natural beauty of the black pear and the human vanity of a character like Hilda. This vanity causes individuals like her and all of the people of "Will You Tell Me?" to make a mockery of love and those they love in passing. In the final lines of the tale, Paul and Hilda embrace in the snows of Montreal, questioning whether their love is as true and wonderful as love should be. If so, how can they be sure, what does wonderful mean, and might not their feelings for one another be an illusion?

This story examines a society so blanketed by falsely sophisticated knowledge that its members have forgotten the most basic approaches to communication. In their insatiable pursuit of new places and escapes, their spurious belief that the devices of literature appear in life, and their failure to understand that a simple word like "wonderful" lacks an objective correlative, these people destroy their sympathy for one another and their capacity for love. At first obscure, the title, "Will You Tell Me?" finally seems the perfect name for a story that charts the course of a rudderless society. Its citizens drift through the wrecked fragments of their world relinquishing the effort to know or love those with whom they collide. Yet the plea "will you tell me?" remains, if not on their lips, foremost in their minds.

The entire modern world has become a wasteland playground for the society dissected in "Will You Tell Me?" In both "Edward and Pia" and "A Few Moments of Waking and Sleeping," the auxiliary stories, two characters attempt to make a society of their own from their fragile, uncertain relationship. Like "The Explanation" and "Kierkegaard Unfair to Schlegel," these stories function as a paired set involving the same protagonists and many of the same issues. Their connections and affinities alone, however, do not justify their place on the typology. Rather, certain dominant qualities in both stories indicate their appropriateness for this position. Edward's nagging determination to know the world of Pia's mind, the futility of his quest, and the associationistic collage it forms on the page make these stories fitting auxiliary tales to "Will You Tell Me?" Moreover, all three stories portray characters who roam the globe searching for some confirmation of themselves and their relationships with others. Yet these two auxiliary stories also show differences from "Will You Tell Me?"

Published in 1964, "Will You Tell Me?" with its sudden leaps in thought, setting, and tone, suggests an Americanized prose version of Eliot's *The Waste Land* tailored to the waifs and dropouts of the sixties.[5] On the other hand, "Edward and Pia" and "A Few Moments of Waking and Sleeping" unfold with the limpid grace and control of Hemingway's descriptive passages in "Big Two-Hearted River." Unlike "Will You Tell Me?" these two tales also possess the careful surface attention to described objects and detail that enables Gertrude Stein to link unlikely commodities in a tightly self-contained linguistic world. Edward and Pia feel the pain which these modernist writers describe and which the characters of "Will You Tell Me?" experience in their inability to know one another, their society, or their capacities for love. Yet Edward masks his fears beneath his preoccupation with physical activity, with reading, and with the question he asks repeatedly of his wife: "What are you thinking about?"[6] At the same time, Pia hides her apprehension be-

5. Jerome Klinkowitz, "Donald Barthelme: A Checklist, 1957–1974," *Critique*, XVI (1975), 52.
6. Barthelme, "Edward and Pia," in *Unspeakable Practices, Unnatural Acts*, 80.

hind her constant change of physical appearance and the discomfort she experiences in pregnancy. Analyzing first "Edward and Pia" and then "A Few Moments of Waking and Sleeping" demonstrates the futility Edward and Pia discover in attempting to know a society that has fragmented into a collage of different voices, desires, and beliefs. In abandoning their efforts to know anyone but each other, Edward and Pia show similarities to characters in "Will You Tell Me?" This connection and the following synopses further reinforce the logic of these stories' location on the typology.

"Edward and Pia," from *Unspeakable Practices, Unnatural Acts* (1968), transports the aimless wandering of American expatriate fiction of the teens and twenties to the homogenized, bourgeois Europe of the sixties. Seeking to escape the vulgarity of an America corrupted by political assassinations and involvement in Vietnam, Edward drifts across Europe with Pia, a Swedish woman several months pregnant by him. Edward and Pia find Europe no alternative; rather, it is a crassly commercialized society with all the consumerism, materialist propaganda, and disrespect for clear thought and speech one might find in America. Therefore, Edward resolves to transcend all societies by envisioning a world based solely on his ability to understand his mistress, Pia. Edward desires to know this woman sexually, emotionally, and intellectually. Yet as the cities and countries they cross begin to blur into one, Edward and Pia fail to communicate on any level. Unable to distinguish Wednesday from Sunday or noon from midnight, Edward can no longer hide his fears that his attempt has failed and he may never know Pia, his world, or himself. With its self-consciously flat, declarative sentences, "Edward and Pia" records a listless yet hypnotic music whose static, searching melody refers only to the present tense. "Edward and Pia" projects a society without past or future, a world in which time has always been now.

The monotony and inertia of this timeless society emerge in detailing the itinerary and activities of Edward and Pia as they travel through Europe. In no discernible pattern and in random sentences and paragraphs, Edward and Pia move between London, Sweden, Amsterdam, and Copenhagen, and on to Berlin, France, and Russia.

They eat, sleep, dress, cook, and perform many other routine physical activities. Edward drinks frequently and always wants sex with Pia, but until midway in the story she refuses his advances. Reading constantly and indiscriminately, Edward buys everything from Ross MacDonald mysteries to *The Penguin English Dictionary* and the *Dansk-Engelsk Ordbog*. Fleeing America and all things American including American English, Edward nonetheless fears that not only the English language but all language will soon grow as mysterious and meaningless to him as it seems to have become to the Europeans around him. Ironically, Pia, the increasingly enigmatic center of his life, has only a faltering control of English. Though Edward devours copies of *Time* and *Newsweek* from seeming boredom or an expressed urge to read something in English, these superficial motives actually camouflage his basic rootlessness and estrangement as a man without a country or a language. In flight from an America that has failed to honor its ideals but still deeply infatuated with his country's best intentions, Edward finds further signs of American blunders on every European street corner. He hears American protest music wherever he goes. He tells troubled Europeans his views on Vietnam or explains to an insistent Swede that he bears no responsibility for John Kennedy's death. He even cooks for Pia the southern fried chicken he continues to adore. Thus "Edward and Pia" refashions the tale of expatriate angst to the age of Vietnam and reestablishes its image as an often American, deeply divided form. Barthelme's variant of this story portrays an individual who, escaping an America he loves because he feels it has betrayed him, ironically rediscovers fragments of his country in European garb.

"Edward and Pia" evokes one man's need to resist the bonds of country and citizenship so he can form a private image of society through a total knowledge of his lover. The tale artfully reproduces the static, timeless displacement the protagonist experiences in his failure to achieve his ideal realm. In disconnected, elliptical sentences and paragraphs, the tale jumps across a continent and through a man's mind as he maps the landscape of a modern world. Edward charts a terrain on which nationalities have blended and languages have grown garbled from misuse. Though men stay in exile and in despair because of their countries' chauvinism, they lack the precision of speech to articulate their malaise. The resulting collage of Edward's impressions forms a mosaic of associations that expresses the futility of a life lived in the effort to understand and form a world.

In the second auxiliary story to "Will You Tell Me?" "A Few Moments of Waking and Sleeping," also from *Unspeakable Practices, Unnatural Acts* (1968), the sojourns of Edward and Pia continue. Edward, still rejecting the concept of country or government, remains committed to making his world from a complete knowledge of Pia's mind. Rather than cross the cities of Europe together as in "Edward and Pia," here the couple remains in an apartment in Copenhagen and Edward travels through Pia's thoughts and imagination by interpreting her dreams. A dreamlike, filmic quality binds the two stories together. If "Edward and Pia" with its attention to the naturalistic details of daily routine has the quality of a documentary film edited as a succession of rapid, disjointed cuts, "A Few Moments of Waking and Sleeping" maintains the slower, fluid rhythm of a series of surreal dreams. These tales consciously use cinematic technique to establish their conception of reality, as Edward's and Pia's lives seem even to them like dreams that move across their minds as scenes on a movie screen.

Although "A Few Moments of Waking and Sleeping" successfully imagines a dream world somewhere between these states, the story also dramatizes Edward's failure to understand Pia's interior life. Pia clearly resents Edward's efforts to delve into her thoughts and imagination. Though she frequently relates her dreams to Edward, the reader wonders how many dreams she intentionally ignores, how many she changes or distorts, and if those dreams which she has "silently rehearsed" are simply her own inventions.[7] As soon as Edward begins to probe Pia's unconscious, he encounters a wily, elusive woman, who regards his quest to understand her psyche with the same mischievous evasion with which A greets the psychologi-

7. Barthelme, "A Few Moments of Waking and Sleeping," in *Unspeakable Practices, Unnatural Acts*, 98.

cal needling of Q in "The Explanation" and "Kierkegaard Unfair to Schlegel." Edward's use of Freud to interpret Pia's dreams further confuses his efforts to find meaning in her nightly thoughts. In this tale even more than in "Edward and Pia," Pia exists as a woman obsessed with her appearance. She spends an hour combing her hair and smudges dark circles of varnish around her eyes to make herself more attractive. Her ludicrous attention to superficials, coupled with her shallow responses to questions about her feelings, suggests a woman who tries to forget her inner emotional life.

Yet Edward is persistent. The vivid, creative replies she makes to his queries function partially as Pia's effort to refute his desire to know her thought process and partially as the workings of her own imaginative energies, which even she cannot always control. The latter unpredictable qualities emerge in the final dream vision of the story, which Pia experiences somewhere between sleeping and waking. In her description Pia tells how an old woman riding a bicycle knocks her down on a street corner in Copenhagen. The woman dumps the bag Pia is carrying into the gutter and rides away. Finding no parallels with her past in this meaningless situation nor wishing any in her future, Pia attempts to banish this dream from the repertoire of her nightly, dreaming cinema: "Pia thought, These things have no significance really. Pia thought, If this is to be my dream for tonight, then I don't want it." [8]

These concluding lines of "A Few Moments of Waking and Sleeping" only reemphasize the irony implicit in the story. Edward's design to unearth the exact nature of Pia's subconscious as reflected in her dreams may well be an impossible task. Since Pia does not believe her dreams have manifest connection with her personality, since she seems to invent some of them and tries to prevent others from recurring in her sleep, Pia's dream world seems highly suspect. Edward may be attempting to extract repressed Freudian truths from a woman dominated by surface appearances and lacking many subconsicous motivations.

In "A Few Moments of Waking and Sleeping" Edward pursues

8. Barthelme, "Moments," 100.

knowledge of another mind and its world more ardently than he does in "Edward and Pia." The prose patterns of this story describe what happens to the perceptions of individuals whose search for knowledge has become so acutely self-conscious that they willingly obliterate distinctions between dreams and reality. All of the story has the dreaming, filmic quality of a Bergman or Buñuel movie. The tale juxtaposes Pia's baroque, embellished dreams and Edward's probing questions with Edward's reading of Freud or the couple's trips to the movies and their arguments about movies they remember imperfectly. The resulting collage destroys the difference between dreams and reality, film and experience, while denying that Edward's obsessive hunt for Pia through her dreams produces anything more than futility and frustration.

Neil Schmitz, a commentator on Barthelme, examines characteristics of Barthelme's writing apparent not just in these tales but throughout his stories. As Schmitz acknowledges, Barthelme disdains the connective tissue that a long narrative requires. He neglects characterization in his short stories and ignores conventional dramatization of the events he explores:

Barthelme has consistently treated the novel as an artifact, a fossilized object. In *Come Back, Dr. Caligari*, there is a formulary roman de société with all the interstitial packaging removed, the connective tissue gone. "Will You Tell Me?" moves through two generations in several pages. Barthelme's primary tense is the present. . . . By displacing the value of linear structure, Barthelme necessarily dislocates the centrality of characterization. It is the quality of situations, not points of view, that Barthelme presents. . . . It is what they have read, which books and magazines, and what they have seen, which movies and exhibitions, that define their posture in the world. . . . The stories dealing with Edward and Pia in *Unspeakable Practices, Unnatural Acts*, stories in which Barthelme reverses the priorities of narrative selection, are exemplary. Disjunctive stacks of abrupt sentences methodically record the random movement and banal talk of the two deracinated lovers. What is customarily left out of such romances is here scrupulously presented. It is the dramatic that is sardonically cramped within the text.[9]

9. Schmitz, "Satire," 110–12.

Granting that this lack of well-defined relationships, characterizations, and dramatization typifies these stories, one may have difficulty determining what constitutes a sense of society in them. If, as Schmitz contends, their characters' lives become a series of unrelated, contemporaneous situations, the reader can question the meaning of any event. Yet Schmitz also implies that the artifacts of a diffused popular culture—the books and magazines these people read and the movies and exhibitions they see—connect them to one another and define their positions in this world.

Similarly, critic Mark L. Krupnick in assessing Barthelme's career through *City Life* (1970) feels that Barthelme's idea of popular culture consciously parallels the wasteland visions that Eliot, Pound, and Hemingway created in the teens and twenties. The literary clichés of the sixties and seventies incorporate not only the inanities of the media and advertising but the ideas of a modern classicist like Eliot as well, although Eliot's vision in its adulteration by mass education, misunderstanding, and time has become a parody of itself. Krupnick demonstrates how the original wasteland of modern culture has degenerated further in Barthelme's tales into the wasteland of postmodern popular culture:

In general the serious themes of the classical modernists reappear in the writing of the contemporary avant-garde as farce. . . . The sustaining images and ideas of earlier literature including the idea of the religion of art, all reach Barthelme as shards from a dead past, and these disenchanted images from history have the same status as junk—as the banalities issuing now from the mass media. Together all these fragments of consciousness make up what Barthelme calls dreck, the "trash phenomenon" which is contemporary culture. . . . After fifty years of the age of Eliot, Barthelme's stories are too often merely parodic footnotes to *The Waste Land*.[10]

Krupnick's interpretation explains the appearance of Eliot's wasteland vision and his hyacinth girl in "Will You Tell Me?" as well as the literary, self-conscious emptiness of the Edward and Pia stories. Yet Krupnick still doubts that Barthelme transforms farcical footnotes into a literature of substance. Although many critics recog-

10. Mark L. Krupnick, "Notes from the Funhouse," *Modern Occasions*, I (Fall, 1970), 110, 112.

nize Barthelme's sometimes negative attitude toward the canon of literary modernism, few analysts take such a harsh view of his limitations. Krupnick's limited vision results from his inability to recognize Barthelme as anything but an avant-garde writer. Even if he is regarded only as an avant-garde sensibility, an aging enfant terrible thumbing his nose at *The Waste Land* and other sources of literary modernism, Barthelme certainly attains to literary purposes. For him the concept of the religion of art seems bogus not because it reveres tradition but because contemporary reality's grotesque immediacy surpasses modern art's ability to depict the ongoing world. Barthelme also believes the established works of literary modernism have falsified their audiences' perceptions of both art and reality. Therefore, Barthelme uses Eliot's hyacinth girl in "Will You Tell Me?" as a suitable image for his comic pop culture graveyard. Similarly, in "Will You Tell Me?" when Barthelme's characters pretend to answer each other's questions with smiles, the story ridicules literature's long-standing reliance on resolving realistic dilemmas with artistic conventions, which only confuse the relationships between life and art.

As rendered in this story, the world of wandering, rootless Americans scurrying across the European Continent emerges as a disconnected, disassociated social image surpassing those created by Hemingway, Stein, and other chroniclers of expatriate existence. Furthermore, "A Few Moments of Waking and Sleeping" produces a world without functional relationships in which reading and books become instruments in Edward's obsessive quest to know the world of Pia's dreams. Thus the story frequently confuses reality with dreams and art. The surreal, trancelike state the tale evokes, however, seems a highly original realm distinct from the worlds charted by the modernists of the teens and twenties. Barthelme jokingly mimics the religion of modernist art to show that its writers and their techniques can only partially suggest the fragmented chaos of life fifty years after the publication of *The Waste Land*; nor, he believes, should generations of readers continue to respond to his and others' postmodern art in the ways that an earlier generation of writers conditioned audiences to react to works.

Recognizing that a debased popular culture filled with the diluted aesthetics of literary modernism comprises both the rubbish and the adhesive force of Barthelme's society, the reader understandably seeks confirmation of a vision of society Barthelme honors unreservedly. Tony Tanner, one of the critics who values his originality, argues that a consistent dialectic pitched between an urge to play and an urge to know gives Barthelme's tales a unique tension:

But the mood that finally comes across is finally very different from the sort of trash-happiness which Barthelme's work seems at times to be purveying. . . . There is a strong feeling of being distinctly not at home in the trash age; though since all the usual modes of complaint, dissatisfaction, nostalgia, etc. are registered as being part of the very trash they seek to repudiate, themselves helping to top up the contemporary plenum, this feeling of not-at-homeness necessarily comes through in indirect ways. . . . This inclination to play with "beautiful dreck" and the countering instinct to get away from matter altogether—a profoundly American combination of feelings—provides the tensions which hold Barthelme's best work together and gives it a distinct vibrant strangeness.[11]

The sense of homelessness Tanner recognizes here pervades these three society stories. The protagonists in each play with the dregs of their societies and yet remove themselves from this refuse by escaping their worlds and briefly forming imperfect societies of their own. Consequently, escape serves as a dominant theme in all three tales. Homeless, wandering exiles gather in shabby apartments in indistinguishable cities to explore one another's minds and dreams. Exchanging signs of recognition but unable to communicate, these individuals quickly flee to other cities and other communities of disaffected travelers.

Turning to those stories colored by a sense of repetition brings us to "Perpetua," from *Sadness* (1972), a tale that illustrates the failure of its protagonist to shape an original society for herself. Repeatedly seeking the self-consciously new and unique, Perpetua achieves only the faddish and the vulgarly popular. Suddenly realizing she no longer wants to be married, Perpetua leaves her husband and contemplates taking seven lovers, one for each day of the

11. Tony Tanner, *City of Words: American Fiction, 1950–1970* (New York, 1971), 402, 404.

week. Without commitment, she freely roams the corridors of a chaotic modern city searching for people and experiences that represent to her the truly distinctive and spontaneous, everything her married life failed to be. But Perpetua does not consider that little originality can exist in a world that exploits and markets it. Therefore, her meanderings become repetitive encounters with consciously eccentric people like herself, trapped into performing ludicrous behavior as their only means of rejecting a vacuous society. Perpetually seeking the incomparable, she repetitively witnesses the conformity of rebellion.

The society that Perpetua seeks and momentarily forms through her unvarying search for individuality suggests the transience and disposability of much of modern life. Such an environment contains many individuals who, like her, have been trained or educated to respond to situations with certain discrete techniques and who repeat these actions, whether or not they yield desired results. Perpetua's transformed life soon proves static, and her story details the ridiculousness of her life and those around her.

Harold, her former husband, demonstrates the failure of a man who invariably consults a guide to reality before venturing into it. While Perpetua has her urban adventures, Harold tries to adjust to single life by traveling across the world using the maps he has always needed to find his way. Like "Me and Miss Mandible," a central identity story also developed through repetition, "Perpetua" mocks those who attempt to live according to a map, plan, or guidebook to experience. The story contends that social reality has the contours of a wilderness. Only by recognizing the world as such can an individual make his own path through it. Using a map, Harold becomes lost in the desert in his Land Rover and wonders what went wrong. In a parallel incident before his expedition, Harold sees the shapely back of a famous model, Sunny Marge, in a men's magazine and writes the publication requesting her name and address. The magazine responds by sending Harold the woman's measurements. Harold takes delight in this information for he believes that possessing the grid coordinates of anything means possessing the thing itself. Harold represents what critic John Leland terms the modern confusion between what the signs of contemporary culture promise and the actual realities those signs grant.[12]

Of all the people she meets in the city, Perpetua's newly found friend, Sunny Marge, best personifies the stylish originality Perpetua seeks from a completely uncharted existence. Yet at the time of their meeting, Sunny Marge's life is filled with unexpected redundancy. Her back, as photographed in Harold's men's magazine, has become an international sensation. To refocus this attention, Sunny Marge has her back tattooed with a portrait of the head of Marshal Foch. Although it makes her unique, this art work also makes her perpetually the same. "Perpetua," particularly in its portrayal of the relationship between Perpetua and Sunny Marge, examines those grotesquely contemporary individuals whose passion for distinctiveness ironically makes them part of the masses and whose worship of the present fashion totally blurs their sense of a past. In the following passage Perpetua removes her orchestra uniform, dons her bohemian, free-spirit uniform, and discovers Sunny Marge. In the process one sees how the lives of these women parallel and contrast.

After the concert she took off her orchestra uniform and put on her suede jeans, her shirt made of a lot of colored scarves sewn together, her carved-wood neck bracelet, and her D'Artagnan cape with its silver lining.

Perpetua could not remember what was this year and what was last year. Had something just happened, or had it happened a long time ago? She met many new people. "You are different," Perpetua said to Sunny Marge. "Very few of the girls I know wear a tattoo of the head of Marshal Foch on their backs."

"I am different," Sunny Marge agreed. "Since I posed for that picture in that magazine for men, many people have been after my back. My back has become practically an international incident. So I decided to alter it."

"Will it come off? Ever?"

"I hope and pray."[13]

In trying to change her appearance, Sunny Marge, whose shoulders have inspired men all over the world, becomes absurdly unique. At

12. Leland, "Remarks Re-marked," 796–97.
13. Donald Barthelme, "Perpetua," in *Sadness*, 40.

the same time, Perpetua, seeking a truly individualized existence, wears clothing that conveys her desire to be one of the millions seeking individualized existences. Purportedly wanting change, the two women merely repeat their respective inclinations for flamboyance and conformity. If both women express dismay at the tattoo on Sunny Marge's back, both have the same contradictory impulse: a need for vivid distinction within the narrow bounds of approved convention.

This impulse inevitably causes Perpetua to form anew the world that she has tried to escape. The society that she has fled, at least in the way she describes it, emerges as a world of monotonous, repeated routine. Her husband Harold dressed himself daily for it like an African tribal chieftain readying for mysterious, ritualistic combat. In the following excerpt not only do Harold's preparations, however vivid, bore Perpetua, but the world that Harold envisions to replace Perpetua's outmoded loveliness seems completely derivative of his original attraction to her. Words and vision conspire here to make both characters' imaginings zany and eccentric yet still static and repetitive.

I remember my husband awakening in the morning, inserting his penis in his penis sheath, placing ornaments of beads and feather on his upper arms, smearing his face with ochre and umber—broad lines under the eyes and across the brow. I remember him taking his blowpipe from the umbrella stand and leaving for the office. What he did there I never knew. Slew his enemies, he said. Our dinner table was decorated with the heads of his enemies, whom he had slain. It was hard to believe one man could have so many enemies. Or maybe they were the same enemies, slain over and over and over. He said he saw girls going down the street who broke his heart, in their loveliness. I no longer broke his heart, he said. I had not broken his heart for at least a year, perhaps more than a year, with my loveliness.[14]

Just as Harold slays the same enemies over and over and over and falls in love with variants of the same woman, Perpetua continues her endless search for the current sensation, the most outrageous fad. Their society so educates Perpetua, Harold, Sunny Marge, and all the characters in this story to stay within the constraints of

14. *Ibid.*, 41.

their conventional world that they are forced to repeat the same monotonous acts in fleeing their staid existences. They escape boring lives with static alternatives.

The real dilemma of the story lies in its implications. It portrays a society infatuated with style, living only in the present tense and without permanent values or lasting relationships. As Perpetua's observations in the passage above reveal, this society has filled its streets, bedrooms, and offices with too many repetitions of experience, even with reproductions of similar human beings. Therefore, the temptation always exists to throw away the old model and obtain a new, improved version. Sadly, this society agonizes about only one thing: should its members be bored by the old or the new? Asking this trivial question and no others, "Perpetua" functions as a comedy with moral dimensions. It describes a society seduced by the instant now, a prefabricated art deco world without depth or feeling. Through their actions its citizens imprison themselves in the present moment, the latest static gesture, which, once repeated, becomes as dated as history.

Next, examining the first auxiliary story occupying the same box as "Perpetua," one discovers that this tale, "Critique de la Vie Quotidienne," from *Sadness* (1972), also describes an individual who forms a static society through repetitive acts. "Critique de la Vie Quotidienne" is a long monologue complaint by a harried, upper-middle-class city dweller about the sameness of his life with a petulant, childish wife and a precocious child of nursery school age. His harangue, though much angrier than Perpetua's disavowals, resembles her criticism of the monotony and repetitions of contemporary married life. As the narrator states: "Our evenings lacked promise. The world in the evening seems fraught with the absence of promise, if you are a married man. There is nothing to do but go home and drink your nine drinks and forget about it."[15] Unlike Perpetua, this narrator does not attempt to find a better existence. He merely retreats deeper into his J&B bottle and his awareness

15. Donald Barthelme, "Critique de la Vie Quotidienne," in *Sadness*, 3–4, hereinafter cited parenthetically in the text as "CV."

that a wife, a son, and a decaying brownstone may well be the final fruits of all his labors.

In his constant struggle with alcohol and boredom the narrator shapes a static, compulsive life with his family in his brownstone apartment. Yet despite its repetitions, he considers this society preferable to the vulgar affluence he finds in the world beyond it. Therefore, the narrator uses his monologue and the embattled comic imagination exhibited in it as a barricade against the intrusions of the moneyed, pretentious outside world. Unfortunately, his wife and child bring values from this extravagant reality into his enclave. One evening his son asks for a horse just like his friend Otto has. He assures his father that the animal can stay in a stable in one of the city parks. When the narrator angrily demands that his wife silence the child and serve dinner, she has a temper tantrum. Throwing food and cooking ware on the floor, this infantile, impulsive woman turns their kitchen into a "muck of pork chops, squash, sauce diable, Danish stainless-steel flatware, and Louis Martini Mountain Red" ("CV," 6). Wary of the society that produces such limitless garbage, the narrator continually tries to keep himself and his family safe from the outside world. But because his wife and son pollute the apartment he strives to keep pure with their own indulgences, he feels trapped by attitudes from within his environment as well as those from without. As always, he resorts to monologue and the ceaseless repetitions of painful domestic life it records: "Holy hell," I said. "Is there to be no end to this family life?" ("CV," 8).

"Critique de la Vie Quotidienne" would be only an amusing inventory of materialistic domestic confinement if the story did not incorporate an intimation of mortality that his prescient son gives to the narrator. The son's prophecy effectively answers the narrator's rhetorical question by telling his father not how his family life will end but why. The child informs his father that his class at school has been making death masks. The narrator, curious yet wary, asks his son what he could possibly know of death at his age. Smiling smugly, the child says, "You'll find out" ("CV," 7). This exchange haunts the protagonist and gives the story a resonance that measurably adds to its critique of society. The child learns at school about death, a force the narrator has attempted to purge from his hermetically sealed home. At the same time, the vulgar world beyond the brownstone tries to convince its citizens that through buying and spending they can forget death exists. For once in a Barthelme story developed through repetition, education—here the child's nursery school death masks—operates as an influence that serves to disrupt the protagonist's static pattern of continuing an action regardless of whether it produces a desired result. The narrator finally learns that death must end his seemingly endless series of repetitions. Subconsciously he realizes that his own fear of death has made him form his boring, self-contained existence.

The narrator, disquieted by his son's memento mori remark and his family's desire to bring death and a crass world into his artificial domain, decides he has reached the breaking point. He and his wife separate, and he rents a bachelor apartment which he can control without interference. Yet his son's vision of the future almost materializes when his former wife visits him in his new residence. She catches the narrator "touring the ruins" ("CV," 12), as she calls it, examining her aging face to see if any of the beauty or mystery that originally attracted him to her remains. Humiliated by his scrutiny and given false courage by a round of drinks, she draws a horse pistol from her bosom and makes a toast to the dead. Then, seeking to place the narrator in their company, she aims the weapon at him. She fires the gun but misses him, breaking one of his J&B bottles instead. Away from his family and his brownstone, the narrator has as much trouble regulating his world and its constant threat of age and death as he did in their company.

"Critique de la Vie Quotidienne" not only describes the unresolved repetitions of a comfortable, materialistic existence but also examines why such debilitating societies continue to function. The story illustrates that once caught in their society's static, indulgent repetitions, most individuals submit to its compromises. From their brownstone apartments or from tempting, tranquilizing worlds elsewhere, most people so fear age, change, and death that they seldom search for beauty or mystery outside their secure enclosures.

Next, investigating the second of the auxiliary stories sharing a box with "Perpetua," one finds a tale like "Critique de la Vie Quotidienne" in which a narrator also believes he can escape his problems and confusion. In this story, "The Party," from *Sadness* (1972), the narrator attempts to immerse himself in a posh, crowded cocktail party by imitating the gestures and actions of those around him. He soon discovers, however, that his social education fails him. By repeating the rites of these partygoers he forms in his own mind a microcosm of the static, sterile society he wishes to evade. In its narrator's long, glib monologue, "The Party" depicts precisely the sort of brittle, wearily sophisticated soirée that Perpetua might attend in her new life in the city. The tale's constant stream of facetious, disconnected comments, though emitted from one mind, expertly mimics the chatter that resounds at such a gathering. The narrator hopes that by absorbing himself in the atmosphere of this party he will somehow emerge from it a new man. He wants to be free from his unchanging, uncertain relationship with his lover Francesca, whom he escorts to the event. Yet the longer he remains at the party, the more the narrator realizes that its supposed festivities merely reproduce the tensions, noise, and confusion of modern life in a single living room. As he admits: "What made us think that we would escape things like bankruptcy, alcoholism, being disappointed, having children," within the confines of a standard social ritual.[16] "The Party" thus describes the failure of individuals who, attempting to forget themselves at chic social gatherings, merely assert the world of their own imaginations.

Striving to repress his personal problems at the party, the narrator tries to meet the other guests. Like Perpetua, he zealously wants to forget the old and to pursue the new and the unusual. Yet as Tony Tanner recognizes, Barthelme's characters desire to escape

16. Barthelme, "The Party" in *Sadness*, 62, hereinafter cited parenthetically in the text as "TP."

from while simultaneously playing with the refuse of their worlds and minds.[17] As the narrator concedes, recognizing his inability to lose himself in the din and dissonance of the party: "The mind carries you with it, away from what you are supposed to do, toward things that cannot be explained rationally, toward difficulty, lack of clarity, late-afternoon light" ("TP," 54). The minds of the narrator and all the guests move on an endlessly circular track. Forever wanting to give themselves to this celebration, they finally discover nothing but their own visions of reality.

While the narrator and the other party guests chat convivially, they carefully guard their responses to one another. A blasé, lackadaisical attitude pervades these partygoers. Educated by their social training that decorum requires diffidence, they communicate superficially at best and soon drift back to their own thoughts and problems. This acculturated, feigned indifference prevents them from observing how reactionary and passive a society they have formed. Regardless how audacious or surreal the events of the party, these people react to the incidents with unchanging, civilized distance. When King Kong reaches a hairy paw through a living room window, the guests seem unabashed. The giant ape joins the activities, and the guests greet without comment his news that he now teaches art history at Rutgers. Meanwhile, outside the window an ominous, intensifying chorus, first of drums, then of whistles, howls, rattles, and alphorns, sounds. Some of the revelers casually suggest that a revolution may be afoot; others suggest a mere revolution in taste may be signaled, "as when mannerism was overthrown by the Baroque" ("TP," 60).

Ultimately realizing that he can never completely obliterate his sense of self, the narrator believes he can best continue his repetitive, static participation in the party if he merely keeps talking. Societies built on this narrator's model or that of the speaker of "Critique de la Vie Quotidienne" function as linguistic facades. Moreover, the narrator uses the people he meets solely as targets for his speech rather than ever listening to their conversation in re-

17. Tanner, *City of Words*, 402, 404.

turn. The narrator and all the party guests exhaust one another with words. The moment any of these people stop talking and begin to listen, thoughts of their own lives overwhelm them. The narrator frankly admits that his logorrhea serves this purpose: "When one has spoken a lot one has already used up all of the ideas one has. You must change the people you are speaking to so that you appear to yourself, to be still alive" ("TP," 61).

Surprisingly, the speaker's efforts at self-deception still fail. Though he continues to exchange the trivial witticisms and adopt the pretentious sparring of the other guests, he cannot forget his tormenting relationship with Francesca. Their affair remains as tentative and unresolved as before he entered the room. In the concluding line of the story the narrator offers an honest assessment of the party as a means of transcending and changing his world: "Wonderful elegance! No good at all!" ("TP," 62). These two phrases describe the empty style of a man who incessantly tries to form a new society through repetition of approved public behavior, his own mental concentration, and his continuous use of words. Because his mind, his problems, and the world beyond the party prove far livelier than its contrived entertainment, the narrator's drive to disavow his own reality ironically returns him to his own obsessions. Seeking escape and originality, he produces only stasis.

In his perceptive analysis of Barthelme's narrative style, John Ditsky defines Barthelme's linguistic conception of escape in ways that relate it to the repetitive technique of "The Party," "Critique de la Vie Quotidienne," and "Perpetua." According to Ditsky, the idea of escape operates largely as a linguistic goal in Barthelme's tales. He sees Barthelme's protagonists as men and women trapped within the pampered confinement of affluent surroundings and elitist educations. He feels they have two methods of limited escape: they can use articulate language to criticize their worlds; or they can imagine themselves as genuinely privileged people, honored and protected by the expensive accumulations of their environment. Thus, for Ditsky, Barthelme's stories serve as acts of distraction and escape. The tales allow their protagonists to forget themselves in the intensity of their embittered monologues, or they depict their characters as momentarily realizing those dreams which their material lives promise but do not lastingly grant. Ditsky uses Barthelme's identity story "Daumier" as an example. For Ditsky this tale contends that the self can never be completely escaped but it may be repeatedly distracted:

Escape. Distraction. The Barthelme man is the prisoner of language, using that very fire against itself in the hope of a brief release from his cage, an even briefer flight. . . . The substance of a Barthelme fiction is the stock of a gift shop in a fashionable suburb, the timely drivel of a smart intellectual journal. It is all that is faddish, is cliché. Indeeed, it is no wonder that Barthelme appears in *The New Yorker*; his tales are *The New Yorker* and what it represents in modern American society. I am referring, of course, not to the magazine's written content but to its true content—its advertising—the expensive dreck of which one's surrogate existences are made. The rich appeal of a life style studded with objects of implied preciousness is the chance to use those objects, like Donald Barthelme's stories themselves, so that the self can briefly be "with ingenuity and hard work, distracted."[18]

Each of the three society stories developed through repetition adheres to Ditsky's definition of escape. Escape in "The Party" represents the narrator's effort to adopt a new surrogate existence. The party serves as the perfect verbal vehicle for the realization of the narrator's shimmering, ephemeral dreams.

Ditsky's interpretation does not dwell exclusively on the fantasies of Barthelme's characters. It also insists that the expensive waste that clutters this party, these society stories, and many other Barthelme tales evokes the processes of change in contemporary society by which the refuse of the world has developed a life and force of its own. In the following passage he refers to the rearrangement, realignment, and refashioning of this debris in Barthelme's stories. Ditsky believes these changes produce surreal artistic effects, which parallel the actual upheavals of a society whose refuse threatens to consume it: "Thus the rearrangement of dreck, junk—is the basis of a realignment of objects and events which, though (as I have said) surrealistic, produces effects as telling as

18. John M. Ditsky, " 'With Ingenuity and Hardwork Distracted': The Narrative Style of Donald Barthelme," *Style*, IX (Summer, 1975), 398–99.

those produced by the conventional display of 'original' materials. By taking his matter from the familiar, even the waste, Barthelme creates a collage as moving and meaningful (in its way) as the art of the new, whatever that may be. In so doing he holds fast to the recognition that such a refashioning is in fact going on, is in process."[19] Ditsky acknowledges that many of Barthelme's stories function as collages. Though this study has identified chiefly the tales developed through the effort to know as collages, Ditsky observes that Barthelme restructures the reader's perceptions of the relationships between objects and events throughout his writing. The familiar and the exotic refuse of a junk-strewn world lie side by side in Barthelme's tales. This debris forms collages that evoke the uncertain, charged tensions of a world torn between change and entropy, movement and inertia.

Moving to the final horizontal block, one enters the realm of art and artists, and this optimistic, creative world again contrasts with the stasis, futility, and mockingly humorous tones of the other society stories. "City Life," the central society story concerned with the creative process, affirms urban experience. The story also values the human consciousness that shapes the city and the art that results from the tension between a metropolis and its inhabitants. Like so many other Barthelme stories, the tale has the form of a collage of vignettes, but it also views New York City as one gigantic collage in which millions of units of human energy intersect and interact. Stressing the recurrence of this technique in much art in the twentieth century, Barthelme in an interview has called New York City a collage, not a huge tribal village in which all the huts duplicate one basic hut design.[20] Thus in "City Life" New York functions as an art object in its own right, and the artful inhabitants of the city learn to create their own society and their own art by accepting the possibilities the city offers.

The story follows the adventures of two new arrivals to the city, Elsa and Ramona, good friends who come to New York, rent an apartment, and enter law school. Elsa represents the passive woman,

19. *Ibid.*, 393.
20. Klinkowitz, "Donald Barthelme," 51.

who interprets the man-made laws and directives of the city too literally. Becoming pregnant, she leaves law school. By contrast, Ramona so independently and imaginatively pursues her study of the law and the relationship between men and women that she believes she has conceived a child without intercourse. Undaunted, she carries her newborn infant at her hip while continuing to attend law school classes. Ramona, however fanciful her views, has transformed her life, her studies, and her refusal to be manipulated by conventional male laws into artful, creative expression.

It is these views, particularly Ramona's insistence that her child was conceived without intercourse, that constitute the story's vision of the relationship between city life, the receptive human consciousness, and the possibilities for artistic expression. Her vision affirms the force of her imagination to create its own reality and justifies positioning "City Life" in its box on the typology. Nonetheless, Ramona wonders which of several men has looked at her with lust and inspired her pregnancy. Ultimately, she decides that their combined glances, her acceptance of their desire, and the city as the perfect environment for this imaginative act each had its role in planting a seed within her: "Upon me their glance has fallen. The engendering force was perhaps the fused glance of all of them. From the millions of units crawling about on the surface of the city, their wavering desirous eye selected me. The pupil enlarged to admit more light: more me. They began dancing little dances of suggestion and fear. These dances constitute an invitation of unmistakable import—an invitation which, if accepted, leads one down many muddy roads. I accepted. What was the alternative?"[21] Ramona's ability to accept diverse lives and others' desires stimulates her imagination and creativity. She feels that only by embracing her society unreservedly can these impulses be nurtured in her. Moreover, Ramona thinks that the best possible atmosphere for accepting life lies in the city, where seas of humanity continually inundate one another. In the preceding passage she affirms the necessity of acceptance over rejection, of teeming urban society over the

21. Barthelme, "City Life," in *City Life*, 167–68, hereinafter cited parenthetically in the text as "CL."

controlled individual consciousness. The story throughout examines Ramona's interpretation of her philosophy, its application to her friend, the rock musician Moonbelly, and the interrelationship between art, human consciousness, and city life.

At the conclusion of "City Life," Ramona clearly decides to subsume her own aspirations within the city's needs and passions. In a statement immediately preceding this declaration, however, Ramona demonstrates that her spiritual impregnation represents the birth rather than the destruction of her individual force and personality. In the following excerpt she explains her willingness to assume the city's concerns before her own. She believes that New York takes the forms of the collective individual consciousness of its millions of residents. For Ramona, the city exists as merely the projection of all its inhabitants' attitudes toward it. Therefore, in accepting city life she finds her special role in it. She chooses to be an artist who molds and transforms her society by affirming her affinity of feeling with as many of her fellow city dwellers as she can. By momentarily denying her individual concerns, Ramona lastingly aligns herself with the cares of the city and millions of its residents. In the following paragraph Ramona empathizes with Moonbelly, a phenomenally popular rock singer, who writes music about city life, and with that artist—maybe herself—who could convince all nine million New Yorkers to ignore their outrageously expensive Con Edison electric bills.

Ramona thought about the city. I have to admit we are locked in the most exquisite mysterious muck. This muck heaves about and palpitates. It is multi-directional and has a mayor. To describe it takes many hundreds of thousands of words. Our muck is only a part of a much greater muck— the nation-state—which is itself the creation of that muck of mucks, human consciousness. Of course all these things also have a touch of sublimity—as when Moonbelly sings, for example, or all the lights go out. What a happy time that was when all the electricity went away! If only we could recreate that paradise! By, for instance, all forgetting to pay our electric bills at the same time. All nine million of us. Then we'd all get those little notices that say unless we remit within five days the lights will go out. We all stand up from our chairs with the notice in our hands. The same thought drifts across the furrowed surface of nine million minds. We wink at each other, through the walls. ("CL," 167)

As these fragments demonstrate, few other Barthelme stories so closely equate art and creativity with a specific social context or with the power of human consciousness. The enormous collective act of telepathy that Ramona wants to initiate would assert the triumph of humanity over technology, the achievement of calculated will over the chaotic failures of city life that repeatedly plunge New York into darkness. Yet in her hypothetical violation of scientific law, Ramona wishes to transform the rules and dictates of society just as she violates biological law with her belief that she has given birth without having had intercourse. Like Paul Klee or the protagonists of "Daumier" and "A Shower of Gold," Ramona clearly affirms that the human consciousness can create its own art forms in its own society. Moreover, Ramona feels that the turbulent modern city serves as the best possible social laboratory for her experiments.

Nonetheless, Ramona remains as much an experimenter as an artist, more of a mystic than a craftsman. Therefore, "City Life" turns to Moonbelly, the acknowledged popular artist among its cast of characters, to illustrate once more the vital relationships between creativity and human consciousness in an urban environment. "City Life" depicts Moonbelly in the act of composing a hymn in honor of the miraculous birth of Ramona's son. This vignette dissects Moonbelly's creativity as a series of steps by which he considers, adjusts, and appropriates his talents to the subjects at hand: the miraculous conception of a child by Ramona and Moonbelly's contradictory conception of cities as centers of sexuality.

Moonbelly was fingering his axe.
    A birth hymn? Do I really want to write a birth hymn?
    What do I really think about this damn birth?
    Of course it's within the tradition.
    Is this the real purpose of cities? Is this why all these units have been brought together, under the red, white, and blue?
    Cities are erotic, in a depressing way. Should that be my line?
    Of course I usually do best with something in the rage line. However—
    C . . F . . C . . C . . C . . C . . G7 . .
    Moonbelly wrote "Cities are Centers of Copulation."
    The recording company official handed Moonbelly a gold record mark-

ing the sale of a million copies of "Cities are Centers of Copulation."
("CL," 165)

Various stages of contemporary pop art creation appear before the
reader in this passage, as do the key issues of the story. Between
the first descriptions of Moonbelly as a quizzical artistic inves-
tigator and the final sentence, which records Moonbelly receiving a
gold record for his finished composition, Moonbelly's consciousness frequently intervenes. This force tells the musician he must
adhere to the rules of his craft but he must also blend his individual
skills with certain requirements. Like Ramona, Moonbelly alters
his city's conception of what an artist can accomplish. Unlike her,
he manages to fuse his own idiosyncrasies with the conventions of
his music, rather than wrenching his society's definition of the artist to fit the demands of his own consciousness.

Though both Moonbelly and Ramona evoke essentially affirming, optimistic conceptions of city life and of the artist's ability to
create his or her own ideal society, creativity represents several processes in "City Life." As in all the stories on the typology centering
upon the creative act, creativity in "City Life" incorporates the
other three processes of development listed on the grid—play,
the effort to know, and repetition—and these other modes appear
throughout the story. Yet the characters in "City Life" apply each of
the processes to their lives randomly, in isolation from the other
modes and without any effort to discover originality in themselves.
Consequently, these people quickly fail to produce worlds in which
they can live contentedly. Many futile attempts at creativity occur
in "City Life" before Ramona experiences her immaculate conception or Moonbelly composes his birth hymn in her honor.

Yet just as Ramona's annoyance at the unproductive play and repetition around her peaks, she experiences her virgin conception.
Metaphorically, Ramona becomes pregnant with the possibilities
of her society. Her act incorporates a preposterous sense of play and
the effort to transcend logical knowledge. Moreover, the birth of
her son Sam affirms her startling originality and opens unforesee-
able possibilities for society. Like Peterson in "A Shower of Gold,"
who creates a mythic past for himself on national television, she is

the artist who in recreating a myth and believing in it makes it true for herself and her society.

Throughout "City Life" Ramona aspires only to be a lawyer. Moonbelly's story, however, offers a portrait of the way a working artist uses creativity to affirm his own vision of the city. He anxiously strives to make something from nothing, to produce interest from indifference, originality from tradition, and chords from mere notes. His consciousness affirms the role of an environment, that of the city, to his art. Furthermore, Ramona and Moonbelly create by shaping their visions in obvious conflict with the realities of city life. In these characters' ability to assimilate and reply to much of urban experience, "City Life" becomes Barthelme's most optimistic short story. It recognizes that the artistic process constitutes mystical, intuitive leaps of faith and feeling, which create a society whose unity remains far more than the sum of its parts.

As surreal or whimsical as its episodes, "City Life" is one of Barthelme's most important stories. In Ramona's absurd virgin birthing the story finds a unique metaphor for the power of the individual human consciousness to create a sense of wonder throughout a society. As one character tells another, the great contemporary social problem "is not angst but lack of angst" ("CL," 165), and "City Life" sees modern urban society as dangerously polluted by laws, conventions, and technology that inhibit art and communication among its citizens. The story's final vision is of a preindustrial paradise without Con Ed, a world in which men and women accept the possibilities of city life without acquiescing to the tyranny of those who attempt to control the lines of power in this chaotic, corrupt society. The tensions and collisions of this world make it a gigantic collage in which Ramona can be imaginatively impregnated by men who pass her in the street, and Moonbelly can create a pop song from the mishaps and miracles that befall her. "City Life" contends that the modern metropolis, unlike any other environment, offers its citizens unlimited access to creativity and humane relationships if men and women could only learn to fuse their energy with their individual human consciousness.

Two auxiliary stories, "The Indian Uprising," from *Unnatural Practices, Unspeakable Acts* (1968), and "Paraguay," from *City Life* (1970), describe the effects of the loss of individual human consciousness on a city or an entire country. Like "City Life," they affirm the dynamic relationship between the artistic process, human consciousness, and urban existence. Unlike the other stories on this vertical row, however, these tales do not affirm or praise the societies they create. Atypically, they contend that the artist can create a vital society from the refuse of the modern city only if his sensibility remains alive to the dangers of technology, totalitarianism, and the erosion of meaningful communication. Moreover, although they do not present an optimistic picture of city life, they do insist that men and women will be trapped unless they keep themselves constantly alerted to these risks. Both "The Indian Uprising" and "Paraguay" describe societies in which the failure of individual consciousness has debased language and all forms of communication and art have failed.

The narrator of each tale attempts to compensate for the confusion and misery around him. Like the voice of "The Party," he tries to create a society of his own by using the debris of his world to compose a perfect artistic rendering of this world. Yet by the nature of their art, these narrators use words—continually changing, volatile commodities—to describe a society undergoing transformation. Therefore, each story functions as a linguistic facade in which the juxtaposition of incongruous objects and bizarre, unexplained events ultimately produces feelings of fear and doom. Whereas "City Life" shows the possibilities for a telepathic utopia within the industrialized chaos of the city, "The Indian Uprising" and "Paraguay" carefully examine two false utopias created when men attempt to form ideal urban societies without respect for the individual's mind or integrity. These stories depict Orwellian civilizations in which the human consciousness has foundered, communication has ceased, and art corrodes. In "The Indian Uprising" the reader stands at the center of this apocalyptic whirlwind in a world of flying objects and assaulting forces. "Paraguay," on the other hand, describes the deadening existence of a society paralyzed in the aftermath of such a storm. Together, these stories emphasize the necessity of the individual human consciousness for artistic creation.

In "The Indian Uprising" a trained army of Comanche Indians attacks a modern city. Long before this onslaught, the residents have surrendered their minds and spirits to the convenient technology of urban life, to the use of words and language that have become meaningless to them, and to the subtle but pervasive forms of totalitarian control they exert over minority groups in the city. Accordingly, their indolence, lack of communication, and fear of the red men make them easy prey to these aggressors. The Indians quickly destroy the white men's street barricades made of cognac bottles, job descriptions, corkscrews, can openers, and assorted bourgeois commodities. By the end of the story, the Comanches have vanquished their enemy and won the city. In the process the narrator of the tale, a metropolitan white, details the blurring of his consciousness during the apocalyptic rush of this alien but historically inevitable force on the city. He realizes that whatever education or knowledge he possesses proves worthless before the rampage of this fierce, determined tribe. Yet as one representative of the failure of the city's collective consciousness to arouse and defend itself, the narrator remains typically ignorant of the city's responsibility for its chaos. As he observes: "There was a sort of muck running in the gutters, yellowish, filthy stream suggesting excrement, or nervousness, a city that does not know what it has done to deserve baldness, errors, infidelity." [22]

"The Indian Uprising" exudes the terrified paralysis of a city and a society that has lost its moorings but lacks the self-consciousness to explore the causes of its racism. When the Comanches invade the ghetto, the minorities offer no resistance and soon join the Indians in terrorizing and burning the city. The narrator diffidently explains how he and many city dwellers react to the recalcitrance of these subcultures and how they have always reacted: "We sent more heroin into the ghetto, and hyacinths, ordering another hun-

22. Barthelme, "The Indian Uprising," in *Unspeakable Practices, Unnatural Acts*, 6, hereinafter cited parenthetically in the text as "IU."

dred thousand of the pale, delicate flowers" ("IU," 6). His and other whites' rejection of any political solution and his personal abdication of consciousness explain the destruction of the city at the hands of this primal force.

The narrator senses that the world he understands is approaching collapse. Nearing psychological exhaustion himself, he still attempts to create a beautifully artful world by placing the debris that rapidly fills his society in creative juxtapositions. Thus he sends hyacinths as well as heroin to the ravaged slums of the ghetto. His effort to aestheticize the ugliness of his world functions as a purely imaginative act, however, for this attempt fails even as a creative ideal. The fragments of reality that the narrator mentally conjoins during the Indian attack prove more prettified, but hardly more surreal, or artistic, than the actual dislocations of objects and events that the Indian uprising produces. Moreover, like the commodities in the street barricades which the Indians quickly burn or mutilate, or the words he uses to describe them, the pieces of the narrator's reality refuse to stay fixed in his sight or in his imagination. The narrator cannot create an artistic world because his society is in chaos and his distorted perception of this world only magnifies its confusion. His uncertainties and vacillations, found to similar degrees in all the whites around him, have caused this social apocalypse. Even language, the basis of his artistic voice, rapidly changes shape and color in the midst of this upheaval.

In his distress the artist turns to Miss R., an instructor in counterinsurgency techniques. She insists on the value of a litany as a means of restoring psychological calm to the narrator. She tells him he may put any combination of words in liturgical form; the content of his litany signifies nothing. But she demands that he intone and repeat these lists of words as if they were the names of saints or religious attributes. She vows that only a litany will restore confidence and authority to the individual who recites it or to those who hear it recited. This observation disturbs the narrator almost as profoundly as the Indian uprising he sees before him. This speaker values words and language, not for any specific form they take, but for their endless suggestibility within an unlimited variety of forms and contexts. The narrator thus expresses his philosophy of art: "Strings of language extend in every direction to bind the world into a rushing, ribald whole" ("IU," 11).

Despite his concept of art, he instantly understands the choice Miss R. has given him. To be an artist he must create his aesthetic world from her litany or accept the confusion of the apocalyptic chaos of forms descending upon him, like the Indians attacking his society. To reestablish order and tranquillity, Miss R. implores the narrator to limit and control his consciousness and his art. When the narrator resists her urgings, he discovers that Miss R. no longer represents counterinsurrectionist forces and perhaps never did. She works for the Comanche Clemency Committee. As the story ends, Miss R. turns the narrator over to the enemy.

In essence, "The Indian Uprising" describes the artistic confusion of a creative voice who attempts to imagine a world without committing himself to the concept of society which his artistic vision presupposes. The narrator chooses the pluralism of forms that binds the world into a rushing, ribald, but ever-changing whole, but his lack of human consciousness invites the Indian uprising that a society which abuses language, technology, and its own minorities produces. Unlike Ramona, the narrator of "The Indian Uprising" never accepts the full possibilities of city life. This aesthete's inability to create, to use and control the writer's gift of words describes the fate of language in a society in which individual human consciousness has died. In this world the teacher demanding a litany as the only art form soon becomes the barbaric Comanche destroying all the art the civilization has produced.

In "Paraguay," the matching auxiliary story to "The Indian Uprising," the totalitarian forces of Paraguay, a futuristic society, have destroyed what contemporary civilization regards as art. This civilization's scientists have replaced art with technological facsimiles of aesthetic expression and valid communication with an empty computer language that justifies their deception. No other Barthelme story so vividly demonstrates how subtle forms of mind control can use technology and language to brainwash an entire society. The tale is narrated by a visitor to this society who takes the reader on a tour of it. His travelogue could be a description of a scientifically advanced planet in a science fiction story. Yet on a less literal level, "Paraguay" becomes a metaphor for an attempted human utopia. In this emotionless world, the state induces and controls every human activity from sleep to sex by regulating the temperature maintained in Paraguay's hermetically sealed environments. Ultimately, these conditions hypnotize the narrator of the tale. He represents the artist, or the man intrigued with art in his own world, without the heightened consciousness to see the grave dangers of this exotic society. The apocalyptic storm that consumes the city in "The Indian Uprising" has already passed through "Paraguay." If Paraguay's artists earlier tried to combat this chaos by insisting on the individual sensibility as the basis for all art, they were destroyed in their struggle. In describing a society created from the debris of a scientifically destructive world, the narrator of "Paraguay" ironically praises a world that would deny his own right to self-expression.

Nonetheless, the narrator fails to see the threat Paraguay poses to his artistic integrity, and he speaks uncritically of the huge doses of art this welfare state provides each citizen. He describes the mass production of art in Paraguay's factories which makes such distribution possible: "Each citizen is given as much art as his system can tolerate. . . . Sheet art is generally dried in smoke and is dark brown in color. Bulk art is air-dried and changes color in particular historical epochs."[23] Tragically, the narrator does not realize that this unequivocally collectivist vision of art completely negates any role for the individual human consciousness. A populace sated with art designed by committees and manufactured on assembly lines would be a society of tepid individual response. Its citizens' inability to respond to art would effectively destroy the basic communicative function of all creativity. In his fascination with Paraguay the narrator jeopardizes his own individuality.

Consistent with its vision, this strange new world demands conformity from its inhabitants. The narrator rapidly emerges as a pro-

23. Barthelme, "Paraguay," in *City Life*, 23.

ponent of the imprecision of language which this society sanctions as its correct tone of discourse. He advocates the state's official "softness" of speech as a proper response to an overly stimulated society crowded with people and ideas. To use the narrator's own euphemistic idiom: "Similarly, the softening of language usually lamented as a falling off from former practice is in fact a clear response to the proliferation of surfaces and stimuli. Imprecise sentences lessen the strain of close tolerances."[24] In his intoxication with this society the narrator apparently fails to realize what George Orwell insists in his essay "Politics and the English Language": a government that consistently uses language filled with clichés and obfuscation wishes to subvert and control its populace.[25] The narrator's adoption of this society's sophisticatedly treacherous jargon accommodates its totalitarian goals. His fluency in double-talk coined from computer terminology and communications theory reveals how technological totalitarianism can debase the language and drug the consciousness of an artistic sensibility. Barthelme, the jocular *New Yorker* writer, in his concern in these stories with the fate of language and human values creates visions of dystopia worthy of Aldous Huxley's *Brave New World* and Orwell's *1984*.

The problems posed for the legitimately creative sensibility in a lifeless society give "Paraguay" its tension as a short story. In suggesting how an outsider to Paraguay might use language to depict that society, the story raises one of the central dilemmas of contemporary literature. The tale asks whether any writer can transcend the corruption of a world he knows to create a critical vision of that society. The narrator's problem here becomes that of all modern writers. In attempting to understand a society, a writer can become dangerously susceptible to the confusions, prejudices, and lack of consciousness he wishes to expose in it. "Paraguay," like the identity story "Brain Damage," depicts the artist as unable to describe the state without assimilating its language and beliefs into his own system of values. Just as "City Life" and "The Indian Up-

24. *Ibid.*, 24.
25. George Orwell, "Politics and the English Language," in *Shooting an Elephant and Other Essays* (New York, 1950), 77–92.

rising," the other society stories describing the creative process, "Paraguay" emphasizes the vital relationships between a society, the human consciousness which defines that society, and the artistry which records that consciousness. It dramatizes the suppression of the human spirit which deforms a society's politics, personal relationships, and possibilities for art. With the death of the individual sensibility, the artistic narrator explores a society that expounds the beauty and perfection of a subtly totalitarian world. Like the narrator of "The Indian Uprising," the narrator of "Paraguay" fails to use the debris of a society to form a better world or to criticize the existing social order. But his example insistently acknowledges the dangers of societies and art created without respect for the dignity of the individual human spirit.

Many Barthelme critics in assessing stories like "City Life," "The Indian Uprising," and "Paraguay" have noted similarities between Barthelme's depictions of modern life, his mosaics and collages filled with fluid, transforming images, and the world of contemporary pop art. Alan Wilde appraises Barthelme's superficially uncritical acceptance of objects and goods that links his writing to pop art:

If Barthelme's fictions are to be compared with painting, the comparison ought more properly to take as its point of reference not modernist but Pop art. A number of reviewers have drawn the analogy casually but it is worth pursuing further. . . . In his admirable study Laurence Alloway describes Pop art as "essentially, an art about signs and sign systems." "The attitude of the Pop artists toward the signs and objects they use," he writes, "is neither one of simple acclaim, celebrating consumer goods, nor of satirical condemnation of the system in favor of some humanistic norm of conduct. On the contrary, they use the objects of the man-made environment with a sense of meaning in process."[26]

Wilde's comments have strong affinities to John Leland's observation that many of Barthelme's stories describe the discrepancy between the promise of signs and the rewards they actually grant, or to John Ditsky's view that the realignments of debris and detritus

26. Alan Wilde, "Barthelme Unfair to Kierkegaard: Some Thoughts on Modern and Postmodern Irony," *Boundary 2*, V (Fall, 1976), 53–54.

that Barthelme's stories so consistently display reflect the actual re-shaping of a society in the process of turbulence and change. More-over, Wilde's interpretation serves to unite these opinions, finding Barthelme's tales similar to pop art in portraying the unpredictable sign systems of a society in constant ferment.[27]

Yet despite its insights, Wilde's criticism does a disservice to the tone of the best of Barthelme's writing. In the above excerpt Wilde sees many of Barthelme's stories as pop art which neither praises nor condemns the mass-produced trash of our civilization. This in-terpretation robs Barthelme's writing of a moral dimension which the best of his work forcefully demonstrates. A fallacy lies in seeing Barthelme's stories as an extension of the principles of pop art in prose, for many of the tales contain far more than the ambivalent irony of a Jasper Johns or an Andy Warhol painting. They dramatize the moral conflict between an environment in turmoil and the in-dividuals who attempt to understand and control it. In the last sen-tence of "City Life," Ramona fully accepts her immaculate concep-tion and the city that has made this miracle possible. In the process of the story, she learns to channel the energy and the corruption of this society to create her own sense of power and originality. In di-rect contrast, "Paraguay" describes a society that anesthetizes the individuals within it. "Paraguay" portrays a false utopia whose citi-zens relinquish any concern with the world around them.

Accordingly, at their most eloquent, "Paraguay" and "The Indian Uprising" become morality tales, which contend that the trash and junk of our pop art lives are ruling us, destroying our feel-ing and our ability to change the society that is rapidly changing us. This cataclysm looms vividly in "The Indian Uprising." Its nar-rator must choose between a repressively formal litany or chaot-ically formless strings of language as his only two possible medi-ums of expression. Multiple options and pluralistic solutions have become as threatening as uniformity because this storyteller lacks the discipline or control to shape his words into a coherent vision of a constantly changing society. In turn, the society challenges the

27. Leland, "Remarks Re-marked," 796–97; Ditsky, "'With Ingenuity and Hard-work Distracted,'" 393.

artist's neglect and guilt. Just as strings of language extending in every direction strike the narrator's consciousness, Comanches attack the center of the city in red waves. "The Indian Uprising" thus invokes the moral responsibility of the writer to commit himself to a compassionate, holistic vision of this society. This tale may resemble pop art in its presentation of unreliable signs cluttering a confused, eruptive canvas. Yet, unlike pop art, it does not remain equivocal about its subject and materials. "The Indian Uprising," as well as "City Life" and "Paraguay," demands that the artist take control of his environment and make it more humane and self-aware before the environment takes control of him.

A similar cognizance of the empty pop art values of contemporary life appears in Neil Schmitz's analysis of "The Indian Uprising." Schmitz feels that the decadent commodities of this vulgar society will eventually destroy it. The litter forming the barricades the white men have erected to stop their Indian attackers could be from a Jasper Johns or an Andy Warhol painting; this refuse delineates the distance between a grossly indulged environment and a harsh, primitive one. Yet, ironically, it also stresses that the real differences between collage and litany, freedom and repression, civilization and barbarism disappear in a society that abdicates its consciousness to an excessive concern with objects. Schmitz argues his view persuasively:

The "woven straw basket" wedged into the barricade, grotesque in its jarred familiarity, describes distance, not essence. It exists with the pregnant solitude of Jasper Johns' flag or Andy Warhol's cans of soups, neutral and amodal, yet profoundly socio-political. . . . Stacked in piles, the garbage of a trashed civilization, they are in "The Indian Uprising" the only constant and veritable things to be noted. Which side are you on? the narrator cries after a friend at one point in the piece, and the question is left hanging. There are no sides, the loyalties of class and race have become confused, ideological politics do not exist, a Hobbesian jungle thrives in the streets.[28]

Thus the problem posed by the synthetic pop art vision of stories like "City Life," "The Indian Uprising," and "Paraguay" crystal-

28. Schmitz, "Satire," 114.

lizes. These tales question whether any artist can create and affirm a humane vision from the garbage of a trashed civilization. They leave the solution to the spirited consciousness of a maverick like Ramona in "City Life," or its dire consequences to the failures of an entire society in "Paraguay" and to a misguided aesthete in "The Indian Uprising." Therefore, of all the stories analyzed in this chapter, only "City Life" offers hope for the creation of a productive, energized society.

"City Life" accomplishes what none of the other society stories on the typology does. It imagines a livable world and then offers the ingredients from which an artistic sensibility might compose such a society. It presents a theory not only of society but of art and creativity as well. The story contends that though art rises from the tensions between an urban society and its residents, the role of the artist is ultimately to shape her own art in her own imaginative world. Though art presumes an affinity of feeling between creator and audience, the canny artist shapes the rules and expectations by which her imagined society lives so that her public experiences the social vision she wishes to evoke. Reciprocally, the greatest art may even change the society it attempts to reflect.

Accordingly, Barthelme's art comprises both the affirmation of Moonbelly's "Cities are Centers of Copulation" and Ramona's belief that her child was conceived without sexual contact. Yet because his art remains strongly committed to the integrity of his individual human consciousness, however original or perverse his views, it must frequently be at odds with society; Barthelme's art has a moral function beyond specific social concerns. Above all, his art stands beyond empirical knowledge. Containing mystical or intuitive elements, his artistic process can even be telepathic. Thus Barthelme's concept of society rests in the eye and the consciousness of his artists. Not only in "City Life" but in "To London and Rome," "Will You Tell Me?" and "Perpetua," the artists are individuals who attempt to create a society in their own images. Only in "City Life," however, does Barthelme create a society in which his protagonist can live happily while aiding, and not manipulating, her fellow human beings.

Chapter IV

The Art Stories

       This chapter examines Barthelme stories that describe the place of art in contemporary life. All the stories interpreted here examine the role of the artist and the reaction of the audience when art becomes a massive object in the landscape, a museum piece, or an insurmountable obstacle. Though all twelve stories appear unconcerned about what their art works mean, some ask from what materials contemporary art can be formed; others question whether human beings are the proper subject matter for art, what should be the goals of art, or how the artist may create in a restless, exhausted world. The highly whimsical art objects created raise still other questions about the function and utility of art in a pragmatic world frequently indifferent or hostile to aesthetic considerations.

       Art in these stories hardly constitutes mimesis. Rather, as long as an audience believes in their art, the artists represented here seem free to create people or human abstractions that could not in all likelihood exist. The stories imply that the effort to know another human being may well be futile and art as representation of facets of the personality may be a sham. All art in these stories is a poor likeness, a stand-in, or a bodyguard for reality. Yet the stories also acknowledge that the only means to make art in their cynical, confused worlds is through painstaking, repetitive destruction of reality's fallacious signs and symbols. Thus each tale forms its own artistic vision by denying that it is creating art, by redefining the symbolic nature of reality so that the artistic and the symbolic include elements of life that lie within the range of common experience. The narrators of these stories attempt to make art no less exciting but less privileged and exclusive than conventional concepts have allowed. Ironically disdaining all claims for aestheticism, Barthelme's creators insist on a different, more meaningful vision of art than the art objects around them provide. They transcend this art with an art of their own.

To assure this creativity, the artistic narrators encountered in this chapter regard art as a self-contained object without necessary meaning beyond its surface appearance or assumed reference to a world outside itself. The narrators of these stories construct original, inventive works because they are acutely aware that the modern audience for their works has grown jaded with conventional, predictable artistic experiences and the traditional responses that most works want to elicit. Accordingly, these stories sometimes attempt to involve the reader in the very processes by which they are created.

Turning to the major story in the first block of art stories, "The Balloon," from *City Life* (1970), we discover a story that directly asks what the materials of modern art should be. As critic Richard Schickel has observed, the balloon that suddenly appears over forty-five blocks of Manhattan in this story serves as a metaphor for the problems of modern art and the public's reaction to it.[1] Imitating the style of environmental and conceptual art seen in New York art galleries in the sixties and seventies, the story presents readers with a superficially meaningless, self-referential object, which offers a variety of interpretations to its public. The narrator of the story shapes a work of art rich in sense of play. This playfulness exists in the childlike whim that prompts him to inflate the airy fabric of the balloon over many city blocks, the joyous spontaneity that a seemingly purposeless object produces in spectators who leave the streets and climb onto the balloon, and the comic tension

1. Richard Schickel, "Freaked Out on Barthelme," *New York Times Magazine*, August 16, 1970, p. 15.

between the obvious form of this enormous toy and its ambiguous content and meaning.

"The Balloon" has no plot and shows no intensification of theme or language as it progresses. The story becomes merely a catalog of public responses to the presence of this huge, rubbery plaything. The clash between the soft, undifferentiated form of the balloon and the hard-edged contours of the city buildings and skyscrapers on which it rests illustrates another of the many conflicts between fluid content and solidified form that appear throughout the story. Similarly, critic Tony Tanner sees Barthelme's balloon as representing a contemporary, abstract art object and its contradictions as embodying the dominance of its form over its content: "But take it as a kind of free-form artistic product, flexible, plastic and ephemeral, and it exemplifies the sort of art which Barthelme and many other American writers are increasingly interested in. It represents an invitation to play, a gesture against patterning, a sportive fantasy floating free above the rigidities of environment; and the invitation and the gesture are more important than the actual material of which the balloon is composed."[2] If the invitations and gestures which the form of the balloon induce in an audience are more important than its content or material, the persona of the story has been canny nonetheless in shaping an art work whose flexibility encourages a wide range of speculation about its contents. This malleability leads Jerome Klinkowitz to a somewhat different view of "The Balloon" from Tanner's: "Barthelme appreciates form, but he never allows it to define content."[3]

Not only does the balloon suggest endless play between its form and content, but it prompts a return to a childish sense of play among those who watch it. Realizing that the balloon can never suggest meaning in the limited terms that more respectable works of art do, the narrator describes the sense of gaiety and freedom the balloon generates among members of its audience:

There was a certain amount of initial argumentation about the "meaning" of the balloon; this subsided, because we have learned not to insist on

2. Tanner, *City of Words*, 405.
3. Klinkowitz and Behrens, *Life*, 73.

meanings, and they are rarely even looked for now, except in cases involving the simplest, safest phenomena. It was agreed that since the meaning of the balloon could never be known absolutely, extended discussion was pointless, or at least less purposeful than the activities of those who, for example, hung green and blue paper lanterns from the warm gray underside, in certain streets, or seized the occasion to write messages on the surface, announcing their availability for the performance of unnatural acts, or the availability of acquaintances.[4]

For the narrator, art must be a source of play as well as inspiring play in those who experience it, and such art defies exact interpretation. Yet the narrator does not explain until near the end of the story the mysterious hold an object of pure, purposeless speculation has on many observers below: "This ability of the balloon to shift its shape, to change was very pleasing, especially to people whose lives were rather rigidly patterned, persons to whom change, although desired, was not available. The balloon, for the twenty-two days of its existence, offered the possibility, in its randomness, of mislocation of the self, in contradistinction to the grid of precise, rectangular pathways under our feet" ("B," 21). Thus the narrator offers his view that the appeal of the balloon lies in its perpetual indeterminacy, its ability to lose and consume those individuals who examine it. By extension, the story offers a theory of the appeal of much modern art: its elusiveness and random qualities allow the casual visitor to the gallery as well as the knowledgeable art student to forget momentarily the utilitarian regularity of his own life.

Just as suddenly as the narrator first had the balloon inflated over Manhattan, he turns off its supply of helium, the balloon expires, and the story ends. As in many Barthelme stories developed through play, the protagonist is a mischievous, hiding man who withholds his motives or identity from the reader. Only in the last paragraph of the story does one learn that the narrator has used the balloon to forget his loneliness and his sexual longing for his lover while she was out of the country. With her return he no longer needs his sub-

4. Barthelme, "The Balloon," in *Unspeakable Practices, Unnatural Acts*, 16–17, hereinafter cited parenthetically in the text as "B."

limatory toy. Just as this story, an example of modern art in its own right, reaches an arbitrary conclusion, so does the balloon; yet the demise of neither story nor balloon supplies a satisfactory meaning for the tale. The story suggests that though contemporary art may evolve out of a state of longing or deprivation, these specific, documented emotions fail to explain the work or the audience's fascination with it.

This droll tale argues that in a utilitarian world, frequently suspicious of art, many modern art works do not evoke reducible meaning. Rather, the balloon encourages the individual to lose the self in its surfaces, to relish a work's refusal to be interpreted, and to experience not only a continuing sensation of change and process but also an uninhibited sense of play that the intellectual demands of other forms preclude. "The Balloon" demonstrates that modern art, germinating in an incidental emotion of the artist, can be constructed from any object, toy, or plaything as long as it causes an audience to participate in a full array of its possibilities.

Critic Jerome Klinkowitz understands the force of the balloon as an art object. In his discussion of Barthelme's early essay, "The Case of the Vanishing Product," in which Barthelme contends that much modern advertising gives "not so much as a clue as to what is being advertised," Klinkowitz concurs that the "very novelty of presentation effaces the product itself."[5] In "The Balloon," the narrator creates an artful advertisement that is total wish fulfillment, a complete Rorschach for each observer's fantasies and desires. Like a Goodyear blimp without a message written on its side, the balloon nurtures frustration, awe, and imaginative wonder in its audience because of the advertising slogans it omits. As the narrator slyly acknowledges: "The apparent purposelessness of the balloon was vexing (as was the fact that it was 'there' at all). Had we painted, in great letters, 'LABORATORY TESTS PROVE' or '18% MORE EFFECTIVE' on the sides of the balloon, this difficulty would have been circumvented. But I could not bear to do so" ("B," 18).

Nor does Barthelme add a label to "The Police Band," the first

5. Klinkowitz and Behrens, *Life*, 73–74.

auxiliary story in this category. Here the quality of play remains intact, and the tale does not yield to easy interpretation. In "The Police Band," from *Unspeakable Practices, Unnatural Acts* (1968), the narrator, a former Detroit mailman and jazz musician, is sent to New York as part of the mayor's special police band. The mayor believes that whenever the rage of the city spills into the streets, the police band will go into the conflict and the soothing sound of its jazz will quell the disturbance. In practice, the mayor's plan proves a disaster. The rage of the city remains much too strong for the police band's music to tame. The mayor and his police commissioner are not reelected, and the city's rage remains unchecked by his artistic antidote.

For all its whimsicality, the parable of "The Police Band" raises interesting questions not only about the obvious inadequacy of music to appease urban turmoil but also about the impossibility of any art form to conquer the ugliness of reality. The story's playful juxtaposition of anguish and art, of policemen turned into artists, and of force used to beautify, illustrates the jocular intermingling of form and content that these three playful stories see as one of the functions of the contemporary art object.

"The Police Band" is also play because it is narrated by an amusing, unnamed critic of society, who joins the band believing that art can briefly transform the despair of reality. Unlike the balloon, however, the police band fails to claim its ghetto audience with the surface of its sounds, to convince them their lives can change or even that the playing of its music can momentarily transcend their cramped existence. The other art object on view, however, the Barthelme story itself, does succeed in reaching a quite different audience. First published in the *New Yorker*, "The Police Band" forced its audience of largely affluent, self-consciously sophisticated readers to question what it meant or even if it had meaning.[6] That question defines these stories' concept of the modern art object. "The Police Band" exists as an object of endless play, and its audience can well wonder whether the sardonic band member who

6. Klinkowitz, "Barthelme: A Checklist," 52.

narrates the story believes his own description of these musicians as representing "a triumph of art over good sense."[7] Art here does thrive on emotion, however, and has little use for good sense. The despondent narrator laments that the city dwellers, like the members of his band, remain angry. Sublimation frequently generates art in these stories, but the tales also demonstrate that one must have a balloon or music to quell one's longing or anger before art will emerge. The police band, though an object of play, differs from the balloon in failing to sublimate the desires of either its maker or its audience. It shares this dual sense of frustrated play with "The Policemen's Ball," the second auxiliary story in this grouping.

"The Policemen's Ball," from *City Life* (1970), depicts forceful, authoritarian policemen attempting to relax at an elaborate dance hall decorated with the theme of Camelot. The art object presented here, a ludicrously prettified social gathering of men and women dedicated to law and order, gives the form of their party an absurdly incongruous content because it contradicts the highly rigid form of these policemen's daily lives. These officers and their wives consistently adapt all their activities to some form of coercion and control. The men turn sex into compliance and submission to their will, and the women see their acquiescence as instrumental in keeping their men fit to protect them from the violence and lawlessness lurking in the streets. Even forms of reason acquire the content of force in this tale. The Pendragon, leader of all the policemen, makes a speech during the ball urging caution in pursuing those who wish to disrupt the law and incite the police: "But I must ask you in the name of force itself to be restrained."[8] Yet long before his words are spoken, whatever pleasure and exuberance the ball might possess have taken on the regimented, military bearing of its dancers.

The minimalist plot of "The Policemen's Ball" concerns the efforts of Horace, a young policeman, to use the sexual overtones of

7. Donald Barthelme, "The Police Band," in *Unspeakable Practices, Unnatural Acts*, 75.
8. Donald Barthelme, "The Policeman's Ball," in *City Life*, 55.

this sumptuous event to entice his girl friend, Margot, into his bed. Sex represents protection and control to both Horace and Margot, yet the story insists on the uncertainty and vulnerability of modern life and modern art. The tale most resembles its matched stories on the typology in its reliance on the mysterious, subversive voice that describes the ball and injects its own opinions on it into the narrative. As in "The Balloon," the voice of this hiding man brings the story to an abrupt, artificial conclusion. Consummating their relationship after the ball, Horace and Margot are locked safely in Horace's apartment. Yet as the narrator asserts in the absurdly melodramatic final sentence of the story: "The horrors had moved outside Horace's apartment. Not even policemen and their ladies are safe, the horrors thought. No one is safe. Safety does not exist. Ha ha ha ha ha ha ha ha ha ha!"[9]

The failure of the policemen and their ladies to escape their fears in the festivities of this beautiful, completely unmilitary ball or its aftermath parallels the failure of the ghetto residents to be cajoled by the police band. Both reactions show the hostility of the contemporary audience to purely playful art forms and the inability of this art to overcome the tensions of modern life. Yet both tales as examples of modern prose art exert just the sense of play, of the continual flux between form and content, that the police band and the policemen's ball fail to exert on their audiences. Nonetheless, the narrator's laughter at the conclusion of "The Policemen's Ball" contains a final irony. The reader can ask if these stories suggest interpretations beyond their sense of play; or, perhaps the nervous, theatrical laughter signifies that the narrator and the horrors themselves are pursued by similar goblins. Regardless, in a world of constant change and process nothing remains inviolable. Yet these stories about enormous sublimatory toys—balloon, band, and ball—provide ways to return art to pleasure while in each case suggesting the fear with which such pleasure is frequently viewed.

If these three stories developed through the process of play ask what forms innovative art might take in the contemporary world,

9. *Ibid.*, 56.

the three tales of knowing or of desiring to know ask why famous human beings or the glorification of humanity have become objects of art. The three tales analyzed here, "Robert Kennedy Saved from Drowning," "The Genius," and "On Angels," examine in exacting detail a charismatic political hero, a famous media-conscious intellectual, and the concept of angels as instruments of God and man, respectively. Each story's technique divides the qualities of its man or idea into specific properties and elements. In each case the resulting assessment forms a collage of contradictory poses and impressions which reveal that even highly public human beings remain unknowable.

However rigorously one attempts to investigate the enigma of the human personality, these tales demonstrate the futility of conclusively defining an individual temperament. Yet the stories that evolve from the effort have the quality of modern art in the jarring, contradictory impressions they render of the surfaces they superficially explore. Art emerges from the effort to know in these portraits of a modern politician, a contemporary intellectual, and a humanized religious image because their sense of incompletion and ellipsis allows the observer to participate in the visions formed. The reader can bring his limited knowledge and imaginative resources to shape a sense of unity and coherence in these pictures where none may actually exist.

The central art story developed through the effort to know, "Robert Kennedy Saved from Drowning," from *Unspeakable Practices, Unnatural Acts* (1968), resembles the central art story developed through play, "The Balloon." Both stories take familiar objects, a balloon and the external, well-publicized behavior of Robert Kennedy, and inflate them to grotesque proportions. Through the irregularities and flexibility of the surfaces of the balloon and Kennedy the stories offer these objects as works of art. But whereas "The Balloon" asserts that play rather than interpretation should be the fruit of art, "Robert Kennedy Saved from Drowning" suggests that a desire to understand the art object might be the goal. "The Balloon" consists of the catalog of an audience's spontaneous responses to a huge air-filled toy, while "Robert Kennedy Saved from

Drowning" seeks to construct a collage of Robert Kennedy's contradictory traits, impulses, and reactions in his role as a political figure. The audience for "Robert Kennedy Saved from Drowning" contains all those readers of the story who attempt to do as the narrator does in the last of the story's many short, disconnected segments. There the narrator tries to rescue Kennedy from the sea of publicity that always threatens to submerge him. Throughout the tale he uses his artistic invention to unify as best he can all these discordant snapshots of this awesome man into a complex portrait of a three-dimensional hero.

Simultaneously the story gives the reader all the evidence necessary to pronounce Kennedy a great, selfless humanitarian or to condemn him as a sham, a totally shallow political charlatan. Yet, deferring to the endless mystery of the human personality and the power of modern art to create a wide range of responses in its audience, the story never commits itself to either point of view. The reader sees Kennedy's role as a husband and father and his relations with an administrative assistant, an old friend, a secretary, a former teacher, and the young people who make up a significant part of his growing constituency. Some of these individuals speak of his warmth and compassion, while others emphasize his impulsiveness and sudden unpredictability. We hear Kennedy's own words describing his massive work load, his views on urban transportation, his feelings about the immense crowds that continually follow him, and his responsibilities as a political leader. These hollow, stereotypical responses could be the stock phrases of an insincere fraud trying to give the electorate what it wants to hear. Or they could represent the efforts of a guileless, striving statesman attempting to break free of the clichés of the political jargon expected by the media and the public.

In the twenty-four separate fragments of this story, Kennedy resembles nothing so much as a huge collage, a mosaic of all the paradoxical characteristics that a contemporary leader must possess to succeed. Robert Kennedy embodies so many perspectives and facets that the story suggests even the famous photographer, Karsh of Ottawa, can never find the right pose, the key shot that will capture the real Robert Francis Kennedy. Kennedy emerges as the ultimate art object, and one segment of the story entitled "Gallery-going" describes Kennedy, the politician as art object, visiting a modern art gallery.

Gallery-going

K. enters a large gallery on Fifty-seventh Street, in the Fuller Building. His entourage includes several ladies and gentlemen. Works by a geometrist are on show. K. looks at the immense, rather theoretical paintings.

"Well, at least we know he has a ruler."

The group dissolves in laughter. People repeat the remark to one another, laughing.

The artist, who has been standing behind a dealer, regards K. with hatred.[10]

The ironic effect produced here juxtaposes Kennedy, a living, three-dimensional political art object, against a superficially more severe two-dimensional one, the geometrical painting. Since his function as a politician is to draw a satisfied response from his audience, Kennedy jokes about the rigidity of the other art object on view. As expected, his audience approves, establishing that they understand and appreciate his political art. Yet Kennedy, in a different sense from the angry artist standing behind him, frequently uses a hard edge. Conditioned to make sardonic quips to further his image, he disregards taste and sensitivity to please his followers.

As becomes a skilled contemporary politician, the Robert Kennedy of this story reaches for an intellectual element within the voting public. In a concluding segment Kennedy discusses a 1949 study by the French writer Georges Poulet of a character type Poulet identifies in the drama of eighteenth-century French writer Pierre Marivaux.[11] This personality obviously represents Kennedy's own ideal of the totally adaptable political chameleon. As Kennedy relates Poulet's vision of the Marivaudian man:

10. Donald Barthelme, "Robert Kennedy Saved from Drowning," in *Unspeakable Practices, Unnatural Acts*, 41.

11. James R. Giles, "The 'Marivaudian Being' Drowns His Children: Dehumanization in Donald Barthelme's 'Robert Kennedy Saved from Drowning' and Joyce Carol Oates' *Wonderland*," *Southern Humanities Review*, IX (Winter, 1975), 63.

The Marivaudian being is, according to Poulet, a pastless, futureless man, born anew at every instant. The instants are points which organize themselves into a line, but what is important is the instant, not the line. The Marivaudian being has in a sense no history. Nothing follows from what has gone before. He is constantly surprised. He cannot predict his own reaction to events. He is constantly being overtaken by events. A condition of breathlessness and dazzlement surrounds him. In consequence he exists in a certain freshness which seems, if I may say so, very desirable.[12]

In choosing the condition of the Marivaudian being as his own goal, Kennedy again invites comparison with works of art. He resembles a pointillist painting, but one in which the arrangement of dots forming the picture becomes less important than the markings themselves. Kennedy's comments suggest that the reader might see each of the twenty-four points of reference of this story as existing without continuum or totality but still having fascination as isolated elements in their own right. In the final fragment of the story, Kennedy nearly drowns in the flood of so many discontinuous points of view. At just this moment the narrator intervenes. Attempting to know Kennedy in some immediate, human, and nonpolitical way, he slips a rope around his waist and throws it into the ocean to save Kennedy from inundation. Kennedy eventually grasps the narrator's rope, but, emerging from the water with a mask still covering his face, he offers the narrator only an impersonal "thank you."

The story consistently presents a potentially frightening portrait of Robert Kennedy as a pastless, futureless man constantly surprised by his own reactions. This man might well be a political leader without commitment to anyone but himself or to anything but the present moment. Consequently, the tale has divided its critics into those who feel that it indicts Kennedy as a hopeless egomaniac obsessed with his own continually shifting image and those who believe that it offers an elliptical portrait of a deeper, more complex man, which emerges when the reader imaginatively connects the dots—Kennedy's contradictory traits—with other implicit, positive attributes. Critic Neil Schmitz belongs among the former commentators:

12. Barthelme, "Robert Kennedy," 46.

The journalistic profile which seeks to humanize the great man by revealing the trivial and the intimate succeeds only in declaring the one-dimensional enormity of the figure's self-consciousness, an ego that has rigorously stylized behavior into a series of gestures. Yet this same Kennedy, master of the stock response, humorlessly quotes Poulet at the end of the piece on the Marivaudian man "born anew" in each instant of experience constantly "overtaken by events." It is scathing picture of the human surface.[13]

Although the reader may agree with Schmitz that Robert Kennedy develops into a blatantly vapid figure in this story, Schmitz's appraisal does not consider that the tale chooses to define Kennedy almost exclusively through his surface actions, however transparent their one-dimensionality. Therefore, Schmitz fails to calculate the demands of Kennedy's audience, which insists that he control and stereotype his behavior if he wishes to remain a public icon and an art object.

Balancing Schmitz's denunciation of the image of Kennedy in the story, William Stott feels that the final triumph of "Robert Kennedy Saved from Drowning" lies ironically in its failure to produce a believable human being from so many mutually exclusive tendencies and attitudes. Stott finds the story a parody of feature article technique which reveals the limitations of journalism to explore the interior life of any human being. Kennedy emerges as a manipulative automaton because any human personality remains, at depth, unknowable, particularly one subjected to such intense scrutiny. But Stott does value the narrator's effort to rescue Kennedy, his desire to know the art object even though it refuses to lower its mask:

K. can't be explained in a news magazine: his public aspect has too little coherence. K.'s self is exactly what the mock notes and the article that will come from them must leave out—what they can't touch, treat, predict. . . . And Barthelme has saved K.—the K. whom Kafka taught us to recognize as Everyman—and Robert Kennedy and similar public figures, from drowning in the sea of publicity by simply insisting that the sea, though it has K.'s body, his acts, his words, even certain of his past dreams and thoughts, doesn't have the real man.[14]

Is Kennedy's nature then all surface or all depth? The truth proba-

13. Schmitz, "Satire," 112.
14. Stott, "Donald Barthelme and the Death of Fiction," 385.

bly lies somewhere between these critical extremes. Still, Schmitz and Stott do not disagree on some of the qualities that make Robert Kennedy, like the balloon, an art object. Both critics see Kennedy as a figure who refuses to explain or give meaning to the world around him. He becomes an aesthetic object because of the fascination his pliable surface has for an audience wary of conventional art, exhausted with literary interpretations and deeper significance. Comparable to the balloon's inability to have a purpose or an advertising function, Kennedy's directly opposite quality, his completely utilitarian goals as a political object, confirms for Stott the extensive interior life the man must possess. These two modern art objects may contain in abundance just those qualities they appear to lack. The seeming uselessness of the balloon disguises the need for the sense of play, spontaneity, and change it prompts, and the total pragmatism of Kennedy's external character may hide the humanity and confusions beneath. Moreover, "Robert Kennedy Saved from Drowning" functions as an excellent modern art object itself, a short story which suggests that a famous politician acquires aesthetic force if, following the narrator of the story, the reader attempts to apprehend the collage formed from the elements of Kennedy's personality. Always ending in some degree of futility, this effort nonetheless demonstrates that a human being shares all the intricacy and contradiction of art if the reader allows his own human nature to participate in the mystery of another personality.

Two auxiliary stories, "The Genius" and "On Angels," evoke the extreme loneliness and isolation experienced by a man or, in the case of angels, spiritual beings who have become art objects in their society. Unlike "Robert Kennedy Saved from Drowning," these stories encompass the points of view of the genius and various angels. Consequently, both tales lack a narrator who futilely tries to know how the diverse strands of a genius's or several angels' personalities have made them art objects esteemed by their society. In each tale, however, the genius or the angels are filled with self-doubt, and the stories evolve as investigations of the means by which these figures can know themselves and explain their power as art.

Of the two tales, "The Genius," from *Sadness* (1972), shows the greater similarity to the themes and structure of "Robert Kennedy Saved from Drowning" and frequently seems merely an extension of that story. In "The Genius," however, the Kennedy parallel appears as an intellectual resembling Marshall McLuhan or Buckminster Fuller, whose ideas, misinterpreted by the oversimplifications of the media, have moved beyond a strictly academic audience and into voguish public acceptance. Similarly, the structures of the two stories are analogous. "The Genius" consists of a series of sentences, descriptions, or anecdotal fragments, which portray the genius as a cantankerous, inconsistent man given to arbitrary, moody poses and responses. These elements of the genius's personality form the collage of his character, which makes him an art object both to those individuals who observe his public behavior and to the readers of the story. The chief difference between this story and "Robert Kennedy Saved from Drowning" arises in the genius's troubled self-consciousness. Unlike Kennedy's impassivity, this trait causes the genius himself, and not a narrative voice, to doubt, question, and challenge his right to be regarded as a significant thinker and an art object.

Throughout the story the genius's quest for self-knowledge serves as a motif uniting its fragments and demonstrating the artistry of the tale. The elements of this collage include an aphorism from Valéry noting that every man of genius also contains a false man of genius. The genius freely acknowledges that he may be a sham, and immediately following Paul Valéry's remark, he describes the contemporary age as a time of ignorance in which no one knows what others know and no one knows enough. "The Genius" depicts a world in which men's and women's efforts to know and their fascination with increasingly higher planes of abstraction, including the concept of genius, have only increased individuals' failures to communicate. Indeed, this struggle has torn and separated people from one another and from themselves. Accordingly, in another fragment the genius speaks of his frustration in attempting to define the sources of his genius. He has no clue as to what makes him a great thinker: "The mystery remains a mystery."[15] If a genius can-

15. Donald Barthelme, "The Genius," in *Sadness*, 27.

not explain genius, the story suggests that the riddle of the human personality may never be solved.

Yet the futility of his task does not prevent the protagonist from seeking an answer. Reminiscent of the segment in "Robert Kennedy Saved from Drowning" in which Kennedy, a political art object, confronts another art object in a gallery, "The Genius" reveals its hero as an intellectual art object who reads Theodore Dreiser's novel *The Genius* to gain self-awareness. Curious to know whether the florid descriptions of the genius in Dreiser's prose resemble his own demeanor, the genius puts the novel down and walks to a mirror. "The Genius," like "Robert Kennedy Saved from Drowning," functions as an endless plane of mirrors in which the popular idol sees himself reflected in the adulation of his audience. In "The Genius," however, the intellectual savior attempts to search for the causes of his acclaim.

By the conclusion of the story the genius realizes that he will never know his meaning or significance as an artistic phenomenon. Yet in a world of monotonous conformity he understands his hold on the public. He attracts an audience by constantly questioning all the events, data, and circumstances it takes for granted. Without solutions to the problems he poses, the genius as an art object nonetheless allows his public to participate in the possibilities for thought he opens to them. Petulant, gnomic, unable to communicate with other people and frightened of other geniuses, the genius constitutes a calculated human puzzle whose pieces defy unity or coherence. By attempting to understand how his own fragments might align, this Marivaudian being saves himself from drowning and presents a picture of both his surface and his depths. In the process, the readers of "The Genius" are free to construct their own genius from this genius's personal, fragmented self-exploration.

The second auxiliary story, "On Angels," from *City Life* (1970), is Barthelme's most whimsical examination of man's potential to become an art object. If the other two stories in this square demonstrate that politicians such as Robert Kennedy and intellectuals such as McLuhan and Fuller develop many of the qualities of a work of art for a contemporary audience, this tale suggests that any object of man's imaginative speculation assumes some of the qualities of art and that the intense effort to know eventually becomes an artistic endeavor. Specifically, the story investigates the fate of the angels after the presumed death of God, and it poses several questions about their threatened existence. If the omnipotence and assured presence of God have vanished from the earth, what, the tale asks, will happen to His divine messengers and servants? Moreover, if angels appear as men in perfect form, what will become of them once men stop believing in godlike perfection and omniscience? Furthermore, should anyone expect artistic perfection in a world in which men can know so little?

"On Angels" rhetorically dismisses its own doubts by quickly asserting that men will continue to believe in art, perfection, and the human possibilities for attaining these qualities regardless of the existence of God, certainty, or final knowledge. To illustrate its view, the story cites three items from the vast literature on angels. Using Emanuel Swedenborg's study of angels, Gustav Davidson's *Dictionary of Angels*, and "The Psychology of Angels," a contemporary essay by Joseph Lyons, the tale demonstrates the enormous force angels have had on the human imagination.[16] The news of the death of God should have made this literature meaningless, but since men and women will always wonder if they can become more perfect and more beautiful, angels will continue to offer a vision of human perfection that traditional art sometimes neglects. The narrator of this essayistic story thus concedes that much writing about angels is actually writing about human beings in angelic forms.

After surveying the literature on angels, the tale concludes by discussing the angels' attempt to find a new role for themselves following the death of God. Once various suggestions are overruled as unworthy of angelic skill and perfection, one faction of the angels proposes that their new function should be to celebrate their refusal to exist. Not only is this alternative immediately rejected by the other angels as a sign of spiritual pride, but the moral force of this story also makes it immediately unacceptable. The tale insists

16. Donald Barthelme, "On Angels," in *City Life*, 127–28.

throughout that the human quest for perfection will never die despite the impossibility of mankind ever knowing whether angels, God, or certainty exists. Consistent with the aesthetic vision that the preceding art stories have taken, angels are perfect Barthelme art objects. Inviting an audience to know their frequently changing shapes and to attempt an understanding of their play of form and content, angels in addition serve as intellectual abstractions that may totally be a product of the artistic imagination. Paralleling angels as an art form, this short story becomes a fitting art object itself. The tale develops as a collage of references, scholarship, and angelic views on some of the human forms angels may acquire. The reader, attempting to know all possibilities for his own aesthetic expression, never discovers whether angels actually exist. Yet in this endless search he can be persuaded of his potential for spiritual perfectibility and angelic form.

Turning now to stories of stasis developed through repetition, we find three tales: the central identity story, "The Glass Mountain," and the two auxiliary stories, "Nothing: A Preliminary Account" and "Concerning the Bodyguard." Rather than questioning what contemporary art should be, or if men and women can achieve aesthetic perfection as the past art stories have, these tales examine the artistic process itself. They recognize it as a quest, an endless, repetitive search, which insistently tries to shape some vision or make some statement from the confusions, uncertainties, and contradictions of experience. In these tales art exists as a venture that always ends in some degree of failure because the artist realizes he has been falsely educated to regard many of the misleading signs and symbols of his world as faithfully designating reality. Accordingly, the artist in these stories acts as a translator and interpreter of reality, attempting to lessen the distance between the artistic symbol and the reality it represents, between the claims of art and its actual possibilities in an often debased, ugly world. Art in these stories becomes a catalog of all that contemporary art cannot achieve, thereby enabling the audience to understand what the contemporary artist seeks from the artistic process. These stories represent the struggle of the artist to express a reality greater than his world yet a reality that still does not exclude a pragmatic assessment of his world. Though raising more questions than they can answer, these investigations of the artistic process are never completely nihilistic because they reveal that the conflict between reality, art, and ideas will always continue even though its terms are always changing.

Turning to the typology, we find the central art story, "The Glass Mountain," from *City Life* (1970), developed through Barthelme's sense of repetitive concern. Superficially, it appears to be one of his most straightforward tales. In one hundred numbered statements the story relates the quest of its artist-protagonist to climb a steep glass mountain, which has suddenly risen at the corner of Thirteenth Street and Eighth Avenue. Once again, a Barthelme story presents its readers with an enormous art object, like the balloon or Robert Kennedy. In this instance, however, the reader is encouraged neither to play with the object nor to understand it, but to conquer the mountain by slowly, painstakingly scaling it. The aesthetic goal to be gained here is not a final prize or reward but the sheer process of accomplishing a very difficult task, even if the odds against completing the climb seem formidable. Many brave knights have tried to scale the mountain, but their dying bodies, groaning in pain, circle its base. Furthermore, the mountain air is bitter cold, and the protagonist has strapped climbing irons to his feet and holds an incongruous tool, a plumber's helper, in each hand. If these physical conditions are not enough to deter the hero, the street below is full of his acquaintances shouting abusive taunts as he inches his way to the summit.

"The Glass Mountain" neatly functions as a metaphor for the plight of the modern artist. Striving to achieve an impossible task, to scale heights others have attempted and failed, the contemporary artist here is a Don Quixote figure. He represents the incurable romantic, who wants to climb the glass mountain to make the world better, not only for himself but for his society. The numbering of each sentence in this story emphasizes the static, repetitive nature of his quest while conveying the numbing despair of the lives of those in the street below. They envy this adventurer because he attempts to do what they cannot: overcome misery through art. As he crawls up the side of the mountain, the narrator describes the city he has left behind. He pictures a world full of senseless violence and fear in which alcoholic, failed artists and drugged teenagers walk on sidewalks caked with dog shit. A vandal wantonly saws down a row of elm trees on a city street as people pass by, nervously observing the incident but doing nothing to stop it.

Consequently, the narrator journeys up the mountain to find artistic values a contemporary audience can still revere. He has heard in a childhood nursery story of a castle of pure gold at the top of the glass mountain. The story says that in a room in the castle tower sits a beautiful, enchanted symbol. Several hundred feet above the city the narrator contemplates his chances for artistic transcendence of the pain and failure of city life. At this point he reconsiders his motives for undertaking this quest. He realizes that though men still need symbols, the harshness of the reality around them should force artists to disenchant the symbol, to bring it down to earth, and to make art more conversant with reality and mankind.

54. It was cold there at 206 feet and when I looked down I was not encouraged.
55. A heap of corpses both of horses and riders ringed the bottom of the mountain, many dying men groaning there.
56. "A weakening of the libidinous interest in reality has recently come to a close." (Anton Ehrenzwieg)
57. A few questions thronged into my mind.
58. Does one climb a glass mountain, at considerable personal discomfort, simply to disenchant a symbol?
59. Do today's stronger egos still need symbols?
60. I decided that the answer to these questions was "yes."
61. Otherwise what was I doing there 206 feet above the power-sawed elms, whose white meat I could see from my height?[17]

In examining this passage, critic Alan Wilde sees "The Glass Mountain" as a radical effort not only to disenchant the idea of the symbol in Barthelme's storytelling but also as his challenge to the givens of much American popular culture.

17. Donald Barthelme, "The Glass Mountain," in *City Life*, 61–62.

The project of the story, and of others like it, is in fact precisely one of demythifying, or disenchanting— . . . the cultural imperatives (scientific, religious, psychological, governmental, and aesthetic) of the present and the past: of everything, in short, from Batman to the American Dream. As compared with the enchanted symbol, the narrator's acquaintances, shouting throughout the climb a volley of obscene discouragements and standing on the sidewalks below—which the narrator sees with a curiously radiant intensity as "full of dogshit in brilliant colors: ocher, umber, Mars yellow, sienna, viridian, ivory black, rose madder" ("CL," 66)—are pure disenchanted, phenomenal reality, and, so the story implies, all the better for that.[18]

Though Wilde's criticism values the story's intention to deflate the authority of symbols in contemporary narrative, his assessment ignores what the passage in question clearly, unambiguously tells the reader. The narrator may climb the mountain to disenchant the symbol, but he also realizes that contemporary men and women need symbols, if not grandiose ones like the glass mountain. The problem of his quest and of contemporary art is in finding symbols that stimulate the modern imagination without completely falsifying deprived, quotidian existence. Contemporary art must somehow mediate between its former lofty perspectives and a harsh modern world, which makes idealized artistic insights ludicrous. The chorus of street people who revile the mountain climber with their discouragement does, as Wilde says, represent phenomenal reality, yet their lives are depicted as brutal and limited. Only through the eyes of the thoroughly romantic narrator, and not through any vision of the people themselves, does the dog shit lining the streets acquire the rainbow of color of the artist's palette.

Therefore, the story suggests that much of this dilemma in modern art arises in the vision of the artists themselves. Miseducated to believe their endless supply of signs and symbols will still produce the aesthetic responses in contemporary audiences this shorthand has always evoked, many contemporary artists continue to build castles of gold filled with enchanted symbols, regardless of how squalid the conditions of the contemporary world may be.

18. Wilde, "Barthelme Unfair to Kierkegaard," 57.

Moreover, the romantic who climbs the glass mountain learns that reality destroys the efforts to discriminate made by artists, literary critics, and semiologists. Consulting *A Dictionary of Literary Terms*, which he carries with him as he climbs, the protagonist finds a distinction made between symbol and sign, which is immediately invalidated by the world around him. The situation explains why contemporary men and women can make so little sense of either their own battered lives or the badly outmoded terminology of literature.

70. In the streets were people concealing their calm behind a facade of vague dread.
71. "The conventional symbol (such as the nightingale, often associated with melancholy), even though it is recognized only through agreement, is not a sign (like the traffic light) because, again, it presumably arouses deep feelings and is regarded as possessing properties beyond what the eye alone sees." (*A Dictionary of Literary Terms*.)
72. A number of nightingales with traffic lights tied to their legs flew past me.[19]

At last the explorer nears the summit and the golden castle containing the enchanted symbol. He dares to disenchant the symbol, to give it new meaning for those trapped in the street below. Approaching the symbol with its many layers of interpretation, he reaches to touch it. To his disgust, his touch transforms the symbol into a beautiful princess. Furious, he throws the princess down the mountain to his vulgar, vengeful friends, who will know what to do with her.

In this conclusion the artist ironically fails both himself and his audience. Searching for an art uncontaminated by his fraudulent literary terms or his overeducated conception of what art should be, this artist wants to reach an audience whose hostile physical environment makes the ethereal symbols of traditional art ridiculous. Yet when the narrator transforms the enchanted symbol into a beautiful princess—a hopelessly commonplace symbol even for people starved for beauty—he becomes enraged at the striking unoriginality of his art. Torn by his conflicting desires to reach his au-

19. Barthelme, "Mountain," 63.

dience and to achieve the high standards he sets for himself, the protagonist can be true to neither goal. Though he is an emissary of art to the people and an interpreter of their artistic reality, the protagonist's soaring standards ironically prevent him from disenchanting the symbol to satisfy his own aesthetics or theirs.

If the narrator's final anger suggests the failure of this artistic process to fulfill either the contemporary artist or his audience, as an art work itself, "The Glass Mountain" demonstrates the ability of new forms of art to transcend the limitations and worn conventions of the old. This story, as a parody of the fairy tale, actually adheres to and reveres the romance form it superficially ridicules. The repetitive, static listing of the one hundred steps necessary to disenchant the symbol finally makes the new symbol, however hackneyed, worth attaining. Moreover, this artistic quest becomes an art unto itself. As Alan Wilde states, this distinctive, numbered technique for composing a short story ultimately represents not just an unsuccessful effort to disenchant the narrative symbol but an examination of Barthelme's aesthetic motivations for writing a story in this form: "But what one senses in the best of his work is an effort to use art to overcome art (as the moderns characteristically employ consciousness to move beyond consciousness)—or, better still, an attempt parallel to that in 'The Glass Mountain' to disenchant the aesthetic, to make of it something not less special but less extraordinary."[20]

This effort to overcome established art forms with less conventional and predictable ones appears also in "Nothing: A Preliminary Account" and "Concerning the Bodyguard," the two auxiliary stories. These tales illustrate the power of the artistic process to shape something—some object, vision, or statement—from the nondescript character, the nothingness, a situation or concept possessed before the artist examined it. Like "The Glass Mountain," both stories are quests that become catalogs of all the ways their particular subject cannot be defined or categorized. Developing through a static sense of repetition, both stories fail to exhaust or

20. Wilde, "Barthelme Unfair to Kierkegaard," 60.

limit their subject, thereby suggesting the endless aesthetic possibilities of the art object or artistic conflict each explores.

Of the two stories, "Nothing: A Preliminary Account," from *Guilty Pleasures* (1974), more directly questions the purpose of the artistic process. The tale consists totally of a run-on list of many objects and ideas, which, occupying space, time, or both, refuse to be merely nothing. In this tale nothing represents the emptiness or void in which all art originates and to which most imperfect art, outliving its inspiration only by a few years or decades, returns. Accordingly, the artistic process in this story becomes the effort to make something of permanence from nothing. Nothing also describes the feelings of despair and incompetence that the effort to produce art characteristically evokes in the artist who realizes that anything he makes will fall short of the complete verisimilitude he seeks to depict in it. Yet the tale functions as well as an effort to trap this destructive quality of nothingness, to exorcise and dispel it from the artist's work. Try as he might, however, nothing eludes this list maker. He decides that to capture nothing permanently and rid it from his art he must compose a compilation of everything that nothing is not. Thus this survey forms the story. Nevertheless, before the tale ends the narrator recognizes that, if given eternity to complete his catalog, he could still find items to include in it. If, miraculously, he could finish his inventory, the tabulation itself would remain, and this endless scroll would not be nothing.

Rather than causing the artist to become nihilistic, his growing awareness that nothingness can never be contained within the artistic process only renews his gleeful sense of possibility characteristic of the story's slapdash tone from the beginning. Realizing that the greatest art endures many centuries and his own life will be infinitely short, the narrator rushes through the thought of philosophers from Gorgias to Heidegger, Kierkegaard, and Sartre for their views on nothingness and being. Finally perceiving that his list of contradictory opinions and data will never be finished, he chooses to see it as a constant beginning, a series of approximations that, even if he could live indefinitely, would still keep him waiting forever for its conclusion. From this perspective, all art and artistic process become a constant correction and reshaping of the partial ideas, philosophies, signs, and symbols that have encouraged men to believe in permanence, conventions, and finite truths.

The story adds to its compendium of thoughts about nothingness such works as Dylan Thomas' "Do not go gentle into that good night" and Samuel Beckett's closing words from Krapp's beckoning of death, "Burning to be gone."[21] Yet as his own storytelling time expires, the narrator understands that death is hardly nothing despite the loss it imposes and neither is that art which tries to deny or embrace the sense of death. Nothing in this story represents the void from which all art emerges and to which most art drifts, as well as the feelings of inadequacy artistic effort generates in those who attempt it. In his concluding lines the narrator makes an ecstatic discovery: nothing also signifies the impossible purity and perfection to which all art aspires and fails: "What a wonderful list! How joyous the notion that, try as we may, we cannot do other than fail and fail absolutely and that the task will remain always before us, like a meaning for our lives. Hurry. Quickly."[22] Consequently, "Nothing: A Preliminary Account" asserts the value of the failed artistic product and contends that the static, repetitive artistic process, however fruitless, gives value to the artist's vision. This story attempting to climb its own glass mountain, to disenchant the aesthetic of nothingness, finds that its own repetitive technique reveals that nothing can never be known and, hence, the denial of nothingness, like its affirmation, will always be a source of art.

The second auxiliary story, "Concerning the Bodyguard," from *Great Days* (1979), which shares a box on the typology with "The Glass Mountain" and "Nothing: A Preliminary Account," also attempts to disenchant the aesthetic of nothingness. In a series of static, repetitive, unanswered questions, the story examines the relationship of a bodyguard to the wealthy, internationally famous man he watches and protects. The bodyguard serves as a function-

21. Donald Barthelme, "Nothing: A Preliminary Account," in *Guilty Pleasures* (New York, 1974), 165.

22. *Ibid.*

ary whose only role is to follow, surround, and symbolize another, implicitly superior individual. Therefore, the artistic process of the story becomes the quest to make something of this human nothing, to transform the bodyguard into an art object, a symbol worthy of the esteemed man he represents. Art in this tale quickly takes the role of duplication, reproduction, and repetition. The artistic process or quest here can be likened to an act of substitution in which the bodyguard must assume many of his employer's habits and routines.

Interestingly, the artistic metaphors implicit in "Concerning the Bodyguard" develop complexity as the story proceeds. The story is concerned not just with the relationship between a human symbol and the reality he represents but with the quality of art in a repressive, class-conscious society. As the list of its insinuating questions continues, this story becomes a repetitive catalog of the indifference and subtle abuse the arrogant industrialist shows his lower-class, poorly educated bodyguard. The story insistently asks about the bodyguard's low pay, shabby clothing, and poor benefits; and these questions reveal the increasing contempt he feels for the man he follows. Consequently, the bodyguard as a symbol can have only strained relationships to his employer's world. This man's art of replication seems a poor stand-in, a contemptuous, disdainful reproduction of the realities of his society. In "The Glass Mountain" the artistic process attempts to disenchant the romantic, elevated symbol and to bring it to the level of the people in the street. In contrast, the artistic process in "Concerning the Bodyguard" questions the purpose of art in a society whose symbols must shield and honor a corrupted, callous humanity.

Eventually, "Concerning the Bodyguard" envisions a society in which art or artistic symbols can slowly transform the world that first adopted them. The tale, like "Nothing: A Preliminary Account," demonstrates that the concept of nothingness, in its absolute aesthetic purity, can never exist. Consequently, the story and its questions are continually making something from nothing, giving distinctive, individualized life to the emptiness of the bodyguard's symbolic function as another man's double. The reader learns that the bodyguard has a wife and two children in another country far away, that he lives in a cramped efficiency apartment and enjoys pornographic films and magazines. Although the bodyguard appears largely ignorant of politics or of the ways his employer exploits workers all over the world, he grows steadily more resentful of the man's displays of personal power. He has mixed feelings of camaraderie and jealousy for the other bodyguards who surround this magnate. He hears the complaints of his fellow workers that their job is dangerous and boring, and he wonders about the loyalty and reliability of the newest bodyguard in their ranks. The story's questions end with a report that, much to the joy of the general public, the industrialist has been assassinated and presumably the bodyguard, or one of his counterparts, bears some responsibility.

All the story's unceasing, unanswered queries do not actually make us know or understand the bodyguard, but they do present the reader with the man's range of response. Totally shaping the process of the story, these interrogations demonstrate that the art of this tale is all process without results, products, or discoveries, other than the certainty that the symbolic life of narrative dies when the reality it represents becomes abusive and corrupt. The artistic process of the story supplies the goal of the bodyguard's life: to kill through static repetition and negligence the reality that is numbing his existence. With the death of this tyrant the bodyguard no longer serves as a slavish symbol, and art can search for more imaginative, liberating ways to transform reality into symbols. As "The Glass Mountain" attempts to move symbolism closer to reality and "Nothing: A Preliminary Account" makes something from nothingness, "Concerning the Bodyguard" says art will follow life indefinitely only if life shows some signs of vitality and humanity.

Approaching the final three stories on the typology, "At the Tolstoy Museum," "The Falling Dog," and "The Flight of Pigeons from the Palace," one can see these art stories as probing one of the central dilemmas of the modern artist: how does one create in a world in which existing works of literature and art seem to dwarf the potential for contemporary expression? These tales examine

the plight of the modern artist who attempts to affirm his own creativity while acknowledging that the mastery of a writer such as
Tolstoy only accentuates the limitations of his own obsessive images. Complicating his dilemma, the artist senses the flight of the
contemporary audience from works that cease to titillate, shock, or
amuse it. In "At the Tolstoy Museum," the reader observes that
modern art and architecture which only entomb the past. Yet the
story also shows the successful effort of its lyrical, inspired narrator to create art in his own style by imaginatively retelling a story
from Tolstoy. Similarly, "The Falling Dog" reveals an additional
source of a sculptor's creativity after he seems to have exhausted
his personal storehouse of images. Receptive to the world around
him, this contemporary artist allows the objects of his immediate
experience to become the objects of his art. A bizarre event in the
sculptor's life serves as an object of his playful speculation and offers him limitless possibilities for a new artistic image, a wealth of
materials from which it might be composed, and a variety of techniques other artists have used to develop it. His play of mind does
not explain the new work of art the sculptor shapes, but it does predict similar associations that the work might elicit in the audience
that discovers it. "The Falling Dog" demonstrates one means by
which reality may jar the artist into new stages of creativity without giving definitive meaning or interpretation to the work that
results.

The second auxiliary story, "The Flight of Pigeons from the Palace," focuses on the contemporary audience forever in search of
new sensations and experiences. Bored by the traditional values
and proven effects of conventional art, this audience forces the artist to turn his work into a literal circus, a freak show filled with
absurd, unrelated acts. Consequently, the story consists of a collage
of verbal descriptions of each of his performers paired with drawings illustrating and following each novelty he places on view. "The
Flight of Pigeons from the Palace" reflects the extent to which the
contemporary artistic performer feels he must pander to a dwindling
public to appease and satisfy it. Lacking confidence in its own
skills to transcend the art of the past, the sensibility in each of

these three stories crafts a mosaic of words and pictures. These collages demonstrate the powerlessness of many contemporary images, visual as well as written, to evoke an aesthetic response in an audience. Yet a considerable contradiction looms in all three stories. In its audacity and imagination each shows an artist affirming his unique creativity, and a literary artist at that, who flourishes without visualization of his materials when he controls his audience's expectations and not merely reacts to its demands.

Returning to a more complete examination of "At the Tolstoy Museum," the central art story developed through an analysis of its narrator's creative process, the reader finds a story that blends words and drawings. The tale describes an utterly contemporary art object, a modernistic museum containing thirty thousand pictures of Tolstoy. In the story the architectural presence of the museum is juxtaposed with sketches of several pictures within it and with exhibits about Tolstoy on view there. The story serves as a parable on the modern tendency to institutionalize the art and artists of other times and to build mausoleums to honor this deification. In describing the inclination of enthusiasts of contemporary art and contemporary artists themselves to regard great works of other eras as insurmountable art objects, "At the Tolstoy Museum" becomes a museum piece itself. If the tale were nothing more than this it would be only an arid essay. But the story records the account of a Sunday visitor to the Tolstoy Museum. This narrator observes several pictures of Tolstoy, accumulates miscellaneous facts about Tolstoy's life from various displays, reads one short story and two of Tolstoy's social pamphlets on exhibit, and reacts to the grotesque architectural modernism of the museum. Above all, he attempts to dispel the sadness that permeates the museum and consumes the response of all the visitors to what they see. This viewer tries to break through the awesome, monumental grief that Tolstoy's majesty induces in writers or other artists, who feel that whatever they might create would be hopelessly inadequate by comparison. The narrator, haunted by these visions of Tolstoy, nevertheless attempts to form an art work of his own from his experience in the museum. Trapped within the aesthetic and architectural constraints of this building and this story, he can frame his art only from an awareness of Tolstoy's genius. In the most important moments of his trip to the museum, the protagonist retells a short story by Tolstoy he finds in the museum's library. Bringing his unique simplicity and feeling to the effort, he affirms his creativity in the process of recasting another man's fable. With this vignette, "At the Tolstoy Museum" becomes a metaphor for the way a contemporary artist, momentarily blinded by the brilliance of an earlier writer, nevertheless can use the author's basic materials to transcend them and claim his own art.

Before the narrator emerges from Tolstoy's shadow he describes the quality that proves so overwhelming to an artist trying to discover his own identity. This story begins with a full-page drawing of Tolstoy's grizzled beard and long face that stares imperiously at the reader and the visitors to the museum. The same sketch reappears on the next page, but this time it dwarfs the small figure of Napoleon drawn in the lower left-hand corner. This juxtaposition of images and sizes conveys the ability of the epic artist Tolstoy to overshadow even the sweeping, awesome history of Napoleonic conquest he recreates. As the story momentarily turns to prose descriptions of the museum, the narrator tries to demythologize the reverential status of Tolstoy generated by the building. He wonders whether the pictures of Tolstoy on one wall might be lowered. Furthermore, he attempts to know and understand Tolstoy by reading unrelated details about his life. Yet all the information the museum provides makes the personality of Tolstoy, like that of Robert Kennedy or the genius, seem an enigma, a series of formidable contradictions. Seeking to unearth the man this modern art museum has entombed, the narrator discovers only a multilayered, infinitely paradoxical human being. Just as the three cantilevered, tilting floors of the futuristic museum seem ready to topple on those who pass before it, so Tolstoy's enormous spiritual and political force shook his world. Yet the beauty of much of his writing suggests a man of considerable aesthetic delicacy. The narrator obviously cannot resolve this conflict between the strength of Tolstoy's social vision, dramatized in the architecture of the museum, and the poetic fragility of his style.

The entire building, viewed from the street, suggests that it is about to fall on you. This the architects relate to Tolstoy's moral authority.

In the basement of the Tolstoy Museum carpenters uncrated new pictures of Count Leo Tolstoy. The huge crates stencilled FRAGILE in red ink.[23]

Repeatedly, the narrator notes that artists who visit the museum weep profusely at its Tolstoy pictures, exhibits, pamphlets, and stories. Sensing the immense burden this great artist has placed on their own creative powers, they feel Tolstoy's gaze resting on them, like the scrutiny of their fathers or that of any older authority figure. Yet Tolstoy's magnificent artistry, despite its grandeur, has considerable emotional distance from our age and less and less to teach an aspiring contemporary writer. Ironically, the revelatory truth of Tolstoy's social pamphlet proclaiming that children would be better teachers of their elders than the old men who instruct the young is completely lost on these observers of Tolstoy, who are paralyzed by their own grief.

The guards at the Tolstoy Museum carry buckets in which there are stacks of clean white pocket handkerchiefs. More than any other museum, the Tolstoy Museum induces weeping. Even the bare title of a Tolstoy work, with its burden of love, can induce weeping—for example, the article titled "Who Should Teach Whom to Write, We the Peasant Children or the Peasant Children Us?" Many people stand before this article, weeping. Too, those who are caught by Tolstoy's eyes, in the various portraits, room after room after room, are not unaffected by the experience. It is like, people say, committing a small crime and being discovered at it by your father, who stands in four doorways, looking at you. ("TM," 45)

Implicit in the misery that an art object like the Tolstoy Museum causes the contemporary imagination lies some respite from its very claustrophobia. Tolstoy relates in another of his social pamphlets on view how men stupefy and sadden themselves when, lionizing past art and artists, they forget that their own opportunities for creativity exist only in the present. Demonstrating Tolstoy's view, the narrator contrasts a single musician playing a trumpet before two children in the plaza of the museum with the 640,086-

23. Barthelme, "At the Tolstoy Museum," in *City Life*, 45, hereinafter cited parenthetically in the text as "TM."

page Jubilee edition of Tolstoy's collected works for inspection in the building. This musician's skill, though largely unheard and unappreciated, constitutes a means by which a man, creating his own art, frees himself of the past. By contrast, the edition of Tolstoy represents a source of inertia for all potential artists chained to the past, particularly those who would read Tolstoy to charge their own imaginative energies. Thus this museumgoer observes that men sadden and stupefy themselves by looking to the past for their art rather than relying on their own resources for creativity, however modest their talents.

At the Tolstoy Museum, sadness grasped the 741 Sunday visitors. The Museum was offering a series of lectures on the text "Why Do Men Stupefy Themselves?" The visitors were made sad by these eloquent speakers, who were probably right.

People stared at tiny pictures of Turgenev, Nekrasov, and Fet. These and other small pictures hung alongside extremely large pictures of Count Leo Tolstoy.

In the plaza, a sinister musician played a wood trumpet while two children watched.

We considered the 640,086 pages (Jubilee Edition) of the author's published work. Some people wanted him to go away, but other people were glad we had him. "He has been a lifelong source of inspiration to me," one said. ("TM," 49)

As acknowledged, the chief lessons that the Tolstoy Museum has to teach a modern audience are exemplified in the narrator's own version of a simple Tolstoy folk tale, which he reads in the museum. The narrator quickly recounts the story of a bishop who discovers three hermits on a desert island. By substituting the Lord's Prayer for their primitive prayer, the bishop believes he has taught these men greater communion with God. The same evening the bishop sees the hermits floating over the ocean. They tell him they have already forgotten his prayer. Aghast at their miracle and his own ignorance, the bishop says that he has nothing to teach them, that their own message reaches God. Concisely and artfully, this story within "At the Tolstoy Museum" epitomizes and summarizes the themes of the tale. The hermits in this fable stand in the same relationship to the bishop as the writers who come to his mu-

seum stand to Tolstoy, or as the narrator stands in his moving reworking of this parable to Tolstoy's skill in the original. Only by
breaking free of the restraints, conventions, and revered teachers of
the past and using them or rejecting them as needed can an artist
affirm a unique sense of creativity and identity. The agony of influence is endurable if an artist knows when to stop agonizing and
how to start reinventing.

In this story the Tolstoy Museum, like the balloon, the gargantuan Robert Kennedy mannequin, or the glass mountain in the other
central art stories, represents a huge object, which dominates the
landscape and the perceptions of the audience and artists who view
it. In certain respects the Tolstoy Museum is the most complete
and self-referential art object Barthelme has created because it contains other art objects and comments on relationships between the
artifacts housed within. Barthelme critic Jerome Klinkowitz sees a
story like "At the Tolstoy Museum" as representing Barthelme's effort to develop a new plane of vision for contemporary fiction. Using
Barthelme's theory from his 1964 essay "After Joyce,"[24] Klinkowitz
recognizes the author's desire to make the short story an environmental, participatory art form, which, like the Tolstoy Museum,
envelops the reader's world just as do the rooms in which the reader
lives and works:

"Art is not about something but is something. . . . The reader is not listening to an authoritative account of the world delivered by an expert (Faulkner
on Mississippi, Hemingway on the corrida) but bumping into something
that is there, like a rock or a refrigerator." More actively, "the reader recon-
stitutes the work by his active participation, by approaching the object,
tapping it, shaking it, holding it to his ear to hear the roaring within. It is
characteristic of the object that it does not declare itself all at once, in a
rush of pleasant naivete. Joyce enforces the way in which *Finnegans Wake*
is to be read. He conceived the reading to be a lifetime project, the book
remaining always there, like the landscape surrounding the reader's home
or the building bounding the reader's apartment."[25]

Unquestionably, the Tolstoy Museum that the narrator explores
in this tale is just such an environment. Though Barthelme may

24. Barthelme, "After Joyce," 15.
25. Klinkowitz and Behrens, *Life*, 77.

hope the reader returns to this story periodically to puzzle the meanings that its unlimited associations suggest, this story, unlike "The Balloon," does offer certain explicit interpretations or at least definite directives. In "The Falling Dog," however, the first auxiliary story to occupy the final square on the typology with "At the Tolstoy Museum," a sculptor creates an art object that resembles Barthelme's artistic ideal in that it resists meaning or interpretation. Although hardly absorbing his entire physical environment, the dog of the title falls literally into the sculptor's life, and he quickly seizes on this grotesque chance encounter to transform the dog into the latest image for this sculpture. "The Falling Dog" addresses itself to the same problem that vexed the narrator of "At the Tolstoy Museum," but it takes the point of view not of an artist so awed by great writers of the past that he inhibits his own capabilities for creativity but of a productive craftsman who has momentarily depleted his mind of images for his art and waits in limbo for an intruding force to stir his creative spirit.

Watching an artist gather images for his own art rather than observing an artist trapped by the images and architecture of other artists produces a unique investigation of the creative process. In "The Falling Dog" the sculptor freely adapts the events of his collision with the dog, all he knows about dogs and their roles in past art, and his reservations about sculpting a statue of the falling dog in a verbal collage of the artistic possibilities that his clash with the animal affords. As a carefully composed artifact, "The Falling Dog" even more closely resembles Jerome Klinkowitz's view of Barthelme's intention for the perfect art object than does "At the Tolstoy Museum": "The key to Barthelme's new aesthetic for fiction is that the work may stand for itself, that it need not yield to complete explication of something else in the world but may exist as an individual object, something beautiful and surprising and deep. . . . Not just a juggler of fragments, Barthelme is an assembler and constructor of objects."[26]

Accordingly, what little plot "The Falling Dog" contains involves

26. *Ibid.*, 80, 76.

the efforts of its protagonist to make an art object from the sense-less fall of the dog from a third-story window onto his back. The sculptor tries to yoke all his knowledge and information about dogs and dogs in art into a sculpted aesthetic whole. The story that re-sults explores the confusions, anger, and cunning in this artist's mind and creative process as he sits on the sidewalk, dusts the con-crete from his chin, and watches the dog that has quickly jumped off his back and moved several feet down the street. The story cap-tures the extravagant play of mind by which a skillful creator trans-poses a fantastic moment in his life into potential art. "The Falling Dog" thus becomes a story about the creative act of writing its story, and its sculptor, attempting to unify all its pieces into one cohesive falling dog, assembles and constructs a surreal variety of objects before his audience. This assemblage includes lists of puns, clichés, and adages involving dogs, all the artists the sculptor can remember who have painted or made dogs, and all the forms and materials in which they have worked. The resulting montage of phrases, jokes, vignettes, and anecdotes is a collage of variously sculpted language that makes "The Falling Dog" a wildly amusing, self-referential art object in which the narrator affirms his unique identity and creativity.

In the process of choosing his images and rejecting those that fal-sify and distort his intentions, the sculptor invites the reader to participate not in a finished work but in the shaping of his artistic perspective. Unlike "At the Tolstoy Museum," "The Falling Dog" uses no pictures to tell its story. Though always searching for the right image, the sculptor discovers that words, used creatively, sup-ply the audience with all the vision necessary to see the falling dog and to appreciate this aesthetic situation. In the final lines of the story, he rushes up to his canine assailant and, clutching the dog in his arms, takes it back to his studio. The sculptor admits that he wonders what the entire episode means. Yet as long as he and his audience respond to the same image, they both can worry about meaning later.

The final auxiliary story sharing a box on the typology with "At the Tolstoy Museum" and "The Falling Dog," "The Flight of

Pigeons from the Palace," from *Sadness* (1972), concerns the fate of the contemporary creative process, not at the hands of past art or at an artist's own imaginative standards but at the mercy of an easily bored, fickle audience. The tale views traditional art forms and conventional aesthetic effects as elitist, outmoded palace art, which no longer delights the restless contemporary audience. Therefore, like the adventurer climbing the glass mountain, the narrator attempts to disenchant and dethrone the aesthetic of art, to please and excite the pigeons who are rapidly fleeing the palace.

The narrator thus recounts his elaborate devices for reclaiming the dilapidated palazzo, clearing the weeds that have grown around it, and making the art displayed there palatable to a general audience. Before our eyes, the protagonist of the tale turns this amphitheater into cheap summer stock, a continual sideshow that caters to the most obvious vaudeville attractions. He brings onto its stage the Amazing Numbered Man, who exhibits thirty-five demarked, completely movable parts. He hires fools to mumble and wander across the footlights, and he even auditions an enormous explosion. All these performances are described in the narrator's prose and illustrated in witty, detailed ink drawings that only heighten the ridiculousness of the artist's attempt to sate the masses. Once again, a Barthelme story achieves collage effects, juxtaposing words and pictures and suggesting the inability of contemporary language to sustain a modern audience without visual parallels.

Though the narrator believes he must appeal to the lowest common denominator of the contemporary audience for his theatrical tent show to survive, the story also shows him needlessly pandering to his spectators' basest feelings about controversial issues. His vaudeville includes scenes of blatant male chauvinism and, to please all factions, an episode in which a woman murders her husband. In his effort to stay a diminishing audience, the modern artist too often sees his role as combining elements of the burlesque comedian, the carnival barker, and the flimflam man. Frequently, his circus becomes merely an effort to shock or titillate those who watch. Yet despite his audience's demand for the grotesque and the lurid and his willingness to supply these commodities, the show does not succeed. The audience feels so manipulated by this bevy of sensations and sees their own desires so constantly exploited in these vignettes that they give the show only the faintest applause.

The force of this tale rests in its ability to be both joyous and sad, to show the tireless exuberance of this contemporary artist attempting to entice the modern audience back to art with vulgar routines that defy most senses of artistry. The tale portrays the modern artist as a cynical magician, who ironically comes to believe in his own bogus tricks. Yet the real skill of the story emerges in the ability of its collage to ridicule these misguided efforts at a new art form and yet, paradoxically, to produce through its startling juxtapositions and acute self-awareness a new art form all the same. The narrator of "The Flight of Pigeons from the Palace" concludes his dilemma with the recognition that the show must and—as long as human invention prevails—will go on:

It is difficult to keep the public interested.

The public demands new wonders piled on new wonders. Often we don't know where our next marvel is coming from.

The supply of strange ideas is not endless. . . . Some things appear to be wonders in the beginning, but when you become familiar with them, are not wonderful at all. . . . Some of us have even thought of folding the show—closing it down. That thought has been gliding through the hallways and rehearsal rooms of the show.

The new volcano we have just placed under contract seems very promising.

[Drawing of an active volcano.][27]

A fascinating tension exists in these Barthelme stories about art and the creative process. The protagonist of each attempts to return his art to its sources of wonder before the contemporary audience, massive social discontent, and the eminence of other artists convinced him to experiment with the play of form and content or collages of pictures and words. Ironically, the narrator of "The Flight of Pigeons from the Palace," though hardly averse to these techniques, uses them to stimulate his own resilient imagination. Critic Jerome Klinkowitz recognizes that the outlandish formal innovation in this

27. Donald Barthelme, "The Flight of Pigeons from the Palace," in *Sadness*, 139.

and other Barthelme tales, however futuristic in appearance, actually represents the effort of the artist in each to attain a sense of perspective, proportion, and control in his art: "Barthelme's vignettes are, then, not conventional arguments in the dialectics of form, but imaginative volcanoes, radical stopgap measures to save experiences which might otherwise be eroded with our loss of traditional standards. In this sense he is a counterrevolutionary, opposing the new language of technology and manipulation with pleas for old-fashioned interest and imagination."[28]

As Klinkowitz's comments indicate, "The Flight of Pigeons from the Palace" shows Barthelme at his most revealing and most contradictory. Forever the juggler of fragments, fully committed to experimentation with the short-story form, Barthelme is also an entertainer and a *New Yorker* writer who inverts, revises, and rearranges our conceptions of art to show us how much we lose by demanding to be entertained, shocked, and amused. Beneath his surreal trappings and collage structures lies a classically conservative sensibility that insists that the world, however torn apart, can be artfully and responsibly put back together again. The artists in "At the Tolstoy Museum," "The Falling Dog," and "The Flight of Pigeons from the Palace" affirm unique creativities by giving fragmented worlds surprising aesthetic harmony.

This chapter logically concludes with the outlines of a theory of art emerging in the twelve stories examined within it. These tales see their works of art as enormous aesthetic objects, which dramatize the endless play of form and content. For an audience to appreciate this art, it must participate in these objects not by examining their internalized meaning but by exploring their contradictory, surprising surfaces. This theory of art divorces the art work from a specific meaning or interpretation. In these stories art is not about something but is something—a toy, object, person, event, performance, landscape, or environment. Freed to be abstract, art can reflect the contours of the world around it and the varied shapes of experience of the audience whose world intersects its own.

28. Klinkowitz and Behrens, *Life*, 76.

Moreover, art in these tales resists the force of the past. Incorporating the immense vision of a writer like Tolstoy or the magnetism of a political leader like Robert Kennedy, these stories attempt to transcend the limitations these figures impose on their narrator's creative possibilities. Thus these tales consciously strive to disenchant the preeminent symbols, to demythologize the totems of past and present. In so doing, the stories transform our previous conceptions of art with an art of their own. This artistry envisions worlds that partake of the imperfections and uncertainties of contemporary life. This art can still be a romantic quest, however, as exemplified by a story like "The Glass Mountain," in which an idealistic knight ascends a treacherous mountain to bring art to the suffering urbanites below. Often, however, these quests become catalogs and lists of all the ways in which conventional art fails the people it seeks to inspire. These tales contend that for too long art has been obsessed with a grandeur of life which seems incongruous with the debilitating quality of much modern experience or with the chaos of events and circumstances that mirrors reality without illuminating it.

Consequently, these tales seek to disenchant this aesthetic of nihilism, to dissect the confusions of contemporary existence without offering final conclusions or interpretations. These stories eventually realize that art substitutes aesthetic effects for the reality it purports to capture; art offers a surrogate life in place of the phenomena it attempts to record. Therefore, contemporary art becomes a ceaseless search for the legitimate, the genuine, and the creative, which yields no definite products or results. Nonetheless, these stories collectively assert that art should be the effort to bring the symbol closer to reality, to make something from nothingness, and to serve and embody that vision of reality which offers a sense of emotional or spiritual transcendence to its audience.

Rather than projecting a sense of defeat or despair, these stories' view of the fallibility of all art instills a sense of joyous determination in their narrators and artists. Art in these tales functions as the unattainable yet perpetually exhilarating object of life, and the four central art stories in this chapter delight in dramatizing ways by which art may be fleetingly grasped. In "The Balloon" the narrator forgets his personal pain by shaping a huge sublimatory toy, which intrigues and frightens its audience with its lack of constructive meaning. Similarly, in "Robert Kennedy Saved from Drowning" the narrator as audience rescues Kennedy's personality from submerging in a sea of contradictions. At the same time, this story suggests that men's and women's failures to know themselves or others, coupled with their drive for perfection, have transformed artistic and political celebrities into contemporary art objects. Attempting to question the authority of an accepted artistic symbol, the mountain climber of "The Glass Mountain" ironically discovers, not the many-layered symbol he desires but a beautiful princess, whom he throws to the foot of the mountain. This frustration of modern art, torn between the mechanistic symbols of the past and the effort to create an art that functions organically in the present, is vividly illustrated in "At the Tolstoy Museum." Here the narrator destroys the anxiety of much contemporary art by realizing he must accept the past. Acting on his conviction, he immediately uses one of Tolstoy's fables to create a lyrical fable of his own.

The balloon, Robert Kennedy, the glass mountain, and the Tolstoy Museum loom awesomely in the landscapes of the artists in each of these stories. Yet by making their environments endless fields of play, each of these artists shapes a new concept of art. Lacking the purity of a Grecian urn or the authority of a scarlet letter, these tales nonetheless form a vision of art less interested in the object itself than in an audience's perceptions of it. In these stories the art work's environment becomes a huge art object designed for the restless, fickle modern audience encouraged to touch, know, scale, and inhabit a world alive to discovery and change.

Conclusion

These forty-six short stories show Donald Barthelme to be an imaginative and versatile writer. Considered separately from the concerns of the typology, Barthelme's tales reveal a sensibility particularly attuned to questioning the function of contemporary art, the role of art and the artist in society, the value of humor and irony in his own work, literature as an escape from a threatening world, and the importance of collage as a means of affirming and reshaping reality. Investigating these themes throughout his writing and the individual stories in which they appear effectively summarizes Barthelme's career and achievement.

Barthelme often visualizes his tales as canvases on which he places eccentric, caricatured situations. He then develops these sketches with bold swatches of language or delicate strokes of suggestion. Barthelme is a word painter, a literary equivalent of the action painter or abstract expressionist who uses patches of color not to explain his work but to evoke a mood or state of mind. Barthelme recognizes, however, that words have meaning in a way that lines and color never explicitly do, and he feels a writer's responsibility to comment on the conflicts and confusions of modern life he so inventively reproduces.

From these perspectives, "See the Moon" seems one of Barthelme's most important short stories. The tale roughly chronicles

Barthelme's own autobiography, contends that in the modern world all epistemologies and ways of knowing fail, and concludes that even the artist in his own art never knows exactly who he is. In the fragmented collage that emerges from this narrator's effort to connect the discontinuous pieces of his life, Barthelme reveals the methodology of his art. To varying degrees almost all of Barthelme's stories are abstract, expressive mosaics that reflect the riddles and contradictions of lives torn into disjunctive elements by time and eroding beliefs.

In a tale like "The Educational Experience" Barthelme enlarges the perspective of his art. This story becomes nothing less than a work of conceptual art, a three-dimensional art event depicting the origins of the disillusionment and sense of failure that the persona acknowledges in "See the Moon." As in stories like "Me and Miss Mandible," "The Sergeant," and "The School," the tale blames its narrator's educational experience for misleading and brutalizing him. It transforms a four-year college curriculum into an intellectual gymnasium in which students exercise to quotations from history and literature and hurdle over new discoveries in solid-state physics like athletes in a track event. This education rewards speed and efficiency in its students but totally fails to suggest the ways human knowledge might develop their imaginations. Consequently, the students are processed from this assembly line with great cynicism about learning, thinking, and feeling. "The Educational Experience" functions as a story about the dubious process of contemporary education and the confusions it causes in those who manage to survive it. Moving from descriptions of the strenuous obstacles these students encounter to the trivial fragments of information they are made to assimilate, the tale emerges as both a piece of conceptual art and an action painting that uses words from strikingly different vocabularies to instruct, admonish, and direct its students into regimented lives.

The same variety of textures of language appears in "The Indian Uprising," another story central to Barthelme's role as a modernist word painter. If "The Educational Experience" functions as conceptual art, "The Indian Uprising" sees its artist's entire environment as a field of forces in which his conflicting loyalties, ideologies, and aesthetic philosophies collide. The narrator describes a chic, hedonistic urban environment designed by young adults newly graduated from the educational experience. Totally narcissistic and uncritical, this world easily surrenders to a band of savage Indians eager to paralyze the modern city in its strangulating technology. In the process of this attack, the narrator fails to control his art, to gain a humane vision of a society that could revere art without repressing its minority groups. "Strings of language extend in every direction to bind the world into a rushing, ribald whole," says the narrator, maintaining an aesthetic that makes social concerns meaningless.[1] Inevitably, the primitive elements of society that his philosophy abuses will destroy him.

"The Indian Uprising" acts as a forceful corrective to critics of Barthelme who find his vivid murals, his environmental and conceptual art objects, lacking in moral content. This story demands that the artist commit himself to concrete social values or risk being controlled by the constantly changing signs and symbols of a world that he attempts to reproduce. Not merely ambiguous Jackson Pollack or Richard Rauschenberg paintings, many of Barthelme's word pictures make emphatic moral statements insisting that the artist must separate life from art or be consumed by his own artistry.

Barthelme's most significant single definition of art in a dehumanizing modern society occurs in his playful tale, "The Balloon." In this story an enormous art object—a balloon—suddenly appears one morning covering forty-five blocks of Manhattan. The balloon serves as a paradigm of Barthelme's ideal modern art object. Highly artificial, larger than life yet distinctly separate from it, the balloon allows its audience to play and to lose themselves in its changing shapes, textures, and colors. In an increasingly rigid, defined world, the great appeal of the balloon lies in its sheer irrationality, its definite lack of purpose. The balloon enables spectators who luxuriate in its surfaces to mislocate themselves and to forget their social roles for brief periods of time. But this play does not lastingly divert

1. Barthelme, "Indian Uprising," 11.

them from reality. It actually develops their wit and energies for combat with the contemporary technological forces that defy their individuality and humanity. Ironically, by the end of the story, the balloon seems to represent reality, the concrete particular, or the thing in itself, which refuses to mean, stand for, or symbolize any other object. The tale suggests that if men and women made their art from objects in their physical environments, however inflated or incongruous, they might be more attuned to play, spontaneity, and their own personalities.

Accordingly, for Barthelme the great natural artist becomes that individual who composes his art from what his environment and circumstances offer him. Consequently, Barthelme chooses the great modernist painter Paul Klee as his example of a man who in time of war made great art from loss and personal deprivation. Freely adapted from Klee's actual experience as a draftee in the German transport service during World War I, "Engineer-Private Paul Klee Misplaces an Aircraft between Milbertshofen and Cambrai, March 1916," describes Klee's reaction to this traumatic disappearance. Calmly, Klee sketches the beautiful, sculpted pattern made by the folds of the tarpaulin over the empty spaces where the plane had been stored. He then forges the official manifest so that the transport train appears to be carrying the correct number of aircraft. For Barthelme, Klee represents the great artist who finds the textures of art where others would find only loss, emptiness, or humiliation. Under continual surveillance by the secret police, Klee epitomizes the evasive, contemporary creator, who in a world frequently at war discovers ways to subvert authority and forge his own artistry. Barthelme raises such counterfeiting in Klee and other protagonists to the highest levels of art.

Underground hiding men and women appear often throughout Barthelme's stories, and they personify the efforts of individuals to overcome the forces of a tyrannical, technological world with a single weapon: human imagination. Barthelme creates a distinct character type: moody, perverse loners, driven to the outer reaches of society by a world that reveres conformity and fears creativity. The pathos of stories like "Hiding Man," "The Phantom of the

Opera's Friend," "A City of Churches," and "The Temptation of St. Anthony" resides in the lack of imaginative human sympathy that the mundane practical world shows these outcasts and rebels who cannot accept society's values and therefore must live on its fringes. As these characters' imaginations expose the emptiness of social conventions, a mockingly humorous tone develops these stories. Ironically, this humor deflates not only the corruption of bourgeois society but the pretensions and paranoia of the hiding men as well. The reader must certainly question the existence of suffering in the phantom of the opera's luxurious life, with his fine French wine and elegant apartment in the caverns of the Paris Opera Theater, even if his isolation is unmistakable. Correspondingly, how should the reader regard Barthelme's contemporary version of St. Anthony, a man of such holiness that the sexual temptations of mundane suburban life drive him, once more, into the desert? Sadness, as Barthelme titles one of his short-story collections, haunts these stories and all of Barthelme's writing. Yet the real sadness of the human imagination in these tales results from the mind's inclination to rebel from accepted social standards by forming alternative dreams and desires which seem as stereotyped or predictable as the worlds they attack.

Throughout his writing Barthelme aims his humor at the chaos and disruptions of contemporary urban life, but he also chooses to undermine those who attempt to escape their worlds with verbal laments or repressed daydreams. Consequently, he functions as a hiding man in his own stories. Refusing to comment on a tale or assent to his protagonists' complaints, his destructive irony only guarantees that even though his characters' criticisms of their worlds appear cogent, their attempts to change their lives are thwarted by their sadly pedestrian imaginations. Accordingly, many of Barthelme's stories conclude as elaborate, contrived jokes at the reader's expense. He frequently encourages his audience to feel sympathy for a narrator's efforts to break free of the rituals of affluent urban life only to show in his bemusement that few modern men and women have found the means to live creatively and still remain free of social restraints. Therefore, if these stories end as jokes, they at least become jokes with a point of view, reflections on individuals' inability to find an artful way out of the morass of modern life. In "Hiding Man" Burlingame transforms the priest in pursuit of his soul into a dog by means of the magic he has learned from a life spent watching the horror movies. Barthelme does not see the lore of horror movies as a legitimate release from Catholicism. Yet in this comically surprising ending and the audacious humor of its reversal, he looks to comedy and irony as supplying a partial solution to the endless frustrations of contemporary metropolitan life.

Frequently identified as a flippant, insouciant *New Yorker* writer, Barthelme has attempted throughout his career to make from the materials of comedy and irony something artistic, to shape an alternative to the facetious wisecracks of his hiding men and women. He believes that laughter can momentarily defeat the pain of reality. Yet some of his best stories ask if a humorist can go beyond mere laughter, if a comic can become an artist by creating a new reality to replace that which his irony has destroyed. This question is thoroughly analyzed in one of Barthelme's most interesting stories, "Kierkegaard Unfair to Schlegel." In this tale, a long conversation between a scientist and a comic voice, the scientific voice tries to convince the comic speaker that, as Kierkegaard insisted, irony destroys all it touches and thus cannot be an element of art. The comedian refutes the scientist's view and his desire to convince the comic sensibility of the beauty and the necessity of a technological society. By the nature of what it attacks, irony creates values as well as destroying them, the comedian argues. Yet as their increasingly angry dialogue breaks off into bitter silence, the story ends.

Just as the scientist and the comic artist actually begin to communicate, however divergent their views and hostile their skirmish, the art of the story evaporates. If Barthelme's hiding men substitute their attacks on a stultifying society with insipid visions of their own, similarly, he demonstrates that the short story and irony itself have grown too staid and too conventional to depict some of the major conflicts of contemporary life. Barthelme tries in this tale to overcome traditional art with an art of his own, to transform a story that exists only as charges and countercharges into musical rounds of questions and answers, answers and questions. He makes a new art form by destroying old art forms, much as his ironic comedian learns that irony must change and create or it will merely add to the debris and waste of modern life rather than destroying it.

In several dialogue stories Barthelme continues and elaborates this debate between a scientific, totalitarian spirit in contemporary society and an artistic, humanist voice who attempts to escape the other's domination and control. The series of questions and answers that constitute these stories seems the perfect device for conveying the contrast between the rigid, unyielding scientist and the flexible artistic voice who can never completely decide between several options, and for whom one question suggests several answers and one answer spawns still more questions. An elusive game of cat and mouse dominates the exchanges between these two speakers in "The Explanation," "The Catechist," and other Barthelme stories. This war of wills provides a means for the humanist to escape the intrusions of an increasingly totalitarian world. Barthelme's fear of a mechanistic, computerized society subtly controlling its artists with scientific, emotionless reasoning pervades many of his stories.

In a tale like "The Explanation" the scientific speaker desperately tries to persuade the artist that a computer can make his life carefree. Yet at the insistent probing of the artist, the scientist reveals that he dislikes the machine he attempts to extol, and he finds watching a beautiful woman infinitely more exciting than electronic technology. The questions and answers of "The Explanation" ridicule a society obsessed with explanations that still fail to explain why men bored with inadequate scientific solutions persist in pursuing them. False logic continues in "The Catechist." This dialogue in its endless tautology records, for Barthelme, the sound of much contemporary conversation. In a world that pits power against weakness, science against art and humanity, and dogma against rebellion, these stories suggest that language and dialogue provide means for the clever, elastic mind to escape the trammels of needless authority. In another group of stories Barthelme projects a way out of the circularity of much modern communication.

"The Reference," "The Leap," "Morning," and "The New Music" make conversation a new music all its own, filled with incessant jazz rhythms and a staccato beat less interested in communicating than in expressing the intensity and individuality of each conversationalist. While escaping the trap that many dialogues become, conversation in these tales exists as sheer stimulant, reflecting the tempo of a hedonistic society in which everyone talks and no one listens.

Though conversation functions as a means of escape in many Barthelme tales, a majority of the stories analyzed in these chapters can be seen as strategies to escape the boring repetitions, the perpetual sameness of everyday life. All of society, not just contemporary conversation, constitutes an enervating trap for many Barthelme characters, and the writer in some of his best tales envisions techniques by which his characters can escape their society, their minds, even their own language. In "Daumier," one of Barthelme's most striking examples of this need for escape, the protagonist creates two surrogates for himself: one to live in the nineteenth century of an Alexandre Dumas romance, and the other to bring a woman he has fallen in love with in the Dumas landscape into his own twentieth-century reality. The villain in Barthelme stories like "Daumier," "The Party," "Critique de la Vie Quotidienne," and "Perpetua" is the capriciousness of the self and its desire to be soothed, preoccupied, and entertained. Rather than become completely obsessed with their own problems and neuroses, many Barthelme protagonists form surrogate selves or alternative societies to escape the total domination of their egos. Frequently, society or the public world in these tales constitutes a protagonist's imaginative effort to escape his own dilemmas or limitations. As the protagonist of "Daumier" recognizes: "The self cannot be escaped, but it can be, with ingenuity and hard work, distracted. There are always openings, if you can find them, there is always something to do."[2] Similarly, in "The Party" the narrator visits a large, bustling cocktail party trying to forget his own nagging per-

2. Barthelme, "Daumier," 183.

sonal worries. Ironically but inevitably, he discovers that the persistent attempt to evade the self merely becomes a return to the self's own anxieties. At the same time, the social world formed by the cocktail party soon seems, in the narrator's imagination, a microcosm of all the tensions, confusions, and dissonances of society itself. Likewise, in "Critique de la Vie Quotidienne" the narrator barricades himself, his wife, and his son in a decaying brownstone apartment to escape the pretensions of affluent city life. His familial society crumbles, however, when the narrator's wife and son insist on contaminating his enclave with their own requests and fixations. In "Perpetua" as well, the fickle heroine instantaneously decides she no longer wants a conventional life and marriage. Insatiably craving the new, Perpetua initially seems to escape her former society. She moves to a turbulent modern city but quickly, inexorably perpetuates all her old delusions and insecurities in the self-reflecting trends, fads, and fashions of the moment.

The striving of the Barthelme persona to remake the world remains the greatest single common denominator of all forty-six tales. The typical Barthelme narrator exists either by escaping a sense of self or by ingeniously placing the pieces into which the contemporary world has shattered into new forms. Sometimes a Barthelme character achieves both goals. In "A Shower of Gold," the sculptor Peterson concludes that though the modern world may be absurd, this absurdity seems to him equally absurd. Rather than acquiesce to the identity which an insane world wants to impose on him, Peterson affirms his role as a sculptor who will forever explore new possibilities, who will find ways of reconstructing the world rather than further dismantling it. "In this kind of a world . . . absurd if you will, possibilities nevertheless proliferate and escalate all around us and there are opportunities for beginning again. . . . How can you be alienated without first having been connected?"[3]

The buoyant optimism and gaiety of this view permeate much of Barthelme's writing. In an age that exudes alienation, absurdity, and

3. Barthelme, "Shower," 183.

despair, Barthelme's stories ask what individuals and artists can do, beyond alienation, to make sense of their society. Barthelme has intentionally made Peterson a sculptor and not a painter, musician, or writer. Above all, Barthelme's tales function as acts of reconstruction and connection in which his protagonists sculpt, shape, and mold the fragments of a disheveled world into some semblance of coherence. Because the pieces of these stories remain on view even at their conclusion, his tales become active gestures of participation with the audience that encounters them. The tales serve as inviting collages for an audience that chooses to imagine the endless possibilities for creation Barthelme has placed within them. Tales such as "Views of My Father Weeping," "Brain Damage," "The Falling Dog," and "The Flight of Pigeons from the Palace" are essential Barthelme in their juxtaposition of words and pictures, modern art with pop art concerns, and the artist's intuitions with his audience's expectations. These stories, though wildly humorous and filled with an inexhaustible sense of Barthelme's energy and technique, are also deeply rueful. Combining their author's penchant for the ordinary and the outlandish, the joyous and the disheartening, these and all his stories contend that though we may never really understand ourselves, our society, the creative process, or why the modern audience seems so restless and dissatisfied, creative effort remains the best hope to answer our questions.

As I write this, G. P. Putnam's has just published *Overnight to Many Distant Cities*, Barthelme's eighth collection of short stories. This collection, like the previous ones, will doubtless amuse, astound, and annoy short-story lovers, Barthelme aficionados, *New Yorker* subscribers, academics, and even the reader who has never seen a page of Barthelme before. Yet I detect that this volume, and perhaps the last two or three, have elicited fewer shocks of recognition and squeals of delight from reviewers, critics, and even the writer's most ardent fans than did his earliest fiction. Perhaps Barthelme achieved his greatest career growth and development during an era in American arts and letters in the late sixties and early seventies, when there seemed to be a burgeoning audience for the free-form experimentation, deadpan humor, and aestheticized parody that the times demanded and the *New Yorker* supplied. With this readership now in disarray, Barthelme relies on his increasingly solipsistic instincts and echoes from his earlier stories.

Regardless, Barthelme's short-story collections, in their virtuosity and cunning appraisal of the tremors and despair in American life over the last twenty years, seem destined to receive a sizable footnote in American literary history. For their place in the development of the American short story, these tales deserve a chapter of their own. No American writer—with the exception of Poe—has ever toyed so seriously with the form and language of short fiction to embody a society that has lost its moorings but need not completely lose its morality.

Bibliography

Aidrige, John. "Dance of Death." Review of *Unspeakable Practices, Unnatural Acts*, by Donald Barthelme. *Atlantic*, July, 1968, pp. 89–91.

Baker, John F. "PW Interviews Donald Barthelme." *Publishers Weekly*, November 11, 1974, pp. 6–7.

Barthelme, Donald. "After Joyce." *Location*, II (Summer, 1964), 13–16.

———. *Amateurs*. New York, 1976.

———. *City Life*. New York, 1970.

———. *Come Back, Dr. Caligari*. Boston, 1964.

———. Commentary on "Paraguay." In *Writer's Choice*, edited by Rust Hills, pp. 25–26. New York, 1974.

———. *The Dead Father*. New York, 1975.

———. "The Elegance Is Under Control." Review of *The Triumph*, by John Kenneth Galbraith. New York *Times*, April 21, 1968, pp. 4–5.

———. *Great Days*. New York, 1979.

———. *Guilty Pleasures*. New York, 1974.

———. "Mr. Hunt's Wooly Utopia." Review of *Alpaca*, by H. L. Hunt. *Reporter*, April 14, 1960, pp. 44–46.

———. *Overnight to Many Distant Cities*. New York, 1983.

———. *Sadness*. New York, 1972.

———. *Sixty Stories*. New York, 1981.

———. *The Slightly Irregular Fire Engine; or, The Hithering Thithering Djinn*. New York, 1971.

———. *Snow White*. New York, 1967.

———. "The Tired Terror of Graham Greene." Review of *The Comedians*, by Graham Greene. *Holiday*, April, 1966, pp. 146, 148–49.

———. *Unspeakable Practices, Unnatural Acts*. New York, 1968.

Bellamy, Joe David. "Barthelme and Delights of Mind Travel." Review of *Great Days*, by Donald Barthelme. Washington *Post Book World*, January 22, 1979, pp. 1, 4.

———. *Superfiction*. New York, 1975.

Carver, Raymond. Review of *Great Days*, by Donald Barthelme. *Texas Monthly*, March, 1979, pp. 162–63.

Conroy, Frank. "An Explorer's Notes: Donald Barthelme Does It Again." New York *Times Book Review*, June 6, 1971, pp. 4–5.

Dervin, Daniel A. "Breast Fantasy in Barthelme, Swift, and Philip Roth: Creativity and Psychoanalytic Structure." *American Imago*, XXX (1976), 102–22.

Dickstein, Morris. *Gates of Eden: American Culture in the Sixties*. New York, 1977.

Ditsky, John M. "'With Ingenuity and Hardwork Distracted': The Narrative Style of Donald Barthelme." *Style*, IX (Summer, 1975), 388–400.

Donaghue, Denis. "For Brevity's Sake." Review of *Great Days*, by Donald Barthelme. *Saturday Review*, March 3, 1979, pp. 50–52.

Flowers, Betty. "Barthelme's *Snow White*: The Reader-Patient Relationship." *Critique*, XVI (1975), 33–43.

Gardner, John. *On Moral Fiction*. New York, 1978.

Gass, William H. "The Leading Edge of the Trash Phenomenon." Review of *Unspeakable Practices, Unnatural Acts*, by Donald Barthelme. *New York Review of Books*, April 25, 1968, pp. 5–6.

Giles, James R. "The 'Marivaudian Being' Drowns His Children: Dehumanization in Donald Barthelme's 'Robert Kennedy Saved from Drowning' and Joyce Carol Oates' *Wonderland*." *Southern Humanities Review*, IX (Winter, 1975), 63–75.

Gillen, Francis. "Donald Barthelme's City: A Guide." *Twentieth Century Literature*, XVIII (Spring, 1974), 37–44.

Gilman, Richard. *The Confusion of Realms*. New York, 1969.

Graff, Gerard. "Babbitt at the Abyss: The Social Context of Post-modern American Fiction." *Triquarterly*, No. 33 (Spring, 1975), 305–37.

Granetz, Marc. Review of *Great Days*, by Donald Barthelme. *New Republic*, February 17, 1979, pp. 37–38.

Guerard, Albert J. "Notes on the Rhetoric of Anti-Realistic Fiction." *Triquarterly*, No. 30 (Spring, 1974), 3–50.

Harris, Charles B. *Contemporary American Novelists of the Absurd*. New Haven, 1971.

Hassan, Ihab. *Contemporary American Literature*. New York, 1973.

———. *Paracriticisms*. Urbana, 1975.

Hendin, Josephine. "Angries: S-M as a Literary Style." *Harper's*, February, 1974, pp. 87–93.

Johnson, Diane. "Possibly Parables." Review of *Great Days*, by Donald Barthelme. *New York Times Book Review*, February 3, 1979, pp. 1, 36–37.

Johnson, R. E., Jr. "'Bees Barking in the Night': The End and Beginning of Donald Barthelme's Narrative." *Boundary 2*, V (Fall, 1976), 71–92.

Kazin, Alfred. *Bright Book of Life: American Novelists and Story Tellers from Hemingway to Mailer*. Boston, 1973.

Klinkowitz, Jerome. "Donald Barthelme." In *The New Fiction: Interviews with Innovative American Writers*, edited by Joe David Bellamy, pp. 45–54. Urbana, 1974.

———. "Donald Barthelme: A Checklist, 1957–1974." *Critique*, XVI (1975), 49–58.

———. "Innovative Short Fiction: 'Vile and Imaginative Things.'" In *Innovative Fiction*, edited by Jerome Klinkowitz and John Somer, pp. xv–xxvii. New York, 1972.

———. "Literary Disruptions; Or, What's Become of American Fiction?" In *Surfiction*, edited by Raymond Federman, pp. 165–79. Chicago, 1975.

———. *Literary Disruptions: The Making of a Post-Contemporary American Fiction*. Urbana, 1975.

Klinkowitz, Jerome, and Roy R. Behrens. *The Life of Fiction*. Urbana, 1977.

Klinkowitz, Jerome, Asa Pieratt, and Robert Murray Davis. "Barthelme, Donald." *Dictionary of Literary Biography*. Detroit, 1978. II, 34–38.

———. *Donald Barthelme: A Comprehensive Bibliography and Annotated Secondary Checklist*. Hamden, Conn., 1977.

Kostelanetz, Richard. *The End of Intelligent Writing: Literary Politics in America*. New York, 1974.

Kramer, Hilton. "Barthelme's Comedy of Patricide." Review of *The Dead Father*, by Donald Barthelme. *Commentary*, LXII (August, 1976), 56–59.

Krupnick, Mark L. "Notes from the Funhouse." *Modern Occasions*, I (Fall, 1970), 108–12.

Lasch, Christopher. *The Culture of Narcissism*. New York, 1978.

Leland, John. "Remarks Re-marked: What Curious of Signs!" *Boundary 2*, V (Spring, 1977), 796–811.

Lingeman, Richard. "Steal My Name and You Got Trash." *New York Times Book Review*, February 3, 1974, p. 39.

Lodge, David. *The Modes of Modern Writing*. Ithaca, 1977.

Longleigh, Peter L., Jr. "Donald Barthelme's *Snow White*." *Critique*, XI (1969), 30–34.

McCaffery, Larry. "Barthelme's *Snow White*: The Aesthetics of Trash." *Critique*, XVI (1975), 19–32.

McConnell, Frank D. *Four Postwar American Novelists: Bellow, Mailer, Barth, and Pynchon*. Chicago, 1977.

McNall, Sally Allen. "'But Why Am I Troubling Myself about Languages?' Style, Reaction, and Lack of Reaction in Barthelme's *Snow White*." *Language and Style*, VIII (1974), 81–94.

Moran, Charles. "Barthelme the Trash-Man: The Uses of Junk." *CEA Critic*, XXXVI (May, 1974), 32–33.

Oates, Joyce Carol. "Whose Side Are You On?" *New York Times Book Review*, June 4, 1972, p. 63.

Olderman, Raymond. *Beyond The Waste Land: The American Novel in the Nineteen-Sixties*. New Haven, 1972.

Orvell, Miles. "Reproduction and 'The Real Thing': The Anxiety of Realism in the Age of Photography." In *The Technological Imagination: Theories and Fictions*, edited by Teresa De Lauretis, Andreas Huyssen, and Kathleen Woodward, pp. 49–64. 3d ed. Madison, 1980.

Peden, William. *The American Short Story*. Boston, 1975.

Prescott, Peter S. "Sound of Music." Review of *Great Days*, by Donald Barthelme. *Newsweek*, February 5, 1979, pp. 62–63.

———. "The Writer's Lot." *Newsweek*, December 24, 1973, pp. 83–85.

Rother, James. "Parafiction: The Adjacent Universe of Barth, Barthelme, Pynchon, and Nabokov." *Boundary 2*, V (Fall, 1976), 21–44.

Samuels, Charles Thomas. Review of *Sadness*, by Donald Barthelme. *New York Times Book Review*, November 5, 1977, pp. 27–28, 30–31.

Schickel, Richard. "Freaked Out on Barthelme." *New York Times Magazine*, August 16, 1970, pp. 14–15, 42.

Schmitz, Neil. "Donald Barthelme and the Emergence of Modern Satire." *Minnesota Review*, I (1972), 109–18.

———. "What Irony Unravels." *Partisan Review*, XL, No. 3 (1973), 482–90.

Scholes, Robert. "Metafiction." *Iowa Review*, I (Fall, 1970), 100–115.

Shadoian, Jack. "Notes on Donald Barthelme's *Snow White*." *Western Humanities Review*, XXIV (Winter, 1970), 73–75.

Shorris, Earl. "Donald Barthelme's Illustrated Wordy-Gurdy." *Harper's*, January, 1973, pp. 92–94, 96.

Stern, Daniel. "The Mysterious New Novel." In *Liberations*, edited by Ihab Hassan, pp. 25–34. Middletown, Conn., 1971.

Stevick, Philip. "Lies, Fictions, and Mock Facts." *Western Humanities Review*, XXX (Winter, 1976), 1–12.

Stott, William. "Donald Barthelme and the Death of Fiction." *Prospects: Annual of American Cultural Studies*, I (1975), 369–86.

Tanner, Tony. *City of Words: American Fiction, 1950–1970*. New York, 1971.

Whalen, Tom. "Wonderful Elegance: Barthelme's 'The Party.'" *Critique*, XVI (1975), 45–48.

Wilde, Alan. "Barthelme Unfair to Kierkegaard: Some Thoughts on Modern and Postmodern Irony." *Boundary 2*, V (Fall, 1976), 45–70.

Index